BEING TRULY HUMAN

THE QUEST FOR REALITY AND SIGNIFICANCE

Book 1 – BEING TRULY HUMAN:
The Limits of our Worth, Power, Freedom and Destiny

Book 2 – FINDING ULTIMATE REALITY:
In Search of the Best Answers to the Biggest Questions

Book 3 – QUESTIONING OUR KNOWLEDGE:
Can we Know What we Need to Know?

Book 4 – DOING WHAT'S RIGHT:
Whose System of Ethics is Good Enough?

Book 5 – CLAIMING TO ANSWER:
How One Person Became the Response to our Deepest Questions

Book 6 – SUFFERING LIFE'S PAIN:
Facing the Problems of Moral and Natural Evil

MYRTLEFIELD
HOUSE

BOOK 1

BEING TRULY HUMAN

THE LIMITS OF OUR WORTH, POWER, FREEDOM AND DESTINY

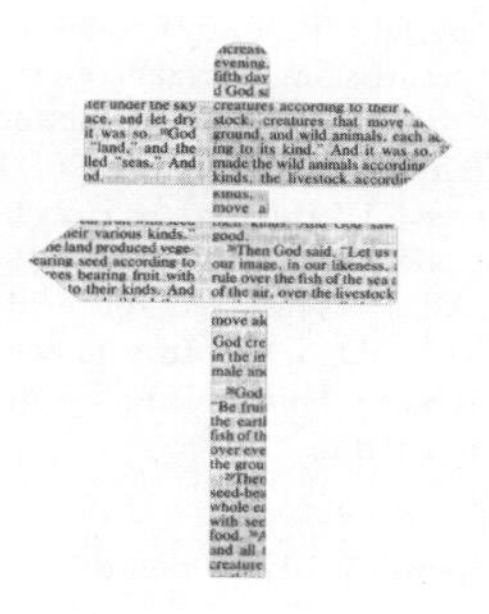

DAVID GOODING
JOHN LENNOX

Myrtlefield House
Belfast, Northern Ireland

Being Truly Human: The Limits of our Worth, Power, Freedom and Destiny
Book 1, The Quest for Reality and Significance
 Italics within Scripture quotations indicate emphasis added. Scripture quotations marked (our trans.) are as translated by David Gooding. Foreign language quotations marked (our trans.) are as translated by John Lennox.

Cover design: Frank Gutbrod.
Interior design and composition: Sharon VanLoozenoord.

Published by The Myrtlefield Trust
PO Box 2216
Belfast, N Ireland, BT1 9YR
w: www.myrtlefieldhouse.com
e: info@myrtlefieldhouse.com

ISBN: 978-1-912721-00-9 (hbk.)
ISBN: 978-1-912721-01-6 (pbk.)
ISBN: 978-1-912721-02-3 (PDF)
ISBN: 978-1-912721-03-0 (Kindle)
ISBN: 978-1-912721-04-7 (EPUB without DRM)
ISBN: 978-1-912721-30-6 (box set)

22 21 20 19 18 10 9 8 7 6 5 4 3 2 1

DEDICATED TO OUR YOUNGER FELLOW STUDENTS,

REMEMBERING THAT WE WERE ONCE STUDENTS—AND STILL ARE

CONTENTS

BOOK 1: BEING TRULY HUMAN

THE LIMITS OF OUR WORTH, POWER, FREEDOM AND DESTINY

ILLUSTRATIONS

SERIES PREFACE

The average student has a problem—many problems in fact, but one in particular. No longer a child, he or she is entering adult life and facing the torrent of change that adult independence brings. It can be exhilarating but sometimes also frightening to have to stand on one's own feet, to decide for oneself how to live, what career to follow, what goals to aim at and what values and principles to adopt.

How are such decisions to be made? Clearly much thought is needed and increasing knowledge and experience will help. But leave these basic decisions too long and there is a danger of simply drifting through life and missing out on the character-forming process of thinking through one's own worldview. For that is what is needed: a coherent framework that will give to life a true perspective and satisfying values and goals. To form such a worldview for oneself, particularly at a time when society's traditional ideas and values are being radically questioned, can be a very daunting task for anyone, not least university students. After all, worldviews are normally composed of many elements drawn from, among other sources, science, philosophy, literature, history and religion; and a student cannot be expected to be an expert in any one of them, let alone in all of them (indeed, is any one of us?).

Nevertheless we do not have to wait for the accumulated wisdom of life's later years to see what life's major issues are; and once we grasp what they are, it is that much easier to make informed and wise decisions of every kind. It is as a contribution to that end that the authors offer this series of books to their younger fellow students. We intend that each book will stand on its own while also contributing to the fuller picture provided by the whole series.

So we begin by laying out the issues at stake in an extended introduction that overviews the fundamental questions to be asked, key voices to be listened to, and why the meaning and nature of ultimate reality matter to each one of us. For it is inevitable that each one of us will, at some time and at some level, have to wrestle with the fundamental questions of our existence. Are we meant to be here, or is it really by accident that we are? In what sense, if any, do we matter, or are we simply rather insignificant specks inhabiting an insubstantial corner of our galaxy? Is there a purpose in it all? And if indeed it does matter, where would we find reliable answers to these questions?

In Book 1, *Being Truly Human*, we consider questions surrounding the value of humans. Besides thinking about human freedom and the dangerous way it is often devalued, we consider the nature and basis of morality and how other moralities compare with one another. For any discussion of the freedom humans have to choose raises the question of the power we wield over other humans and also over nature, sometimes with disastrous consequences. What should guide our use of power? What, if anything, should limit our choices, and to what extent can our choices keep us from fulfilling our full potential and destiny?

The realities of these issues bring before us another problem. It is not the case that, having developed a worldview, life will unfold before us automatically and with no new choices. Quite the opposite. All of us from childhood onward are increasingly faced with the practical necessity of making ethical decisions about right and wrong, fairness and injustice, truth and falsity. Such decisions not only affect our individual relationships with people in our immediate circle: eventually they play their part in developing the social and moral tone of each nation and, indeed, of the world. We need, therefore, all the help we can get in learning how to make truly ethical decisions.

But ethical theory inevitably makes us ask what is the ultimate authority behind ethics. Who or what has the authority to tell us: you ought to do this, or you ought not to do that? If we cannot answer that question satisfactorily, the ethical theory we are following lacks a sufficiently solid and effective base. Ultimately, the answer to this question unavoidably leads us to the wider philosophical question: how are we related to the universe of which we form a part? What is the nature of ultimate reality? Is there a creator who made us and built into us our moral awareness, and requires us to live according to his laws? Or, are human beings the product of mindless, amoral forces that care nothing about ethics, so that as a human race we are left to make up our own ethical rules as best we can, and try to get as much general agreement to them as we can manage, either by persuasion or even, regretfully, by force?

For this reason, we have devoted Book 2, *Finding Ultimate Reality*, to a discussion of Ultimate Reality; and for comparison we have selected views and beliefs drawn from various parts of the world and from different centuries: the Indian philosophy of Shankara; the natural and moral philosophies of the ancient Greeks, with one example of Greek mysticism; modern atheism and naturalism; and finally, Christian theism.

The perusal of such widely differing views, however, naturally provokes further questions: how can we know which of them, if any, is true? And what is truth anyway? Is there such a thing as absolute truth? And how should we recognise it, even if we encountered it? That, of course, raises the fundamental question that affects not only scientific and philosophical theories, but our day-to-day experience as well: how do we know anything?

The part of philosophy that deals with these questions is known as epistemology, and to it we devote Book 3, *Questioning Our Knowledge*. Here we pay special attention to a theory that has found wide popularity in recent times, namely, postmodernism. We pay close attention to it, because if it were true (and we think it isn't) it would seriously affect not only ethics, but science and the interpretation of literature.

When it comes to deciding what are the basic ethical principles that all should universally follow we should observe that we are not the first generation on earth to have thought about this question. Book 4, *Doing What's Right*, therefore, presents a selection of notable but diverse ethical theories, so that we may profit from their insights that are of permanent value; and, at the same time, discern what, if any, are their weaknesses, or even fallacies.

But any serious consideration of humankind's ethical behaviour will eventually raise another practical problem. As Aristotle observed long ago, ethics can tell us what we ought to do; but by itself it gives us no adequate power to do it. It is the indisputable fact that, even when we know that something is ethically right and that it is our duty to do it, we fail to do it; and contrariwise, when we know something is wrong and should not be done, we nonetheless go and do it. Why is that? Unless we can find an answer to this problem, ethical theory—of whatever kind—will prove ultimately ineffective, because it is impractical.

Therefore, it seemed to us that it would be seriously deficient to deal with ethics simply as a philosophy that tells us what ethical standards we ought to attain to in life. Our human plight is that, even when we know that something is wrong, we go and do it anyway. How can we overcome this universal weakness?

Jesus Christ, whose emphasis on ethical teaching is unmistakable, and in some respects unparalleled, nevertheless insisted that ethical teaching is ineffective unless it is preceded by a spiritual rebirth (see Gospel of John 3). But this brings us into the area of religion, and many people find that difficult. What right has religion to talk about ethics, they say, when religion has been the cause of so many wars, and still leads to much violence? But the same is true of political philosophies—and it does not stop us thinking about politics.

Then there are many religions, and they all claim to offer their adherents help to fulfil their ethical duties. How can we know if they are true, and that they offer real hope? It seems to us that, in order to know whether the help a religion offers is real or not, one would have to practise that religion and discover it by experience. We, the authors of this book, are Christians, and we would regard it as impertinent of us to try to describe what other religions mean to their adherents. Therefore, in Book 5, *Claiming to Answer*, we confine ourselves to stating why we think the claims of the Christian gospel are valid, and the help it offers real.

However, talk of God raises an obvious and very poignant problem: how can there be a God who cares for justice, when, apparently, he makes no attempt to put a stop to the injustices that ravage our world? And how can it be thought that there is an all-loving, all-powerful, and all-wise creator when so many people suffer such bad things, inflicted on them not just by man's cruelty but by natural disasters and disease? These are certainly difficult questions. It is the purpose of Book 6, *Suffering Life's Pain*, to discuss these difficulties and to consider possible solutions.

It only remains to point out that every section and subsection of the book is provided with questions, both to help understanding of the subject matter and to encourage the widest possible discussion and debate.

David Gooding
John Lennox

ANALYTICAL OUTLINE

BEING TRULY HUMAN

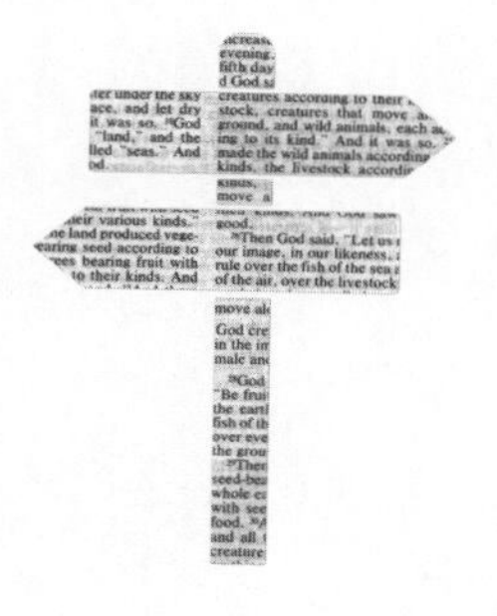

SERIES INTRODUCTION

Our worldview . . . includes our views, however ill or well thought out, right or wrong, about the hard yet fascinating questions of existence and life: What am I to make of the universe? Where did it come from? Who am I? Where did I come from? How do I know things? Do I have any significance? Do I have any duty?

THE SHAPING OF A WORLDVIEW FOR A LIFE FULL OF CHOICES

In this introductory section we are going to consider the need for each one of us to construct his or her own worldview. We shall discuss what a worldview is and why it is necessary to form one; and we shall enquire as to what voices we must listen to as we construct our worldview. As we set out to examine how we understand the world, we are also trying to discover whether we can know the ultimate truth about reality. So each of the subjects in this series will bring us back to the twin questions of what is real and why it matters whether we know what is real. We will, therefore, need to ask as we conclude this introductory section what we mean by 'reality' and then to ask: what is the nature of ultimate reality?[1]

WHY WE NEED A WORLDVIEW

There is a tendency in our modern world for education to become a matter of increasing specialisation. The vast increase of knowledge during the past century means that unless we specialise in this or that topic it is very difficult to keep up with, and grasp the significance of, the ever-increasing flood of new discoveries. In one sense this is to be welcomed because it is the result of something that in itself is one of the marvels of our modern world, namely, the fantastic progress of science and technology.

But while that is so, it is good to remind ourselves that true education has a much wider objective than this. If, for instance, we are to understand the progress of our modern world, we must see it against

[1] Please note this Introduction is the same for each book in the series, except for the final section—Our Aim.

the background of the traditions we have inherited from the past and that will mean that we need to have a good grasp of history.

Sometimes we forget that ancient philosophers faced and thought deeply about the basic philosophical principles that underlie all science and came up with answers from which we can still profit. If we forget this, we might spend a lot of time and effort thinking through the same problems and not coming up with as good answers as they did.

Moreover, the role of education is surely to try and understand how all the various fields of knowledge and experience in life fit together. To understand a grand painting one needs to see the picture as a whole and understand the interrelationship of all its details and not simply concentrate on one of its features.

Moreover, while we rightly insist on the objectivity of science we must not forget that it is we who are doing the science. And therefore, sooner or later, we must come to ask how we ourselves fit into the universe that we are studying. We must not allow ourselves to become so engrossed in our material world and its related technologies that we neglect our fellow human beings; for they, as we shall later see, are more important than the rest of the universe put together.[2] The study of ourselves and our fellow human beings will, of course, take more than a knowledge of science. It will involve the worlds of philosophy, sociology, literature, art, music, history and much more besides.

Educationally, therefore, it is an important thing to remember—and a thrilling thing to discover—the interrelation and the unity of all knowledge. Take, for example, what it means to know what a rose is: *What is the truth about a rose?*

To answer the question adequately, we shall have to consult a whole array of people. First the scientists. We begin with the *botanists*, who are constantly compiling and revising lists of all the known plants and flowers in the world and then classifying them in terms of families and groups. They help us to appreciate our rose by telling us what family it belongs to and what are its distinctive features.

Next, the *plant breeders* and *gardeners* will inform us of the history of our particular rose, how it was bred from other kinds, and the conditions under which its sort can best be cultivated.

---

2 Especially in Book 1 of this series, *Being Truly Human*.

FIGURE I.1. A Rose.

In William Shakespeare's play *Romeo and Juliet*, the beloved dismisses the fact that her lover is from the rival house of Montague, invoking the beauty of one of the best known and most favourite flowers in the world: 'What's in a name? that which we call a rose / By any other name would smell as sweet'.

Reproduced with permission of ©iStock/OGphoto.

Then, the *chemists, biochemists, biologists* and *geneticists* will tell us about the chemical and biochemical constituents of our rose and the bewildering complexities of its cells, those micro-miniaturised factories which embody mechanisms more complicated than any built by human beings, and yet so tiny that we need highly specialised equipment to see them. They will tell us about the vast coded database of genetic information which the cell factories use in order to produce the building blocks of the rose. They will describe, among a host of other things, the processes by which the rose lives: how it photosynthesises sunlight into sugar-borne energy and the mechanisms by which it is pollinated and propagated.

After that, the *physicists* and *cosmologists* will tell us that the chemicals of which our rose is composed are made up of atoms which themselves are built from various particles like electrons, protons and neutrons. They will give us their account of where the basic material in the universe comes from and how it was formed. If we ask how such knowledge helps us to understand roses, the cosmologists may well point out that our earth is the only planet in our solar system that is able to grow roses! In that respect, as in a multitude of other respects, our planet is very special—and that is surely something to be wondered at.

But when the botanists, plant breeders, gardeners, chemists, biochemists, physicists and cosmologists have told us all they can, and it is a great deal which would fill many volumes, even then many of us will feel that they will scarcely have begun to tell us the truth about roses. Indeed, they have not explained what perhaps most of us would think is the most important thing about roses: the beauty of their form, colour and fragrance.

Now here is a very significant thing: scientists can explain the astonishing complexity of the mechanisms which lie behind our senses of vision and smell that enable us to see roses and detect their scent. But we don't need to ask the scientists whether we ought to consider roses beautiful or not: we can see and smell that for ourselves! We perceive this by *intuition*. We just look at the rose and we can at once see that it is beautiful. We do not need anyone to tell us that it is beautiful. If anyone were so foolish as to suggest that because science cannot measure beauty, therefore beauty does not exist, we should simply say: 'Don't be silly.'

But the perception of beauty does not rest on our own intuition alone. We could also consult the *artists*. With their highly developed sense of colour, light and form, they will help us to perceive a depth and intensity of beauty in a rose that otherwise we might miss. They can educate our eyes.

Likewise, there are the *poets*. They, with their finely honed ability as word artists, will use imagery, metaphor, allusion, rhythm and rhyme to help us formulate and articulate the feelings we experience when we look at roses, feelings that otherwise might remain vague and difficult to express.

Finally, if we wanted to pursue this matter of the beauty of a rose deeper still, we could talk to the *philosophers*, especially experts in aesthetics. For each of us, perceiving that a rose is beautiful is a highly subjective experience, something that we see and feel at a deep level inside ourselves. Nevertheless, when we show a rose to other people, we expect them too to agree that it is beautiful. They usually have no difficulty in doing so.

From this it would seem that, though the appreciation of beauty is a highly subjective experience, yet we observe:

1. there are some objective criteria for deciding what is beautiful and what is not;
2. there is in each person an inbuilt aesthetic sense, a capacity for perceiving beauty; and
3. where some people cannot, or will not, see beauty, in, say,

a rose, or will even prefer ugliness, it must be that their internal capacity for seeing beauty is defective or damaged in some way, as, for instance, by colour blindness or defective shape recognition, or through some psychological disorder (like, for instance, people who revel in cruelty, rather than in kindness).

Now by this time we may think that we have exhausted the truth about roses; but of course we haven't. We have thought about the scientific explanation of roses. We have then considered the value we place on them, their beauty and what they mean to us. But precisely because they have meaning and value, they raise another group of questions about the moral, ethical and eventually spiritual significance of what we do with them. Consider, for instance, the following situations:

First, a woman has used what little spare money she had to buy some roses. She likes roses intensely and wants to keep them as long as she can. But a poor neighbour of hers is sick, and she gets a strong feeling that she ought to give at least some of these roses to her sick neighbour. So now she has two conflicting instincts within her:

1. an instinct of self-interest: a strong desire to keep the roses for herself, and
2. an instinctive sense of duty: she ought to love her neighbour as herself, and therefore give her roses to her neighbour.

Questions arise. Where do these instincts come from? And how shall she decide between them? Some might argue that her selfish desire to keep the roses is simply the expression of the blind, but powerful, basic driving force of evolution: self-propagation. But the altruistic sense of duty to help her neighbour at the expense of loss to herself—where does that come from? Why ought she to obey it? She has a further problem: she must decide one way or the other. She cannot wait for scientists or philosophers, or indeed anyone else, to help her. She has to commit herself to some course of action. How and on what grounds should she decide between the two competing urges?

Second, a man likes roses, but he has no money to buy them. He sees that he could steal roses from someone else's garden in such a way that he could be certain that he would never be found out. Would it be wrong to steal them? If neither the owner of the roses, nor the police, nor the courts would ever find out that he stole them, why shouldn't he steal them? Who has the right to say that it is wrong to steal?

Third, a man repeatedly gives bunches of roses to a woman whose husband is abroad on business. The suspicion is that he is giving her roses in order to tempt her to be disloyal to her husband. That would be adultery. Is adultery wrong? Always wrong? Who has the right to say so?

Now to answer questions like these in the first, second, and third situations thoroughly and adequately we must ask and answer the most fundamental questions that we can ask about roses (and indeed about anything else).

Where do roses come from? We human beings did not create them (and are still far from being able to create anything like them). Is there a God who designed and created them? Is he their ultimate owner, who has the right to lay down the rules as to how we should use them?

Or did roses simply evolve out of eternally existing inorganic matter, without any plan or purpose behind them, and without any ultimate owner to lay down the rules as to how they ought to be used? And if so, is the individual himself free to do what he likes, so long as no one finds out?

So far, then, we have been answering the simple question 'What is the truth about a rose?' and we have found that to answer it adequately we have had to draw on, not one source of knowledge, like science or literature, but on many. Even the consideration of roses has led to deep and fundamental questions about the world beyond the roses.

It is our answers to these questions which combine to shape the framework into which we fit all of our knowledge of other things. That framework, which consists of those ideas, conscious or unconscious, which all of us have about the basic nature of the world and of ourselves and of society, is called our worldview. It includes our views, however ill or well thought out, right or wrong, about the hard yet fascinating questions of existence and life: What am I to make of the universe? Where did it come from? Who am I? Where did I come from? How do I know things? Do I have any significance? Do I have any duty? Our worldview is the big picture into which we fit everything else. It is the lens through which we look to try to make sense of the world.

Our worldview is the big picture into which we fit everything else. It is the lens through which we look to try to make sense of the world.

ASKING THE FUNDAMENTAL QUESTIONS

'He who will succeed', said Aristotle, 'must ask the right questions'; and so, when it comes to forming a worldview, must we.

It is at least comforting to know that we are not the first people to have asked such questions. Many others have done so in the past (and continue to do so in the present). That means they have done some of the work for us! In order to profit from their thinking and experience, it will be helpful for us to collect some of those fundamental questions which have been and are on practically everybody's list. We shall then ask why these particular questions have been thought to be important. After that we shall briefly survey some of the varied answers that have been given, before we tackle the task of forming our own answers. So let's get down to compiling a list of 'worldview questions'. First of all there are questions about the universe in general and about our home planet Earth in particular.

The Greeks were the first people in Europe to ask scientific questions about what the earth and the universe are made of, and how they work. It would appear that they asked their questions for no other reason than sheer intellectual curiosity. Their research was, as we would nowadays describe it, disinterested. They were not at first concerned with any technology that might result from it. Theirs was pure, not applied, science. We pause to point out that it is still a very healthy thing for any educational system to maintain a place for pure science in its curriculum and to foster an attitude of intellectual curiosity for its own sake.

But we cannot afford to limit ourselves to pure science (and even less to technology, marvellous though it is). Centuries ago Socrates perceived that. He was initially curious about the universe, but gradually came to feel that studying how human beings ought to behave

FIGURE I.2. ***The School of Athens*** **by Raphael.**

Italian Renaissance artist Raphael likely painted the fresco *Scuola di Atene* (The School of Athens), representing Philosophy, between 1509 and 1511 for the Vatican. Many interpreters believe the hand gestures of the central figures, Plato and Aristotle, and the books each is holding respectively, *Timaeus* and *Nichomachean Ethics*, indicate two approaches to metaphysics. A number of other great ancient Greek philosophers are featured by Raphael in this painting, including Socrates (eighth figure to the left of Plato).

Reproduced from Wikimedia Commons.

was far more important than finding out what the moon was made of. He therefore abandoned physics and immersed himself in moral philosophy.

On the other hand, the leaders of the major philosophical schools in ancient Greece came to see that you could not form an adequate doctrine of human moral behaviour without understanding how human beings are related both to their cosmic environment and to the powers and principles that control the universe. In this they were surely right, which brings us to what was and still is the first fundamental question.[3]

First fundamental worldview question

What lies behind the observable universe? Physics has taught us that things are not quite what they seem to be. A wooden table, which looks solid, turns out to be composed of atoms bound together by powerful forces which operate in the otherwise empty space between them. Each atom turns out also to be mostly empty space and can be modelled from one point of view as a nucleus surrounded by orbiting electrons. The nucleus only occupies about one billionth of the space of the atom. Split the nucleus and we find protons and neutrons. They turn out to be composed of even stranger quarks and gluons. Are these the basic building blocks of matter, or are there other even more mysterious elementary building blocks to be found? That is one of the exciting quests of modern physics. And even as the search goes on, another question keeps nagging: what lies behind basic matter anyway?

The answers that are given to this question fall roughly into two groups: those that suggest that there is nothing 'behind' the basic matter of the universe, and those that maintain that there certainly is something.

Group A. There is nothing but matter. It is the prime reality, being self-existent and eternal. It is not dependent on anything or on anyone. It is blind and purposeless; nevertheless it has within it the power to develop and organise itself—

[3] See Book 4: *Doing What's Right.*

still blindly and purposelessly—into all the variety of matter and life that we see in the universe today. This is the philosophy of materialism.

Group B. Behind matter, which had a beginning, stands some uncreated self-existent, creative Intelligence; or, as Jews and Muslims would say, God; and Christians, the God and Father of the Lord Jesus Christ. This God upholds the universe, interacts with it, but is not part of it. He is spirit, not matter. The universe exists as an expression of his mind and for the purpose of fulfilling his will. This is the philosophy of theism.

Second fundamental worldview question

This leads us to our second fundamental worldview question, which is in three parts: *how did our world come into existence, how has it developed, and how has it come to be populated with such an amazing variety of life?*

Again, answers to these questions tend to fall into two groups:

Group A. Inanimate matter itself, without any antecedent design or purpose, formed into that conglomerate which became the earth and then in some way (not yet observed or understood) as a result of its own inherent properties and powers by spontaneous generation spawned life. The initial lowly life forms then gradually evolved into the present vast variety of life through the natural processes of mutation and natural selection, mechanisms likewise without any design or purpose. There is, therefore, no ultimate rational purpose behind either the existence of the universe, or of earth and its inhabitants.

Group B. The universe, the solar system and planet Earth have been designed and precision engineered to make it possible for life to exist on earth. The astonishing complexity of living systems, and the awesome sophistication of their mechanisms, point in the same direction.

It is not difficult to see what different implications the two radically different views have for human significance and behaviour.

Third fundamental worldview question

The third fundamental worldview question comes, again, as a set of related questions with the answers commonly given to central ideas falling into two groups: *What are human beings? Where do their rationality and moral sense come from? What are their hopes for the future, and what, if anything, happens to them after death?*

Group A. *Human nature.* Human beings are nothing but matter. They have no spirit and their powers of rational thought have arisen out of mindless matter by non-rational processes.

Morality. Man's sense of morality and duty arise solely out of social interactions between him and his fellow humans.

Human rights. Human beings have no inherent, natural rights, but only those that are granted by society or the government of the day.

Purpose in life. Man makes his own purpose.

The future. The utopia dreamed of and longed for will be brought about, either by the irresistible outworking of the forces inherent in matter and/or history; or, alternatively, as human beings learn to direct and control the biological processes of evolution itself.

Death and beyond. Death for each individual means total extinction. Nothing survives.

Group B. *Human nature.* Human beings are created by God, indeed in the image of God (according, at least, to Judaism, Christianity and Islam). Human beings' powers of rationality are derived from the divine 'Logos' through whom they were created.

Morality. Their moral sense arises from certain 'laws of God' implanted in them by their Creator.

Human rights. They have certain inalienable rights which all other human beings and governments must respect, simply because they are creatures of God, created in God's image.

Purpose in life. Their main purpose in life is to enjoy fellowship with God and to serve God, and likewise to serve their fellow creatures for their Creator's sake.

The future. The utopia they long for is not a dream, but a sure hope based on the Creator's plan for the redemption of humankind and of the world.

Death and beyond. Death does not mean extinction. Human beings, after death, will be held accountable to God. Their ultimate state will eventually be, either to be with God in total fellowship in heaven; or to be excluded from his presence.

These, very broadly speaking, are the questions that people have asked through the whole of recorded history, and a brief survey of some of the answers that have been, and still are, given to them.

The fundamental difference between the two groups of answers

Now it is obvious that the two groups of answers given above are diametrically opposed; but we ought to pause here to make sure that we have understood what exactly the nature and cause of the opposition is. If we were not thinking carefully, we might jump to the conclusion that the answers in the A-groups are those given by science, while the answers in the B-groups are those given by religion. But that would be a fundamental misunderstanding of the situation. It is true that the majority of scientists today would agree with the answers given in the A-groups; but there is a growing number of scientists who would agree with the answers given in the B-groups. It is not therefore a conflict between science and religion. It is a difference in the basic philosophies which determine the interpretation of the evidence which science provides. Atheists will interpret that evidence in one way; theists (or pantheists) will interpret it in another.

This is understandable. No scientist comes to the task of doing research with a mind completely free of presuppositions. The atheist does research on the presupposition that there is no God. That is his basic philosophy, his worldview. He claims that he can explain everything without God. He will sometimes say that he cannot imagine what kind of scientific evidence there could possibly be for the existence of God; and not surprisingly he tends not to find any.

The theist, on the other hand, starts by believing in God and finds in his scientific discoveries abundant—overwhelming, he would say—evidence of God's hand in the sophisticated design and mechanisms of the universe.

We pick up ideas, beliefs and attitudes from our family and society, often without realising that we have done so, and without recognising how these largely unconscious influences and presuppositions control our reactions to the questions with which life faces us.

It all comes down, then, to the importance of recognising what worldview we start with. Some of us, who have never yet thought deeply about these things, may feel that we have no worldview, and that we come to life's questions in general, and science in particular, with a completely open mind. But that is unlikely to be so. We pick up ideas, beliefs and attitudes from our family and society, often without realising that we have done so, and without recognising how these largely unconscious influences and presuppositions control our reactions to the questions with which life faces us. Hence the importance of consciously thinking through our worldview and of adjusting it where necessary to take account of the evidence available.

In that process, then, we certainly must listen to science and allow it to critique where necessary and to amend our presuppositions. But to form an adequate worldview we shall need to listen to many other voices as well.

VOICES TO BE LISTENED TO

So far, then, we have been surveying some worldview questions and various answers that have been, and still are, given to them. Now we must face these questions ourselves, and begin to come to our own decisions about them.

Our worldview must be our own, in the sense that we have personally thought it through and adopted it of our own free will. No one has the right to impose his or her worldview on us by force. The days are rightly gone when the church could force Galileo to deny what science had plainly taught him. Gone, too, for the most part, are the days when the State could force an atheistic worldview on people on pain of prison and even death. Human rights demand that people should be free to hold and to propagate by reasoned argument whatever worldview they believe in—so long, of course, that their view does not injure other people. We, the authors of this book, hold a theistic worldview. But we shall not attempt to force our view down anybody's throat. We come from a tradition whose basic principle is 'Let everyone be persuaded in his own mind.'

So we must all make up our own minds and form our own worldview. In the process of doing so there are a number of voices that we must listen to.

The voice of intuition

The first voice we must listen to is intuition. There are things in life that we see and know, not as the result of lengthy philosophical reasoning, nor as a result of rigorous scientific experimentation, but by direct, instinctive intuition. We 'see' that a rose is beautiful. We instinctively 'know' that child abuse is wrong. A scientist can sometimes 'see' what the solution to a problem is going to be even before he has worked out the scientific technique that will eventually provide formal proof of it.

A few scientists and philosophers still try to persuade us that the laws of cause and effect operating in the human brain are completely deterministic so that our decisions are predetermined: real choice is not possible. But, say what they will, we ourselves intuitively know that we do have the ability to make a free choice, whether, say, to read a book, or to go for a walk, whether to tell the truth or to tell a lie. We know we are free to take either course of action, and everyone else knows it too, and acts accordingly. This freedom is such a part of our innate concept of human dignity and value that we (for the most part) insist on being treated as responsible human beings and on treating others as such. For that reason, if we commit a crime, the magistrate will first enquire (*a*) if, when we committed the crime, we knew we were doing wrong; and (*b*) whether or not we were acting under duress. The answer to these questions will determine the verdict.

We must, therefore, give due attention to intuition, and not allow ourselves to be persuaded by pseudo-intellectual arguments to deny (or affirm) what we intuitively know to be true (or false).

On the other hand, intuition has its limits. It can be mistaken. When ancient scientists first suggested that the world was a sphere, even some otherwise great thinkers rejected the idea. They intuitively felt that it was absurd to think that there were human beings on the opposite side of the earth to us, walking 'upside-down', their feet pointed towards our feet (hence the term 'antipodean') and their heads hanging perilously down into empty space! But intuition had misled them. The scientists who believed in a spherical earth were right, intuition was wrong.

The lesson is that we need both intuition and science, acting as checks and balances, the one on the other.

The voice of science

Science speaks to our modern world with a very powerful and authoritative voice. It can proudly point to a string of scintillating theoretical breakthroughs which have spawned an almost endless array of technological spin-offs: from the invention of the light bulb to virtual-reality environments; from the wheel to the moon-landing vehicle; from the discovery of aspirin and antibiotics to the cracking of the genetic code; from the vacuum cleaner to the smartphone; from the abacus to the parallel computer; from the bicycle to the self-driving car. The benefits that come from these achievements of science are self-evident, and they both excite our admiration and give to science an immense credibility.

Yet for many people the voice of science has a certain ambivalence about it, for the achievements of science are not invariably used for the good of humanity. Indeed, in the past century science has produced the most hideously efficient weapons of destruction that the world has ever seen. The laser that is used to restore vision to the eye can be used to guide missiles with deadly efficiency. This development has led in recent times to a strong anti-scientific reaction.

This is understandable; but we need to guard against the obvious fallacy of blaming science for the misuse made of its discoveries. The blame for the devastation caused by the atomic bomb, for instance, does not chiefly lie with the scientists who discovered the possibility of atomic fission and fusion, but with the politicians who for reasons of global conquest insisted on the discoveries being used for the making of weapons of mass destruction.

Science, in itself, is morally neutral. Indeed, as scientists who are Christians would say, it is a form of the worship of God through the reverent study of his handiwork and is by all means to be encouraged. It is for that reason that James Clerk Maxwell, the nineteenth-century Scottish physicist who discovered the famous equations governing electromagnetic waves which are now called after him, put the following quotation from the Hebrew Psalms above the door of the Cavendish Laboratory in Cambridge where it still stands: 'The works of the LORD are great, sought out of all them that have pleasure therein' (Ps 111:2).

We must distinguish, of course, between science as a method of investigation and individual scientists who actually do the investigation. We must also distinguish between the facts which they establish beyond (reasonable) doubt and the tentative hypotheses and theories which they construct on the basis of their initial observations and experiments, and which they use to guide their subsequent research.

> Scientists sometimes mistake their tentative theories for proven fact, and in their teaching of students and in their public lectures promulgate as established fact what has never actually been proved.

These distinctions are important because scientists sometimes mistake their tentative theories for proven fact, and in their teaching of students and in their public lectures promulgate as established fact what has never actually been proved. It can also happen that scientists advance a tentative theory which catches the attention of the media who then put it across to the public with so much hype that the impression is given that the theory has been established beyond question.

Then again, we need to remember the proper limits of science. As we discovered when talking about the beauty of roses, there are things which science, strictly so called, cannot and should not be expected to explain.

Sometimes some scientists forget this, and damage the reputation of science by making wildly exaggerated claims for it. The famous mathematician and philosopher Bertrand Russell, for instance, once wrote: 'Whatever knowledge is attainable, must be attained by scientific methods; and what science cannot discover, mankind cannot know.'[4] Nobel laureate Sir Peter Medawar had a saner and more realistic view of science. He wrote:

> There is no quicker way for a scientist to bring discredit upon himself and on his profession than roundly to declare—particularly when no declaration of any kind is called for—that science knows or soon will know the answers to all questions worth asking, and that the questions that do not admit a scientific answer are in some way nonquestions or 'pseudoquestions' that only simpletons ask and only the gullible profess to be able to answer.[5]

Medawar says elsewhere: 'The existence of a limit to science is, however, made clear by its inability to answer childlike elementary questions having to do with first and last things—questions such as "How did everything begin?"; "What are we all here for?"; "What is the point of living?"' He adds that it is to imaginative literature and religion that we must turn for answers to such questions.[6]

However, when we have said all that should be said about the limits of science, the voice of science is still one of the most important voices to which we must listen in forming our worldview. We cannot, of course, all be experts in science. But when the experts report their findings to students in other disciplines or to the general public, as they increasingly do, we all must listen to them; listen as critically as we listen to experts in other fields. But we must listen.[7]

The voice of philosophy

The next voice we must listen to is the voice of philosophy. To some people the very thought of philosophy is daunting; but actually any-

[4] Russell, *Religion and Science*, 243.
[5] Medawar, *Advice to a Young Scientist*, 31.
[6] Medawar, *Limits of Science*, 59–60.
[7] Those who wish to study the topic further are directed to the Appendix in this book: 'The Scientific Endeavour', and to the books by John Lennox noted there.

one who seriously attempts to investigate the truth of any statement is already thinking philosophically. Eminent philosopher Anthony Kenny writes:

> Philosophy is exciting because it is the broadest of all disciplines, exploring the basic concepts which run through all our talking and thinking on any topic whatever. Moreover, it can be undertaken without any special preliminary training or instruction; anyone can do philosophy who is willing to think hard and follow a line of reasoning.[8]

Whether we realise it or not, the way we think and reason owes a great deal to philosophy—we have already listened to its voice!

Philosophy has a number of very positive benefits to confer on us. First and foremost is the shining example of men and women who have refused to go through life unthinkingly adopting whatever happened to be the majority view at the time. Socrates said that the unexamined life is not worth living. These men and women were determined to use all their intellectual powers to try to understand what the universe was made of, how it worked, what man's place in it was, what the essence of human nature was, why we human beings so frequently do wrong and so damage ourselves and society; what could help us to avoid doing wrong; and what our chief goal in life should be, our *summum bonum* (Latin for 'chief good'). Their zeal to discover the truth and then to live by it should encourage—perhaps even shame—us to follow their example.

Secondly, it was in their search for the truth that philosophers from Socrates, Plato, and Aristotle onwards discovered the need for, and the rules of, rigorous logical thinking. The benefit of this to humanity is incalculable, in that it enables us to learn to think straight, to expose the presuppositions that lie sometimes unnoticed behind even our scientific experiments and theories, to unpick the assumptions that lurk in the formulation and expressions of our opinions, to point to fallacies in our argumentation, to detect instances of circular reasoning, and so on.

However, philosophy, just like science, has its proper limits. It cannot tell us what axioms or fundamental assumptions we should

[8] Kenny, *Brief History of Western Philosophy*, xi.

adopt; but it can and will help us to see if the belief system which we build on those axioms is logically consistent.

There is yet a third benefit to be gained from philosophy. The history of philosophy shows that, of all the many different philosophical systems, or worldviews, that have been built up by rigorous philosophers on the basis of human reasoning alone, none has proved convincing to all other philosophers, let alone to the general public. None has achieved permanence, a fact which can seem very frustrating. But perhaps the frustration is not altogether bad in that it might lead us to ask whether there could just be another source of information without which human reason alone is by definition inadequate. And if our very frustration with philosophy for having seemed at first to promise so much satisfaction, and then in the end to have delivered so little, disposes us to look around for that other source of information, even our frustration could turn out to be a supreme benefit.

The voice of history

Yet another voice to which we must listen is the voice of history. We are fortunate indeed to be living so far on in the course of human history as we do. Already in the first century AD a simple form of jet propulsion was described by Hero of Alexandria. But technology at that time knew no means of harnessing that discovery to any worthwhile practical purpose. Eighteen hundred years were to pass before scientists discovered a way of making jet engines powerful enough to be fitted to aircraft.

When in the 1950s and 1960s scientists, working on the basis of a discovery of Albert Einstein's, argued that it would be possible to make laser beams, and then actually made them, many people mockingly said that lasers were a solution to a non-existent problem, because no one could think of a practical use to which they could be put. History has proved the critics wrong and justified the pure scientists (if pure science needs any justification!).

In other cases history has taught the opposite lesson. At one point the phlogiston theory of combustion came to be almost universally accepted. History eventually proved it wrong.

Fanatical religious sects (in spite, be it said, of the explicit prohibition of the Bible) have from time to time predicted that the end of the world would take place at such-and-such a time in such-and-such a place. History has invariably proved them wrong.

In the last century, the philosophical system known as logical positivism arose like a meteor and seemed set to dominate the philosophical landscape, superseding all other systems. But history discovered its fatal flaw, namely that it was based on a verification principle which allowed only two kinds of meaningful statement: *analytic* (a statement which is true by definition, that is a tautology like 'a vixen is a female fox'), or *synthetic* (a statement which is capable of verification by experiment, like 'water is composed of hydrogen and oxygen'). Thus all metaphysical statements were dismissed as meaningless! But, as philosopher Karl Popper famously pointed out, the Verification Principle itself is neither analytic nor synthetic and so is meaningless! Logical positivism is therefore self-refuting. Professor Nicholas Fotion, in his article on the topic in *The Oxford Companion to Philosophy*, says: 'By the late 1960s it became obvious that the movement had pretty much run its course.'[9]

Earlier still, Marx, basing himself on Hegel, applied his dialectical materialism first to matter and then to history. He claimed to have discovered a law in the workings of social and political history that would irresistibly lead to the establishment of a utopia on earth; and millions gave their lives to help forward this process. The verdict has been that history seems not to know any such irresistible law.

History has also delivered a devastating verdict on the Nazi theory of the supremacy of the Aryan races, which, it was promised, would lead to a new world order.

History, then, is a very valuable, if sometimes very disconcerting, adjudicator of our ideas and systems of thought. We should certainly pay serious heed to its lessons and be grateful for them.

But there is another reason why we should listen to history. It introduces us to the men and women who have proved to be world leaders of thought and whose influence is still a live force among us today. Among them, of course, is Jesus Christ. He was rejected, as we know, by his contemporaries and executed. But, then, so was Socrates. Socrates' influence has lived on; but Christ's influence has been and still is infinitely greater than that of Socrates, or of any other world leader.

[9] Fotion, 'Logical Positivism'.

It would be very strange if we listened, as we do, to Socrates, Plato, Aristotle, Hume, Kant, Marx and Einstein, and neglected or refused to listen to Christ. The numerous (and some very early) manuscripts of the New Testament make available to us an authentic record of his teaching. Only extreme prejudice would dismiss him without first listening to what he says.

History introduces us to the men and women who have proved to be world leaders of thought and whose influence is still a live force among us today. . . . It would be very strange if we listened, as we do, to Socrates, Plato, Aristotle, Hume, Kant, Marx and Einstein, and neglected or refused to listen to Christ.

The voice of divine self-revelation

The final voice that claims the right to be heard is a voice which runs persistently through history and refuses to be silenced in claiming that there is another source of information beyond that which intuition, scientific research and philosophical reasoning can provide. That voice is the voice of divine self-revelation. The claim is that the Creator, whose existence and power can be intuitively perceived through his created works, has not otherwise remained silent and aloof. In the course of the centuries he has spoken into our world through his prophets and supremely through Jesus Christ.

Of course, atheists will say that for them this claim seems to be the stuff of fairy tales; and atheistic scientists will object that there is no scientific evidence for the existence of a creator (indeed, they may well claim that assuming the existence of a creator destroys the foundation of true scientific methodology—for more of that see this book's Appendix); and that, therefore, the idea that we could have direct information from the creator himself is conceptually absurd. This reaction is, of course, perfectly consistent with the basic assumption of atheism.

However, apparent conceptual absurdity is not proof positive that something is not possible, or even true. Remember what we noticed earlier, that many leading thinkers, when they first encountered the suggestion that the earth was not flat but spherical, rejected it out of hand because of the conceptual absurdities to which they imagined it led.

In the second century AD a certain Lucian of Samosata decided to debunk what he thought to be fanciful speculations of the early scientists and the grotesque traveller's tales of so-called explorers. He wrote a book which, with his tongue in his cheek, he called *Vera historia* (A True Story). In it he told how he had travelled through space to the moon. He discovered that the moon-dwellers had a special kind of mirror by means of which they could see what people were doing on earth. They also possessed something like a well shaft by means of which they could even hear what people on earth were saying. His prose was sober enough, as if he were writing factual history. But he expected his readers to see that the very conceptual absurdity of what he claimed to have seen meant that these things were impossible and would forever remain so.

Unknown to him, however, the forces and materials already existed in nature, which, when mankind learned to harness them, would send some astronauts into orbit round the moon, land others on the moon, and make possible radio and television communication between the moon and the earth!

We should remember, too, that atomic radiation and radio frequency emissions from distant galaxies were not invented by scientists in recent decades. They were there all the time, though invisible and undetected and not believed in nor even thought of for centuries; but they were not discovered until comparatively recent times, when brilliant scientists conceived the possibility that, against all popular expectation, such phenomena might exist. They looked for them, and found them.

Is it then, after all, so conceptually absurd to think that our human intellect and rationality come not from mindless matter through the agency of impersonal unthinking forces, but from a higher personal intellect and reason?

An old, but still valid, analogy will help us at this point. If we ask about a particular motor car: 'Where did this motor car begin?' one answer would be: 'It began on the production lines of such-and-such a factory and was put together by humans and robots.'

Another, deeper-level, answer would be: 'It had its beginning in the mineral from which its constituent parts were made.'

But in the prime sense of beginning, the motor car, of which this particular motor car is a specimen, had its beginning, not in the factory, nor in its basic materials, but in something altogether different: in the intelligent mind of a person, that is, of its inventor. We know this, of course, by history and by experience; but we also know it intuitively: it is self-evidently true.

Millions of people likewise have felt, and still do feel, that what Christ and his prophets say about the 'beginning' of our human rationality is similarly self-evidently true: 'In the beginning was the Logos, and the Logos was with God, and the Logos was God. . . . All things were made by him . . .' (John 1:1–2, our trans.). That is, at any rate, a far more likely story than that our human intelligence and rationality sprang originally out of mindless matter, by accidental permutations, selected by unthinking nature.

Now the term 'Logos' means both rationality and the expression of that rationality through intelligible communication. If that rational intelligence is God and personal, and we humans are endowed by him with personhood and intelligence, then it is far from being absurd to think that the divine Logos, whose very nature and function it is to be the expression and communicator of that intelligence, should communicate with us. On the contrary, to deny a priori the possibility of divine revelation and to shut one's ears in advance to what Jesus Christ has to say, before listening to his teaching to see if it is, or is not, self-evidently true, is not the true scientific attitude, which is to keep an open mind and explore any reasonable avenue to truth.[10]

Moreover, the fear that to assume the existence of a creator God would undermine true scientific methodology is contradicted by the sheer facts of history. Sir Francis Bacon (1561–1626), widely regarded as the father of the modern scientific method, believed that God had revealed himself in two great Books, the Book of Nature and the Book of God's Word, the Bible. In his famous *Advancement of Learning* (1605), Bacon wrote: 'Let no man . . . think or maintain, that a man can search too far, or be too well studied in the book of God's word, or in the book of God's works; divinity or philosophy; but rather let men endeavour an endless progress or proficience in both.'[11] It is this quotation which Charles Darwin chose to put at the front of *On the Origin of Species* (1859).

---

[10] For the fuller treatment of these questions and related topics, see Book 5 in this series, *Claiming to Answer.*

[11] Bacon, *Advancement of Learning*, 8.

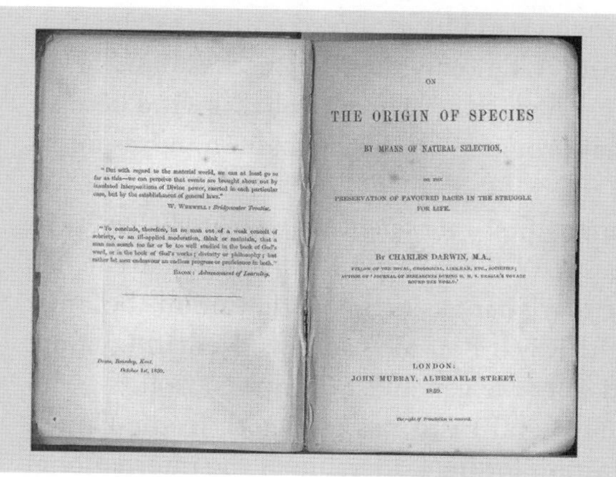

W. Whewell: *Bridgewater Treatise.*

Bacon: *Advancement of Learning.*

ON

THE ORIGIN OF SPECIES

BY MEANS OF NATURAL SELECTION,

PRESERVATION OF FAVOURED RACES IN THE STRUGGLE FOR LIFE.

By CHARLES DARWIN, M.A.,

LONDON:

JOHN MURRAY, ALBEMARLE STREET.

1859.

Figure I.3.
***On the Origin of Species* (1859) by Charles Darwin.**

One of the book epigraphs Charles Darwin selected for his magnum opus is from Francis Bacon's *Advancement of Learning* (1605).

Reproduced from Dennis O'Neil.

Historians of science point out that it was this theistic 'Two-Book' view which was largely responsible for the meteoric rise of science beginning in the sixteenth century. C. S. Lewis refers to a statement by one of the most eminent historians of all time, Sir Alfred North Whitehead, and says: 'Professor Whitehead points out that centuries of belief in a God who combined "the personal energy of Jehovah" with "the rationality of a Greek philosopher" first produced that firm expectation of systematic order which rendered possible the birth of modern science. Men became scientific because they expected Law in Nature and they expected Law in Nature because they believed in a Legislator.'[12] In other words, theism was the cradle of science. Indeed, far from thinking that the idea of a creator was conceptually absurd, most of the great leaders of science in that period did believe in a creator.

Johannes Kepler	1571–1630	Celestial mechanics
Blaise Pascal	1623–62	Hydrostatics
Robert Boyle	1627–91	Chemistry, Gas dynamics
Isaac Newton	1642–1727	Mathematics, Optics, Dynamics
Michael Faraday	1791–1867	Magnetism
Charles Babbage	1791–1871	Computer science
Gregor Mendel	1822–84	Genetics
Louis Pasteur	1822–95	Bacteriology
Lord Kelvin	1824–1907	Thermodynamics
James Clerk Maxwell	1831–79	Electrodynamics, Thermodynamics

[12] Lewis, *Miracles*, 110.

All of these famous men would have agreed with Einstein: 'Science without religion is lame, religion without science is blind.'[13] History shows us very clearly, then, that far from belief in God being a hindrance to science, it has provided one of the main impulses for its development.

Still today there are many first-rate scientists who are believers in God. For example, Professor William D. Phillips, Nobel laureate for Physics 1997, is an active Christian, as is the world-famous botanist and former Director of the Royal Botanic Gardens, Kew in London, Sir Ghillean Prance, and so is the geneticist Francis S. Collins, who was the Director of the National Institutes of Health in the United States who gained recognition for his leadership of the international Human Genome Project which culminated in 2003 with the completion of a finished sequence of human DNA.[14]

But with many people another objection arises: if one is not sure that God even exists, would it not be unscientific to go looking for evidence for God's existence? Surely not. Take the late Professor Carl Sagan and the Search for Extra Terrestrial Intelligence (the SETI project), which he promoted. Sagan was a famous astronomer, but when he began this search he had no hard-and-fast proven facts to go on. He proceeded simply on the basis of a hypothesis. If intelligent life has evolved on earth, then it would be possible, perhaps even likely, that it would have developed on other suitable planets elsewhere in the universe. He had no guarantee that it was so, or that he would find it, even if it existed. But even so both he and NASA (the National Aeronautics and Space Administration) thought it worth spending great effort, time and considerable sums of money to employ radio telescopes to listen to remote galaxies for evidence of intelligent life elsewhere in the universe.

Why, then, should it be thought any less scientific to look for an intelligent creator, especially when there is evidence that the universe bears the imprint of his mind? The only valid excuse for not seeking for God would be the possession of convincing evidence that God does not, and could not, exist. No one has such proof.

But for many people divine revelation seems, nonetheless, an utter

---

13 Einstein, 'Science and Religion'.

14 The list could go on, as any Internet search for 'Christians in science' will show.

impossibility, for they have the impression that science has outgrown the cradle in which it was born and somehow proved that there is no God after all. For that reason, we examine in greater detail in the Appendix to this book what science is, what it means to be truly scientific in outlook, what science has and has not proved, and some of the fallacious ways in which science is commonly misunderstood. Here we must consider even larger questions about reality.

> The only valid excuse for not seeking for God would be the possession of convincing evidence that God does not, and could not, exist. No one has such proof.

THE MEANING OF REALITY

One of the central questions we are setting out to examine is: can we know the ultimate truth about reality? Before we consider different aspects of reality, we need to determine what we mean by 'reality'. For that purpose let's start with the way we use the term in ordinary, everyday language. After that we can move on to consider its use at higher levels.

In everyday language the noun 'reality', the adjective 'real', and the adverb 'really' have several different connotations according to the contexts in which they are used. Let's think about some examples.

First, in some situations the opposite of 'real' is 'imaginary' or 'illusory'. So, for instance, a thirsty traveller in the Sahara may see in the distance what looks to him like an oasis with water and palm trees, when in fact there is no oasis there at all. What he thinks he sees is a mirage, an optical illusion. The oasis is not real, we say; it does not actually exist.[15] Similarly a patient, having been injected with powerful drugs in the course of a serious operation, may upon waking up from the anaesthetic suffer hallucinations, and imagine she sees all kinds of weird creatures stalking round her room. But if we say, as we do, that these things which she imagines she sees, are not real, we

[15] Mirages occur 'when sharp differences in temperature and therefore in density develop between thin layers of air at and immediately above the ground. This causes light to be bent, or refracted, as it travels through one layer to the next. . . . During the day, when a warm layer occurs next to the ground, objects near the horizon often appear to be reflected in flat surfaces, such as beaches, deserts, roads and water. This produces the shimmering, floating images which are commonly observed on very hot days.' *Oxford Reference Encyclopaedia*, 913.

mean that they do not in actual fact exist. We could argue, of course, that something is going on in the patient's brain, and she is experiencing impressions similar to those she would have received if the weird creatures had been real. Her impressions, then, are real in the sense that they exist in her brain; but they do not correspond with the external reality that the patient supposes is creating these sense impressions. The mechanisms of her brain are presenting her with a false picture: the weird creatures do not exist. She is not seeing *them*. They are not real. On the basis of examples like this (the traveller and the patient) some philosophers have argued that none of us can ever be sure that the sense impressions which we think we receive from the external world are true representations of the external world, and not illusions. We consider their arguments in detail in Book 3 in this series, *Questioning Our Knowledge*, dealing with epistemology and related matters.

To sum up so far, then: neither the traveller nor the patient was perceiving external reality as it really was. But the reasons for their failure were different: with the traveller it was an external illusion (possibly reinforced by his thirst) that made him misread reality and imagine there was a real oasis there, when there wasn't. With the patient there was nothing unusual in the appearance of her room to cause her disordered perception. The difficulty was altogether internal to her. The drugs had distorted the perception mechanisms of her brain.

From these two examples we can learn some practical lessons:

1. It is important for us all to question from time to time whether what we unthinkingly take to be reality is in fact reality.
2. In cases like these it is external reality that has to be the standard by which we judge whether our sense perceptions are true or not.
3. Setting people free from their internal subjective misperceptions will depend on getting them, by some means or other, to face and perceive the external, objective reality.

Second, in other situations the opposite of 'real', in everyday language, is 'counterfeit', 'spurious', 'fraudulent'. So if we describe a piece of metal as being 'real gold', we mean that it is genuine gold, and not something such as brass that looks like gold, but isn't. The practical importance of being able to discern the difference between what is real in this sense and what is spurious or counterfeit, can easily be illustrated.

Take coinage, for instance. In past centuries, when coins were made (or supposed to be made) of real gold, or real silver, fraudsters would often adulterate the coinage by mixing inferior metal with gold or silver. Buyers or sellers, if they had no means of testing whether the coins they were offered were genuine, and of full value, or not, could easily be cheated.

Similarly, in our modern world counterfeiters print false bank notes and surreptitiously get them into circulation. Eventually, when the fraud is discovered, banks and traders refuse the spurious bank notes, with the result that innocent people are left with worthless pieces of paper.

Or, again, a dishonest jeweller might show a rich woman a necklace made, according to him, of valuable gems; and the rich, but unsuspecting, woman might pay a large price for it, only to discover later on that the gems were not real: they were imitations, made of a kind of glass called paste, or strass.

Conversely, an elderly woman might take her necklace, made of real gems, to a jeweller and offer to sell it to him in order to get some money to maintain herself in her old age. But the unscrupulous jeweller might make out that the gems were not as valuable as she thought: they were imitations, made of paste; and by this deceit he would persuade the reluctant woman to sell him the necklace for a much lesser price than it was worth.

Once more it will be instructive to study the underlying principles at work in these examples, because later on, when we come to study reality at a higher level, they could provide us with helpful analogies and thought models.[16]

Notice, then, that these last three examples involve significantly different principles from those that were operating in the two which we studied earlier. The oasis and the weird creatures were not real, because they did not actually exist in the external world. But the spurious coins, the fraudulent bank notes, and the genuine and the

[16] See especially in Book 2: *Finding Ultimate Reality.*

imitation gems, all existed in the external world. In that sense, therefore, they were all real, part of the external reality, actual pieces of matter.

What, then, was the trouble with them? It was that the fraudsters had claimed for the coins and the bank notes a value and a buying power that they did not actually possess; and in the case of the two necklaces the unscrupulous jewellers had on both occasions misrepresented the nature of the matter of which the gems were composed.

The question arises: how can people avoid being taken in by such spurious claims and misrepresentations of matter? It is not difficult to see how questions like this will become important when we come to consider the matter of the universe and its properties.

In modern, as in ancient, times, to test whether an object is made of pure gold or not, use is made of a black, fine-grained, siliceous stone, called a touchstone. When pure gold is rubbed on this touchstone, it leaves behind on the stone streaks of a certain character; whereas objects made of adulterated gold, or of some baser metal, will leave behind streaks of a different character.

FIGURE I.4. A Touchstone.

First mentioned by Theophrastus (*c.*372–*c.*287 BC) in his treatise *On Stone*, touchstones are tablets of finely grained black stones used to assay or estimate the proportion of gold or silver in a sample of metal. Traces of gold can be seen on the stone.

Reproduced from Mauro Cateb/Flickr

In the ancient world merchants would always carry a touchstone with them; but even so it would require considerable knowledge and expertise to interpret the test correctly. When it comes to bank notes and gems, the imitations may be so cleverly made that only an expert could tell the difference between the real thing and the false. In that case non-experts, like ourselves, would have to depend on the judgments of experts.

But what are we to do when the experts disagree? How do we decide which experts to trust? Is there any kind of touchstone that ordinary people can use on the experts themselves, or at least on their interpretations?

There is one more situation worth investigating at this point before we begin our main study.

Third, when we are confronted with what purports to be an account of something that happened in the past and of the causes that led to its happening, we rightly ask questions: 'Did this event really take place? Did it take place in the way that this account says it did? Was the alleged cause the real cause?' The difficulty with things that happened in the past is that we cannot get them to repeat themselves in the present, and watch them happening all over again in our laboratories. We have therefore to search out and study what evidence is available and then decide which interpretation of the evidence best explains what actually happened.

This, of course, is no unusual situation to be in. Detectives, seeking to solve a murder mystery and to discover the real criminal, are constantly in this situation; and this is what historians and archaeologists and palaeontologists do all the time. But mistakes can be made in handling and interpreting the evidence. For instance, in 1980 a man and his wife were camping in the Australian outback, when a dingo (an Australian wild dog) suddenly attacked and killed their little child. When, however, the police investigated the matter, they did not believe the parents' story; they alleged that the woman herself had actually killed the child. The courts found her guilty and she was duly sentenced. But new evidence was discovered that corroborated the parents' story, and proved that it really was a dingo that killed the infant. The couple was not fully and finally exonerated until 2012.

Does this kind of case mean, then, that we cannot ever be certain that any historical event really happened? Or that we can never be sure as to its real causes? Of course not! It is beyond all doubt that, for instance, Napoleon invaded Russia, and that Genghis Khan besieged Beijing (then called Zhongdu). The question is, as we considered earlier: what kind of evidence must we have in order to be sure that a historical event really happened?

But enough of these preliminary exercises. It is time now to take our first step towards answering the question: can we know the ultimate truth about reality?

WHAT IS THE NATURE OF ULTIMATE REALITY?

We have thought about the meaning of reality in various practical situations in daily life. Now we must begin to consider reality at the higher levels of our own individual existence, and that of our fellow human beings, and eventually that of the whole universe.

Ourselves as individuals

Let's start with ourselves as individuals. We know we exist. We do not have to engage in lengthy philosophical discussion before we can be certain that we exist. We know it intuitively. Indeed, we cannot logically deny it. If I were to claim 'I do not exist', I would, by stating my claim, refute it. A non-existent person cannot make any claim. If I didn't exist, I couldn't even say 'I do not exist', since I have to exist in order to make the claim. I cannot, therefore, logically affirm my own non-existence.[17]

There are other things too which we know about ourselves by intuition.

First, we are self-conscious, that is, we are aware of ourselves as separate individuals. I know I am not my brother, or my sister, or my next-door neighbour. I was born of my parents; but I am not just an extension of my father and mother. I am a separate individual, a human being in my own right. My will is not a continuation of their will, such that, if they will something, I automatically will the same thing. My will is my own.

My will may be conditioned by many past experiences, most of which have now passed into my subconscious memory. My will may well be pressurised by many internal desires or fears, and by external circumstances. But whatever philosophers of the determinist school may say, we know in our heart of hearts that we have the power of choice. Our wills, in that sense, are free. If they weren't, no one could ever be held to be guilty for doing wrong, or praised for doing right.

Second, *we are also intuitively aware of ourselves as persons, intrinsically different from, and superior to, non-personal things.* It is

[17] We call this law of logic the law of non-affirmability.

not a question of size, but of mind and personality. A mountain may be large, but it is mindless and impersonal. It is composed of non-rational matter. We are aware of the mountain; it is not aware of us. It is not aware of itself. It neither loves nor hates, neither anticipates nor reflects, has no hopes nor fears. Non-rational though it is, if it became a volcano, it might well destroy us, though we are rational beings. Yet we should not conclude from the fact that simply because such impersonal, non-rational matter is larger and more powerful that it is therefore a higher form of existence than personal, rational human beings. But it poignantly raises the question: what, then, is the status of our human existence in this material world and universe?

Our status in the world

We know that we did not always exist. We can remember being little children. We have watched ourselves growing up to full manhood and womanhood. We have also observed that sooner or later people die, and the unthinking earth, unknowingly, becomes their grave. What then is the significance of the individual human person, and of his or her comparatively short life on earth?

Some think that it is Mankind, the human race as a whole, that is the significant phenomenon: the individual counts for very little. On this view, the human race is like a great fruit tree. Each year it produces a large crop of apples. All of them are more or less alike. None is of any particular significance as an individual. Everyone is

FIGURE I.5. An Apple.

Apple trees take four to five years to produce their first fruit, and it takes the energy from 50 leaves to produce one apple. Archaeologists have found evidence that humans have been enjoying apples since before recorded history.

Reproduced with permission of ©iStock/ChrisBoswell.

destined for a very short life before, like the rest of the crop, it is consumed and forgotten; and so makes room for next year's crop. The tree itself lives on, producing crops year after year, in a seemingly endless cycle of birth, growth and disappearance. On this view then, the tree is the permanent, significant phenomenon; any one individual apple is of comparatively little value.

Our origin

But this view of the individual in relation to the race does not get us to the root of our question; for the human race too did not always exist, but had a beginning, and so did the universe itself. This, therefore, only pushes the question one stage further back: to what ultimately do the human race as a whole and the universe itself owe their existence? What is the Great Reality behind the non-rational matter of the universe, and behind us rational, personal, individual members of the human race?

Before we begin to survey the answers that have been given to this question over the centuries, we should notice that though science can point towards an answer, it cannot finally give us a complete answer. That is not because there is something wrong with science; the difficulty lies in the nature of things. The most widely accepted scientific theory nowadays (but not the only one) is that the universe came into being at the so-called Big Bang. But the theory tells us that here we encounter a singularity, that is, a point at which the laws of physics all break down. If that is true, it follows that science by itself cannot give a scientific account of what lay before, and led to, the Big Bang, and thus to the universe, and eventually to ourselves as individual human beings.

Our purpose

The fact that science cannot answer these questions does not mean, of course, that they are pseudo-questions and not worth asking. Adam Schaff, the Polish Marxist philosopher, long ago observed:

> What is the meaning of life? What is man's place in the universe? It seems difficult to express oneself scientifically on such

hazy topics. And yet if one should assert ten times over that these are typical pseudo-problems, *problems would remain.*[18]

Yes, surely problems would remain; and they are life's most important questions. Suppose by the help of science we could come to know everything about every atom, every molecule, every cell, every electrical current, every mechanism in our body and brain. How much further forward should we be? We should now know what we are made of, and how we work. But we should still not know what we are made for.

Suppose for analogy's sake we woke up one morning to find a new, empty jeep parked outside our house, with our name written on it, by some anonymous donor, specifying that it was for our use. Scientists could describe every atom and molecule it was made of. Engineers could explain how it worked, and that it was designed for transporting people. It was obviously intended, therefore, to go places. But where? Neither science as such, nor engineering as such, could tell us where we were meant to drive the jeep to. Should we not then need to discover who the anonymous donor was, and whether the jeep was ours to do what we liked with, answerable to nobody; or whether the jeep had been given to us on permanent loan by its maker and owner with the expectation that we should consult the donor's intentions, follow the rules in the driver's handbook, and in the end be answerable to the donor for how we had used it?

That surely is the situation we find ourselves in as human beings. We are equipped with a magnificent piece of physical and biological engineering, that is, our body and brain; and we are in the driver's seat, behind the steering wheel. But we did not make ourselves, nor the 'machine' we are in charge of. Must we not ask what our relationship is to whatever we owe our existence to? After all, what if it turned out to be that we owe our existence not to an impersonal what but to a personal who?

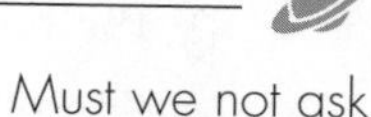

Must we not ask what our relationship is to whatever we owe our existence to? After all, what if it turned out to be that we owe our existence not to an impersonal what but to a personal who?

To some the latter possibility is instinctively unattractive if not frightening; they would prefer

[18] Schaff, *Philosophy of Man*, 34 (emphasis added).

to think that they owe their existence to impersonal material, forces and processes. But then that view induces in some who hold it its own peculiar *angst*. Scientist Jacob Bronowski (1908–74) confessed to a deep instinctive longing, not simply to exist, but to be a recognisably distinct individual, and not just one among millions of otherwise undifferentiated human beings:

> When I say that I want to be myself, I mean as the existentialist does that I want to be free to be myself. This implies that I want to be rid of constraints (inner as well as outward constraints) in order to act in unexpected ways. Yet I do not mean that I want to act either at random or unpredictably. It is not in these senses that I want to be free, but in the sense that I want to be allowed to be different from others. I want to follow my own way—but I want it to be a way recognisably my own, and not zig-zag. And I want people to recognise it: I want them to say, 'How characteristic!'[19]

Yet at the same time he confessed that certain interpretations of science roused in him a fear that undermined his confidence:

> This is where the fulcrum of our fears lies: that man as a species and we as thinking men, will be shown to be no more than a machinery of atoms. We pay lip service to the vital life of the amoeba and the cheese mite; but what we are defending is the human claim to have a complex of will and thoughts and emotions—to have a mind. . . .
>
> The crisis of confidence . . . springs from each man's wish to be a mind and a person, in face of the nagging fear that he is a mechanism. The central question I ask is this: Can man be both a machine and a self?[20]

Our Search

And so we come back to our original question; but now we clearly notice that it is a double question: not merely to what or to whom

[19] Bronowski, *Identity of Man*, 14–5.

[20] Bronowski, *Identity of Man*, 7–9.

does humanity as a whole owe its existence, but what is the status of the individual human being in relation to the race as a whole and to the uncountable myriads of individual phenomena that go to make up the universe? Or, we might ask it another way: what is our significance within the reality in which we find ourselves? This is the ultimate question hanging over every one of our lives, whether we seek answers or we don't. The answers we have for it will affect our thinking in every significant area of life.

These, then, are not merely academic questions irrelevant to practical living. They lie at the heart of life itself; and naturally in the course of the centuries notable answers to them have been given, many of which are held still today around the world.

If we are to try to understand something of the seriously held views of our fellow human beings, we must try to understand their views and the reasons for which they hold them. But just here we must sound a warning that will be necessary to repeat again in the course of these books: those who start out seriously enquiring for truth will find that at however lowly a level they start, they will not be logically able to resist asking what the Ultimate Truth about everything is!

In the spirit of truthfulness and honesty, then, let us say directly that we, the authors of this book, are Christians. We do not pretend to be indifferent guides; we commend to you wholeheartedly the answers we have discovered and will tell you why we think the claims of the Christian gospel are valid, and the help it offers real. This does not, however, preclude the possibility of our approaching other views in a spirit of honesty and fairness. We hope that those who do not share our views will approach them in the same spirit. We can ask nothing more as we set out together on this quest—in search of reality and significance.

OUR AIM

Our small contribution to this quest is set out in the 6 volumes of this series. In this, the first book in the series, we consider questions surrounding the value of humans. Besides thinking about human freedom and the dangerous way it is often devalued, we will consider the nature and basis of morality and how other moralities compare with one another. For any discussion of the freedom humans have to choose raises the question of the power we wield over other humans and also over nature, sometimes with disastrous consequences. What should guide our use of power? What, if anything, should limit our choices, and to what extent can our choices keep us from fulfilling our full potential and destiny?

THE BASIC VALUE OF A HUMAN BEING

If we say that human life is valuable, surely we must mean more than that parents who welcome and love a newborn baby should not destroy it, but parents for whom a newborn child is neither wanted nor loved should be free to destroy it. That would reduce the value of life to a mere matter of arbitrary, personal taste.

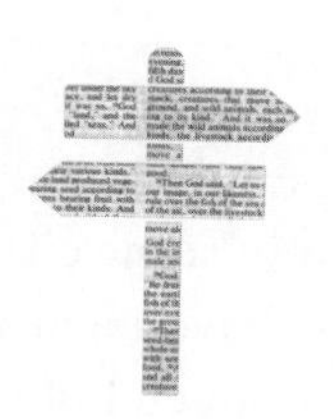

THE VALUE OF LIFE

Without first attempting to define human life—for that could be a long, if not impossible, task—let's begin by asking: what value do we put on human life? After all, we are all human beings, we are all alive, and what is more, we all have direct personal experience of being alive. We ought, therefore, to be able to decide what value we place on human life; our own of course to start with, yet not merely our own, but other people's as well.

And let's be clear what exactly we mean by 'placing value on human life'. We are not asking: how much have we enjoyed living in the past? Or: are we having any rewarding experiences of life in the present? We are asking: what value do we put on human life in and of itself? Is human life, our own or any other person's, so valuable that it would be wrong to mistreat it or to diminish it in any way or to destroy it? The answer to this question is fundamental to our attitude to other people, and likewise to ourselves.

So let's start with a real-life, practical situation that will bring us at once to the heart of the matter.

THE QUESTION OF INFANTICIDE

All of us were newborn babies once, and presumably we are grateful that no one practised infanticide on us. But is there anything wrong with infanticide? And if so, what and why?

In ancient Greece the father (or both parents) of an unwanted child was allowed to take the baby, place it in an open box or jar, and set it on the mountainside to be devoured by wild beasts (they thus tried to salve their conscience by pretending that it was not they who killed the child, but wild beasts). The historians Professor M. Cary and Professor T. J. Haarhoff comment that after 200 BC this way of disposing of unwanted children 'seems to have become frequent enough to keep the Greek population at a stationary level, and even to induce a sharp regression in some cities'.[1] Intentionally or not, infanticide seems not only to have been a means by which a family limited the demands on its budget, but to have become also a way of population control.

The question immediately arises: is such infanticide morally right? The question concerns us, because it is not just an ancient problem. We too were once babies. If for any reason our parents had not wanted us, would it have been morally permissible for them to eliminate us? During the last several decades, hundreds of millions of foetuses, whose brains and nervous systems were already formed, have been aborted because their mothers, or mothers and fathers, did not want them.[2] Were they not also human? And if they were (though many people would deny it), we could ask the same about them: was it morally right to destroy them?

During the last several decades, hundreds of millions of foetuses, whose brains and nervous systems were already formed, have been aborted because their mothers, or mothers and fathers, did not want them.

But to get back to newborn babies, for nobody would deny that they are human beings. Is their life so absolutely valuable that it would be wrong to kill them, even if their parents could not afford to keep them, or if for any reason they did not want them, or if the State wanted to curb excessive population growth?

At the beginning of the last century many people kept a cat to suppress the mice that otherwise would infest the house. Some people still do. If, however, the cat produced a litter of four or five kittens, and the householder did not want them, and nobody else was willing to take them, the householder would put the kittens in a tank of water and drown them. Nobody thought it was morally wrong.

Now many people urge us to believe that human beings are simply animals that by accidental mutation of the genes and subsequent natural selection have by chance evolved further than the other primates. If that is so, on what ground could we say that killing a

1 *Life and Thought in the Greek and Roman World*, 143.

2 This figure is not an exaggeration, as figures from the Guttmacher Institute show. See, for instance, the 2016 article by Dr Gilda Sedgh et al. in *The Lancet*.

newborn kitten would not be morally wrong but killing a newborn human would be? What is so special about a human being?

If, as many hold, there is nothing but matter in the universe, and human beings have no soul or spirit, but just like animals are simply a highly evolved form of matter, then why should newborn humans not be done away with as well as the young of animals? What's the difference?

Someone may suggest at this point: 'The difference is that humans are more valuable than animals, and that's why it would be wrong to kill human babies, or any human beings at all at any time for that matter.'

True: to sense that human life is somehow specially valuable is a good beginning. But the terms 'value' and 'valuable' are commonly used in several different senses. We need, therefore, to examine in what sense human beings may be said to be first valuable, and then more valuable than animals.

THE VALUE OF HUMAN LIFE CANNOT DEPEND ON PEOPLE'S SUBJECTIVE JUDGMENT

Some things have no value in themselves; in regard to value, they are, we say, neutral. They become valuable only when people happen to like them. Take cigarettes, for example. Some people like them; and to these people a packet of cigarettes would be valuable. Other people don't like them; in fact they think they are only worth putting on the fire. To them they have no value at all.

Can that be what is meant, then, when we say that human life is valuable: if people like a certain human being, that human being is valuable to them and they should not destroy him or her; but if people don't like a certain human being, that human being is not valuable to them, and they may eliminate her or him?

That sounds, and is, horrific; but that is how some nations sometimes behave. Many Chinese parents apparently prefer sons to daughters for various reasons. In 1979 the Chinese government, alarmed at the exponential growth of the birth rate, passed a law forbidding parents to have more than one child. There is strong anecdotal evidence that in some remoter parts, if the firstborn child turned out to be a girl, the parents quietly killed her, in the hope that their next child would be a boy. And in ancient times one of the Egyptian pharaohs, wishing to subjugate his serfs, laid it down as government policy that daughters born to the serfs could be saved alive; sons were to be killed at birth by the midwives or drowned in the river.

So if we say that human life is valuable, surely we must mean more than that parents who welcome and love a newborn baby should not destroy it, but parents for whom a newborn child is neither wanted nor loved should be free to destroy it. That would reduce the value of life to a mere matter of arbitrary, personal taste. If human life is valuable at all, one would have thought that it must always and everywhere be equally valuable, no matter whether people like its possessor or not.

But perhaps someone will object: 'Newborn babies and adult human beings are not equally valuable. A fully developed human being is surely more valuable than a newborn, undeveloped baby; and an adult who has, say, brilliant artistic scientific or engineering gifts is more valuable than an adult who has none of these gifts, or may even have a learning disability. Doesn't the general public value a famous footballer or film star more than it does a factory worker, or a disabled child?

Well, we certainly do, and should, value growth in a child, and grieve if a child fails to develop normally; and of course we do, and should, value the skills of a good cook, or trained doctor, and the special gifts of a brilliant teacher, novelist or musician.

But when we acknowledge that we all admire and value gifted people for their gifts, what exactly are we implying? We don't mean, do we, that to qualify for being classed as human, you have to be gifted? Or that the elderly grandmother is less human than a film star? Take the least gifted and least sophisticated person imaginable. Does not that person have human life? And is not that life to be valued and regarded as sacrosanct and inviolable simply because it is human life?

Are we saying that there are different grades of human life, such that the higher grades should be preserved and nurtured, but the lesser grades are scarcely worth preserving and may rightly be neglected or even destroyed?

Or are we saying that there are different grades of human life, such that the higher grades should be preserved and nurtured, but the lesser grades are scarcely worth preserving and may rightly be neglected or even destroyed?

THE VALUE OF HUMAN LIFE CANNOT BE MADE TO DEPEND ON WHAT GIFTS A HUMAN BEING POSSESSES

This, again, is not a merely academic question; for the view that the value of human life varies according to the extent of its evolution has been more than once adopted in the last century on a grand scale with far-reaching results. Let's take some examples.

Hitler's anti-Semitism

Prof. Z. Sternhill has pointed out what value-judgments lay behind and led up to Hitler's extermination of at least six million Jews and several million others. Based on an extreme and perverted view of Social Darwinism (which modern Social Darwinists would decry) people like G. Vacher de Lapouge of France[3] and Otto Ammon in Germany:[4]

> not only asserted the absolute physical, moral and social superiority of the Aryan (which they based on measurements of the skull as well as on other social, anthropological and economic criteria) but also put forward a new concept of human nature and a new idea of the relationships between men. . . . Social Darwinism allied to racism had the immediate effect of desacralizing the human being and assimilating social with physical existence. For such racists, society was an organism regulated by the same laws as living organisms, the human species was subject to the same law as the other animal species, and human life was nothing but an incessant struggle for existence. The world, they believed, belonged to the strongest who was accordingly the best, and there came into being a new morality (which Vacher de Lapouge called 'selectionist') to replace the traditional Christian morality. The idea of the ethnic inequality

[3] *Les Sélections Sociales.*

[4] *Die Gesellschaftsordnung und ihre natürlichen Grundlagen*. See also Biddiss, *Father of Racist Ideology*.

of the different peoples had become prevalent by the turn of the century.[5]

Mixed with Aryan anti-Semitism, it eventually, through a flood of publications in Germany and France, entered Hitler's political thinking, with what results we know only too well.

The massacres in Cambodia

Pol Pot also held the view that some human beings are more valuable, others less. But for him it was the non-intellectuals that were superior and worth preserving. The intellectuals, he considered, were decidedly inferior; and on those grounds he executed about two million of them.

Street children around the world

These are children that are either orphans, or abandoned as youngsters by their parents. They live on the streets, grow up without supervision, make a living by doing simple jobs or stealing, and make a general nuisance of themselves. They are undeniably human. But nobody values or wants them. From time to time the police in some countries drive round the streets and shoot them down like vermin. They are treated as low-grade, and therefore undesirable, human beings.

The physically weak

But we should not confine our attention to these extreme examples. If the value of human life depends on the gifts and abilities of its possessor, or on his or her usefulness to society, and not simply on the sheer fact that it is human life and as such is inviolable, what shall we say about granddad or grandma? They were in earlier life fit and useful members of society. But now their gifts have waned, their health is poor, they can contribute little or nothing to society, they are in fact a burden to their family. In some countries nowadays there is a strong and vociferous lobby that calls on the government to pass legislation to the effect that in these circumstances granddad's or grandma's relatives or doctors or friends are to be permitted to 'help' him or

[5] Miller et al., *Blackwell Encyclopaedia of Political Thought*, 414–16.

her to die. Assisted suicide, it is called. Would that be morally right?

And what about disabled children, or adults with learning disabilities? Does the fact that, though damaged, they are human beings possessed of human life, impose on us, or on the State, a duty to care for them to the best of our ability and resources? Or are we justified in leaving them to rot like animals in squalor?

So far, then, we have raised more questions than we have answered. But already it has emerged:

1. that the value of human life cannot satisfactorily be made to depend on this or that person's, or nation's, subjective judgment. It cannot be left as a matter of someone's arbitrary, personal taste or preference.
2. that it is highly dangerous to make the value of human life depend on the extent of its development or on its 'usefulness' to society.

That being so, let us examine another possibility, namely that the value of human life inheres in life itself and so has objective value.

THE INHERENT VALUE OF HUMAN LIFE AND ITS OBJECTIVE VALUE

If one evening the setting sun paints an unusually magnificent display of colour across the western sky, we might well exclaim, almost involuntarily, 'That is majestic!' What is more we should expect everyone else who saw it to respond to it in the same way. If anyone didn't, we should think that there was something wrong with him or her, colour-blindness, perhaps, or sheer insensitivity. We react in this way because we really do believe that the sunset has intrinsic beauty. It was not our feeling that the sunset was beautiful which bestowed beauty on it. Indeed most of us would maintain that the sunset was beautiful whether we saw it or not.

Moreover we did not come to see it was beautiful by some long, drawn-out process of logical analysis. The sunset by its sheer intrinsic beauty compelled our admiration and acknowledgement of its beauty. Nor did the sunset have to get the consensus-verdict of the majority of our fellow-citizens to the effect that the sunset was majestic, before it could convince us it was majestically beautiful. It convinced us by the unaided power of its inherent beauty.

There are of course many things in nature like that. Some scientists tell us that when they come to perceive how some part of the physical universe works, the sheer sophistication and yet basic simplicity of the laws and processes that govern it fills them with a sense of awe. Their industry, experimentation and logical analysis brought them to the position where they could understand these laws and perceive their elegance. But it was not their industry, experimentation and logical analysis that created these elegant laws. Their beauty was an objective, intrinsic beauty; and it was that beauty that compelled the scientists' awe and wonder. So surely it is with human life: it is life's own objective, intrinsic essence and nature that compels our recognition of its value.

It is life's own objective, intrinsic essence and nature that compels our recognition of its value.

But now we ought to listen to the reductionist explanations of those who would convince us that human life does not actually possess this intrinsic value that we imagine it has.

REDUCTIONIST EXPLANATIONS

Let's go back to the sunset for a moment. The reductionists would tell us that what we took to be its majestic beauty was merely our subjective reaction to material phenomena. They maintain that science can explain how these material phenomena are produced: by solar rays, photons and nerve impulses in the brain; and that science can give a complete explanation of everything about these photons and forces without dragging in ideas of meaning and value and majesty and beauty. And since such things cannot be measured by science, then they have no objective reality. They are merely illusions which we weave around sunsets in our imagination because that helps to soften the impact that the sheer raw, impersonal facts of nature, as revealed by science, would otherwise make upon us.

Reductionists say the same about human life. Human life for them is nothing but animated matter. By its inherent qualities matter spontaneously (though quite unintentionally) produced proteins, cells, genes, chromosomes, that eventually by chance hit upon an arrangement that (without any purpose) produced some lowly form of life, which in turn gradually evolved into human life.

Now this matter and these forces did what they did without any conscious purpose or sense of value. The matter of which genes are composed still has no deliberate aim in mind. Genes have no mind. It is simply that the matter of which they consist has this quality: given a chance, it will blindly take the route of maximising the replication of itself in successive generations.[6]

How then could human life, produced in this way, have any intrinsic value? What is more, if human beings come to feel that human life has some inherent value, they are then told by the reductionists that it is the neurons in their brains that control their emotional reactions and whatever sense of values they have. Sensations of value produced in the human brain by such mindless, impersonal, electrochemical processes—what inherent, objective value could they possibly have?

Not all scientists, of course, are extreme reductionists of this kind.[7] And, in any case, as we approach the central mystery of the human being, that is, how the brain works, how memory functions, the chemical basis of the emotions, and the supreme question of the relation of the brain to the mind, we are grateful for the work of all scientists, whatever their worldview, reductionists included!

On the other hand, when it comes to the understanding of the essential nature and value of human life, we are not dependent solely on science and its empirical methods: we have another, more direct, route to knowledge open to us. We can listen to the voice of intuition.

OUR DIRECT EXPERIENCE OF HUMAN LIFE

An ounce of experience, they say, is worth a ton of theory; and this is especially so when we come to the question of what life is.

---

[6] To describe genes as selfish, as Richard Dawkins does in his famous book *The Selfish Gene*, is highly misleading. In normal language the term 'selfish' implies a self-conscious personality that knowingly asserts itself. Yet this is precisely the quality that Dawkins denies to the matter of which genes are composed.

[7] See the Appendix to this book: 'The Scientific Endeavour', p. 253.

We human beings know by experience what it is to be alive. We do not have to ask the scientist whether we are alive or not, nor what being alive is like. We have direct experience of it. At this level, therefore, philosophical reflection on that experience is more likely to help us grasp its significance than is empirical science. The scientist with his empirical methods endeavours to find out what life is; we live it!

In virtue, then, of this direct experience each one of us knows with utter certainty two things at least. Each can say of himself or herself:

1. 'I am alive', and
2. 'I am conscious that it is I that experience this being alive. I, as the philosophers would say, am the subject of this life; that is, I do the living.'

The same thing is true with thinking. I may feed my brain with information, set it working on a problem, and even when I am asleep it will continue to process this information through its computer-like neurons. But I have to do the thinking and interpret its findings. I cannot leave that to the electrochemical neural processes in my brain. For such reductionism is ultimately suicidal as it destroys rationality, as Professor John Polkinghorne has pointed out. Consider his description of the implications of reductionism:

> Thought is replaced by electro-chemical neural events. Two such events cannot confront each other in rational discourse. They are neither right nor wrong. They simply happen. If our mental life is nothing but the humming activity of an immensely complexly-connected computer-like brain, who is to say whether the programme running on the intricate machine is correct or not? Conceivably that programme is conveyed from generation to generation via encoding in DNA, but that might still be merely the propagation of error. If we are caught in the reductionist trap we have no means of judging intellectual truth. The very assertions of the reductionist himself are nothing but blips in the neural network of his brain. The world of rational discourse dissolves into the absurd chatter of firing synapses. Quite frankly, that cannot be right and none of us believes it to be so.[8]

[8] *One World*, 92–3.

If, then, electrochemical neural events, by their very nature, cannot engage in rational discourse, the 'I', which can and does, cannot be simply a collection of electrochemicals nor indeed matter in any shape or form. The 'I' is what Aristotle saw it was long ago, and what the Bible says it is—soul, or spirit. Human life and the 'I' which is the subject of that life is not reducible to matter; and it is the 'I' within each one of us that asks about the life of which it is the subject: What is human life worth? What am I worth?

And then there is another characteristic feature of what it means to be human. The philosophers call it transcendence; and any one of us can test for ourselves whether this feature really exists.

THE TRANSCENDENCE OF HUMAN LIFE

A moment's reflection will be enough to show us that in our mental life we have the ability to go beyond (for that is what transcendence means) our own life. We can, for instance, forget about ourselves and think about distant galaxies, study them, and not impose our human qualities on them, but allow their characteristics, qualities, functions, the laws of their being, to impress themselves on us, until we come to know them as they are in themselves.

Our love, in the deepest sense, for other people, our respect for them, and our moral behaviour towards them likewise depend on this ability of ours to transcend ourselves, and our own interests and feelings. A dog will respond to you with something that looks very like affection, because it has experienced your kindness and the food you have given it. But as human beings we can admire someone whom we have never met, but only heard about, or seen on television, for what they are in themselves, for their qualities and character, even though they have never done anything for us. In the same way we can admire inanimate things like a sunset or a painting for their inherent beauty.

As human beings we can transcend the matter of which the universe is made, and think mathematically about the laws according to which it functions, acts and interacts.

In thought we can transcend our own present existence. We can envisage the time when we did not yet exist. We can also envisage the time when our life on earth will be over. When we think like that, the question arises: where do we come from? Since our transcendence carries with it an incurable refusal to be content with the brute fact of the present existence of anything, of any activity, or even of ourselves, and irresistibly enquires about the purpose of it, we inevitably find ourselves asking about our own existence, its ultimate purpose, meaning and value. 'Only human beings', say Peter B. Medawar and Jean S. Medawar, 'guide their behaviour by a knowledge of what happened before they were born and a preconception of what may happen after they are dead; thus only human beings find their way by a light that illumines more than the patch of ground they stand on.'[9]

In thought we can transcend our own present existence. We can envisage the time when we did not yet exist. We can also envisage the time when our life on earth will be over. When we think like that, the question arises: where do we come from?

The fact is that we human beings perceive that we are not just matter, we are persons; not just neurons, not just electrochemical events. We are part matter, but also spirit; and because we are spirit we know ourselves to be superior to matter. Any one of us is, in fact, more significant, more valuable than all the mere matter of the universe put together.

It is, then, this transcendence over the universe coupled at the same time with the undeniable awareness that we did not make ourselves, that leads men and women, or at least some men and women, to seek the source of their being in a Creator God who, as the Bible says, is spirit, and who has made us in his image, creatures who are able in part to understand his character, and to love and worship him in a value-response to his perfect goodness.

If this is the truth of the matter it is easy to understand how Jews, Christians and Muslims would answer the question: what is special about human life that gives it its supreme value? It is that man is made in the image of God, by God and for God; man's life is therefore inviolable (Gen 1:26–27; 9:6; Col 1:16–17), and eternally significant (Matt 22:31–32).

---

[9] *Life Science*, 171. As quoted by Karl Popper and John C. Eccles in *The Self and Its Brain*, vi.

Christians would add that the value of a human as a creature of God has been immeasurably increased by the fact that Christ at the cost of his own life's blood has opened up a way by which men and women may be rescued from their deep alienation from God caused by mankind's wrongdoing and sinfulness (1 Pet 1:18–19; Rev 5:9–10).

On the other hand, many people do not believe that human life is anywhere near so valuable as this. Many atheists, in fact, react vigorously against this version of human value. They consider that introducing the concept of a Creator God degrades humans and robs them of their freedom and essential dignity. To that topic, therefore, we must turn in our next chapter.

HUMAN FREEDOM AND THE DANGER OF ITS DEVALUATION

Every human being, man or woman, boy or girl, of whatever race, colour or creed, from whatever part of the world, has a right to be treated as an end in himself or herself, never as a mere statistic, or simply as a means of production, but as a person with a name and a unique identity, born to be free. So we all feel, and so we all say.

FREEDOM: EVERYONE'S BIRTHRIGHT

With all of us, whatever our worldview, freedom ranks among the highest of our ideals. Freedom, we feel, is every human being's birthright: no one has the right to deprive us of it against our will (except, of course, in cases of proven criminality). Even to attempt to remove someone's freedom is a crime against the essential dignity of what it means to be human.

Actually, in the practicalities of life there are situations where we all voluntarily surrender some of our personal freedom for the sake of some common good. We do so in small matters like, say, football (soccer). On the field ten of the players agree to submit to the directions of the captain, and all eleven agree to play according to the rules of the game under the authority of the referee. No player claims the freedom to play according to his own rules: no game would be possible under such conditions. Likewise we voluntarily surrender part of our personal freedom in more important contexts. As citizens of a civilised state, for instance, we voluntarily (in theory, at least) forego part of our freedom as individuals, as do all our fellow-citizens, and submit to the laws of the land for the sake of the higher good of enjoying the benefits of living together in a peaceful and cultivated society.

But when it comes to the right of every human being to his or her essential freedom, all of us, whatever worldview we hold, would agree that this right is, or should be held to be, inviolable.[1] It, therefore, rightly rouses our indignation to see any human being enslaved, treated as nothing more than a cog in a machine, a mere means to the end of another person's pleasure or profit. Every human being, man or woman, boy or girl, of whatever race, colour or creed, from

[1] Perhaps this is an exaggeration. Too often, these basic human rights are not held to be unbreakable, and worthy of respect and protection. In some parts of the world there is still a sorry failure to achieve the four essential human freedoms: freedom of speech and expression, freedom of every person to worship God in his own way and to propagate his faith (or not to worship any god and to propagate atheism), freedom from want, and freedom from fear.

whatever part of the world, has a right to be treated as an end in himself or herself, never as a mere statistic, or simply as a means of production, but as a person with a name and a unique identity, born to be free. So we all feel, and so we all say.

DISAGREEMENT ON THE BASIC CONDITION NECESSARY FOR HUMAN FREEDOM

But when it comes to the basic condition necessary for the realisation of full human freedom, we find that the two major groups of world-views, the theistic and the atheistic, diametrically disagree as to what that condition is.

The fundamental question is this: Is the human race the highest and sole rational authority in our world—or in the universe as far as we know and as far as it affects us? And are humans, as a race, therefore completely free to decide how they shall behave, what is wrong and what is right, what humanity's ultimate values are, what, if any, the purpose of their existence is, and what their ultimate goal, their *summum bonum*, should be? And are they ultimately responsible to none but themselves, with no one to answer to?

Or is there a God who, having created the universe and humankind within it, has the right to lay down, and has in fact laid down, not only the physical laws of nature, the boundary conditions of humankind's existence, but also the moral and spiritual laws that are meant to control their behaviour? And is it so that humanity in general, and individual men and women in particular, are held responsible by this God for the way they behave and will be called upon at last to render account to him?

It is no secret that atheists and theists disagree intensely over this question; but there would be little point or profit in simply noting the fact, or in observing that the disagreement has been accompanied in the past by a certain amount of intolerance. The more rational attitude would be for theists and atheists to attempt to understand each other, not only each other's beliefs, but the deep-seated feelings that lie behind and motivate those beliefs. The resultant growing understanding of each other's position, and of the reasons why those positions are so tenaciously held, should at least remove any blind intolerance and lead to a greater respect for each other as human beings. So let us make the attempt.

THE VARIOUS KINDS OF ATHEISM

The first thing that we ought to do in order to understand the atheistic position is to observe that not all atheists are the same. Atheism, for instance, is not in and of itself necessarily attached to any one particular political philosophy. Some are ardently attached to communism, or socialism, some to democracy of one kind or another, some left wing, some right. In what follows we shall not be concerned with atheists' political preferences, but simply with their atheism.

> The first thing that we ought to do in order to understand the atheistic position, is to observe that not all atheists are the same.

We should next observe that atheists come in different strengths, so to speak.

Some are little more than agnostics who simply don't know for sure whether there is a God or not. They hold that there is no evidence, or not sufficient evidence to justify belief in the existence of a god of any kind; and in the absence of such evidence they style themselves as atheists; and some go further and admit that, if they came across evidence for God's existence that satisfied them, they would accept it and abandon atheism.

Some atheists maintain that it is the scientific attitude to life that compels them to be atheists in spite of the fact that their atheistic interpretation of science attributes a bleak meaninglessness to the universe and to human existence. The humanist Kurt E. M. Baier expresses this attitude well:

> The scientific approach demands that we look for a natural explanation of anything and everything. The scientific way of looking at, and explaining, things has yielded an immensely greater measure of understanding of, and control over, the universe than any other way. And when one looks at the world in this scientific way, there seems to be no room for a personal relationship between human beings and a supernatural perfect

> being ruling and guiding men. Hence many scientists and educated men have come to feel that Christian attitudes towards the world and human existence are inappropriate. They have become convinced that the universe and human existence in it are without a purpose and therefore devoid of meaning.[2]

Other atheists admit that science cannot prove that there is no God; but then they confess that they have an emotional preference for atheism. Isaac Asimov, president of the American Humanist Association from 1985 to 1992, said in an interview:

> I am an atheist, out and out. It took me a long time to say it. I've been an atheist for years and years, but somehow I felt it was intellectually unrespectable to say one was an atheist, because it assumed knowledge that one didn't have. Somehow it was better to say one was a humanist or an agnostic. I finally decided that I'm a creature of emotion as well as reason. Emotionally I am an atheist. I don't have the evidence to prove that God doesn't exist, but I so strongly suspect he doesn't that I don't want to waste my time.[3]

Some atheists are embarrassed by their atheism. The famous French existentialist Jean-Paul Sartre remarked:

> The existentialist, on the contrary, thinks it very distressing that God does not exist, because all possibility of finding values in a heaven of ideas disappears along with Him; there can no longer be an a priori Good, since there is no infinite and perfect consciousness to think it. Nowhere is it written that the good exists, that we must be honest, that we must not lie; because the fact is we are on a plane where there are only men. Dostoievsky said; 'If God didn't exist, everything would be possible.' That is the very starting point of existentialism. Indeed, everything is permissible if God does not exist, and as a result man is forlorn, because neither within him nor without does he find anything to cling to. He can't start making excuses for himself.[4]

Other atheists do not like the term 'atheist', and would prefer some such neutral description as 'non-theist'. The reason is that the

---

[2] 'Meaning of Life', 296.

[3] 'Interview with Isaac Asimov', 9.

[4] *Existentialism and Human Emotions*, 22.

word 'atheism', by its very linguistic formation, contains a reference to, and negation of, theism. It is a negation of (a previously or generally held) belief in God. For that reason Karl Marx disliked the term:

> *Atheism* . . . is no longer meaningful, for atheism is a *negation* of *God* and seeks to assert by this negation *the existence of man*. Socialism no longer requires such a roundabout method; it begins from the *theoretical* and *practical sense perception* of man and nature as essential beings. It is positive human *self-consciousness*, no longer a self-consciousness attained through the negation of religion.[5]

Still other atheists scarcely deserve to be dignified with the term 'atheist', for the simple reason that they have never given any serious thought to the question whether there is a God or not. They have just unthinkingly and without question imbibed a completely secular way of thinking about life and living.

THE MOTIVATION BEHIND DOGMATIC ATHEISM

It is obvious, then, from what we have found so far that it would be unfair to lump all atheists together and to ascribe to all of them the same motivation for their atheistic beliefs, or to suppose that they all hold to their atheism with the same strength of conviction.

On the other hand, when we survey leading atheistic philosophers of the nineteenth and first half of the twentieth centuries, we find a strikingly clear and similar motivation behind their philosophical systems. That motivation has little or nothing to do with science. It is not that science has made belief in God impossible for them, and thereby forced them to work out some completely secular philosophy. It is that they are determined to stand for man's total and absolute freedom and autonomy. To recognise God, or any

> It would be unfair to lump all atheists together and to ascribe to all of them the same motivation for their atheistic beliefs, or to suppose that they all hold to their atheism with the same strength of conviction.

[5] 'Economic and Philosophical Manuscripts', 43.

concept of God as creator and supreme moral authority, would in their opinion degrade man, compromise his freedom and destroy his essential dignity. Therefore, and for that reason, any notion of God must be rejected, and they look to science to confirm them in this stance.

The existentialist Sartre for instance, is very open and honest on the topic. His position is consistently atheistic; but the basis and heart of it is not founded on proofs for the non-existence of God. As we have already noticed, he admitted that for certain reasons the non-existence of God was an embarrassment to him and to existentialists in general. But he makes it clear that even if God existed and were his creator, nevertheless for the sake of man's total freedom to will nothing but his own freedom, in every station of life, man would resolutely stand over against God in radical independence.[6]

It is in this spirit of determined independence of God that in one of his plays Sartre makes Orestes say to Jupiter, 'What have I to do with you or you with me? We shall glide past each other, like ships in a river, without touching. You are God and I am free.'[7]

In other words, it would make no difference for Sartre whether science could or could not prove God's existence or non-existence. The motivating force at the heart of his philosophy is this determination to be absolutely free, in the sense of being utterly independent of God.

But not all atheists were, or are, existentialists like Sartre. So let us look at some characteristic views of other representative atheistic philosophers, drawn from Germany, France and the United States of America; one is pre-Marxist, another is Marx himself, one is another kind of existentialist, and the rest humanist.

Ludwig Feuerbach (1804–72)

> We have reduced the supermundane, supernatural, and superhuman nature of God to the elements of human nature as its fundamental elements. Our process of analysis has brought us again to the position with which we set out. The beginning, middle and end of religion is MAN.[8]

[6] See Sartre, *Existentialism and Humanism*, 51–5.

[7] *The Flies*, 159.

[8] *Essence of Christianity*, 184.

> My fellow-man is *per se* the mediator between me and the sacred reality of the species. *Homo homini Deus est.*[9]

This German philosopher's philosophy had considerable influence on Marx.

Karl Marx (1818–83)

In the Foreword to his doctoral thesis Marx wrote:

> Philosophy makes no secret of it. Prometheus' admission "I hate all gods" is its own admission, its own motto against all gods, heavenly and earthly, who do not acknowledge the consciousness of man as the supreme divinity.[10]
>
> A man does not regard himself as independent unless he is his own master, and he is only his own master when he owes his existence to himself. A man who lives by the favour of another considers himself a dependent being. But I live completely by another person's favour when I owe to him not only the continuance of my life but also its *creation*, when he is its source.'[11]

And, therefore, Marx was not prepared to acknowledge God as mankind's source, creator and sustainer, for to acknowledge any such Being superior to man himself, would be to compromise man's absolute autonomy:

> Religion is only the illusory sun about which man revolves so long as he does not revolve about himself.[12]
>
> Man is the highest being for man.[13]

Maurice Merleau-Ponty (1908–61)

Professor Patrick Masterson comments on the French philosopher Merleau-Ponty's philosophy thus:

---

[9] Latin for 'Man is man's God'. *Essence of Christianity*, 159.

[10] 'Difference between the Natural Philosophy of Democritus and the Natural Philosophy of Epicurus', 15.

[11] 'Difference', 5.

[12] 'Difference', 15.

[13] See 'Difference', 17–19.

> Obviously this metaphysical viewpoint precludes the affirmation of a divine absolute. In particular, Merleau-Ponty points out, it precludes the Christian belief in God the Father as the creator of heaven and earth. Such a belief, he argues, undermines the conception of man as an irreducible source of genuine historical meaning and value and engenders a stoical attitude of unavailing quietism. For it envisages God as an absolute being in whom all knowledge, beauty and goodness have been achieved from all eternity. Human endeavour is rendered meaningless and the *status quo* invested with the stamp of divine approval. No endeavour on our part can add to the perfection of reality since this is already fully realised in an infinite manner. There is literally nothing to do or to accomplish. We are petrified and impotent beneath a divine gaze, reduced to the condition of *visible things*. All our inner resources are alienated by an infinite wisdom which has already disposed all things well.[14]

Christians would doubtless be astonished at this, to them bizarre, description of the effect that belief in God is supposed to have on believers, and will protest that they have never found it so themselves or anything like it. But such a protest is for the moment beside the point. What we should notice in Merleau-Ponty is the recurrence of this idea that belief in God is rejected because it is felt to compromise, restrict, negate and virtually abolish man's freedom and potentiality.

Views of leading modern secular humanists

First, we should notice the significance of the adjective 'secular' in this label 'Secular Humanists'. Humanism of itself stands in an honoured tradition dating from the Renaissance and is exemplified by men like Erasmus and Leonardo da Vinci. It has been, and still is in some countries, applied as a general label to the subjects taught by those who profess 'the humanities', i.e. the study of literature, philosophy, the arts, ancient Greek and Latin language, literature and philosophical anthropology. In a still more general sense nowadays

[14] *Atheism and Alienation*, 143–4.

a sympathetic practical concern for the welfare of others is referred to as humanism. This present series with its 'quest for reality and significance' could rightly be called humanist.

But in the course of the twentieth century, in some countries, and especially in the United Kingdom and the United States of America, the title 'humanist' has been taken over by people in all walks of life—and often in influential academic, teaching, legal and political positions—who hold that mankind can develop its full potential only by denying the existence of God (or, gods), rejecting all religion and supernaturalism, and creating a totally anthropocentric society. Their interpretation of humanism is well summed up by Professor Paul Kurtz: 'humanism cannot in any fair sense of the word apply to one who still believes in God as the source and creator of the universe.'[15]

To save confusion, therefore, throughout the rest of this book the terms humanism and humanist will be used to refer only to this type of secular, atheistic humanism. It is hoped that readers will bear this in mind.

Now let us consider some representative statements of the secular humanist view.

Arthur E. Briggs. '[A] Humanist is one who believes in man as centre of the universe.'[16]

J. A. C. F. Auer (of Harvard University): 'Man would worship God if man felt that he could admire God. But if not, if God fell below the level of moral excellence which he, man, set up, he would refuse his worship. That is Humanism—Man the measure of all things, including religion.'[17]

Blanche Sanders: 'A Humanist has cast off the ancient yoke of supernaturalism, with its burden of fear and servitude, and he moves on the earth a free man, a child of nature and not of any man-made gods.'[18]

Sir Julian Huxley: 'For my own part, the sense of spiritual relief which comes from rejecting the idea of God as a supernatural being is enormous.'[19]

---

15 'Is Everyone a Humanist?', 177.

16 'Third Annual Humanist Convention', 53.

17 'Religion as the Integration of Human Life', 161.

18 *The Humanist* 5 (1945), 226.

19 *Religion Without Revelation*, 32.

It is clear, then, what motivation lies behind these expressions of pre-Marxist, Marxist, existentialist and humanist atheism. Its heartbeat and resolute ambition is human freedom: man completely independent of God and absolutely autonomous; man as the ultimate authority on everything; man as the measure of all things, the centre of the universe. It is this motivation that then demands the denial of God's existence and the banishing of any and every concept of a supernatural creator, since to admit God's existence would compromise man's freedom.

> It is this motivation that then demands the denial of God's existence and the banishing of any and every concept of a supernatural creator, since to admit God's existence would compromise man's freedom.

Here, then, is what many atheists regard as the fundamental, necessary condition for the realisation of man's freedom. What do theists say to that? They do, of course, take it seriously together with its supporting arguments; and we shall presently give a detailed analysis of this 'flight from God', as it appears to theists. But for the moment it might be helpful to make a few comments from a theistic point of view on the atheists' stance so as to clear up some potential misunderstandings before we get down to the detailed analysis.

The cry for freedom

The first thing that theists might want to say is that they, just as atheists, acknowledge, approve of, and value the instinctive desire of the human heart for freedom. In itself that desire is altogether healthy, and, as theists would say, God-given. It is, moreover, both fundamental and central to their experience of God.

Religious Jews, for example, will point to the experience that was the original, formative element in their existence and identity as a nation: their nation's deliverance, which they believe God effected for them, from the slave labour camps of pharaonic Egypt in the second millennium BC. The clarion call of God's prophet Moses to the pharaoh: 'Let my people go that they may worship me' has resounded in Jewish hearts all down the centuries. They have celebrated it ever since in the annual Feast of Passover (Pesach). The faith it has fostered in God as Sustainer and Liberator has maintained their hope during the many oppressions they have since suffered in the course of the centuries at the hands of totalitarian, anti-Semitic governments.

Christians will add that release and freedom are the essential core of the gospel of Christ. They will quote Christ's programmatic statement of his mission:

> The Spirit of the Lord is upon me, because he has anointed me to preach good news to the poor. He has sent me to proclaim liberty to the captives and recovering of sight to the blind, to set at liberty those who are oppressed, to proclaim the year of the Lord's favour. (Luke 4:18–19)

Or they will cite Christ's promise to his disciples:

> If you continue in my teaching, you are really my disciples. Then you will know the truth, and the truth shall set you free. . . . I tell you the truth, everyone who sins is a slave to sin. . . . So if the Son shall set you free, you will be free indeed. (John 8:31–36 our trans.)

> Then you will know the truth, and the truth shall set you free. . . . I tell you the truth, everyone who sins is a slave to sin. . . . So if the Son shall set you free, you will be free indeed.
> —John 8:32–36

It would be pointless for atheists to object that Christ is simply talking about moral and spiritual freedom, whereas what atheists are interested in is real freedom, that is, social and political freedom. If you survey again the quotations from the atheistic philosophers which we cited a moment ago, you will see that when they demand independence of God, it is precisely moral and spiritual freedom that they are claiming for autonomous man. Marx is objecting to God being his creator. Marx demands to be his own master who owes his existence to himself. Julian Huxley is expressing his sense of spiritual relief, which comes from rejecting the idea of God as a supernatural being, not relief at being free to change his political party.

And as to Christians' ongoing relationship with God, and what it feels like to them as they experience it, Christians will affirm as true what the Apostle Paul says:

> For you did not receive the spirit of slavery to fall back into fear, but you have received the Spirit of adoption as sons, by whom we cry, 'Abba! Father!' The Spirit himself bears witness with our spirit that we are children of God, and if children, then heirs—heirs of God and fellow heirs with Christ. (Rom 8:15–17)

When, therefore, Christians hear an atheist like Blanche Sanders talking about casting off 'the ancient yoke of supernaturalism with its burden of fear and servitude', they might well want to ask precisely what version of supernaturalism or religion she is referring to. More of that in a moment.

But with that there comes into focus one major point in the debate between atheism and theism. Both promise freedom. But what does each of them mean by 'freedom'? And which promise carries the greater likelihood of practical fulfilment?

Atheists' criticism of religion

Underlying the atheists' determination to throw off any concept of a Creator God is often their criticism of religion—born out of personal experience, who knows?—as an oppressive enslavement of the human spirit, and a cause of man's alienation from his true self.

The response of a Christian would be to agree with the criticism, to this extent at least, that mere religion, as distinct from a living personal faith in the living God, easily degenerates into a form of slavery. It is most important to notice that the Bible itself points out the danger of this happening. When the Apostle Paul exhorts his fellow Christians: 'For freedom Christ has set us free; stand firm therefore, and do not submit again to a yoke of slavery' (Gal 5:1), the yoke of slavery he refers to is a form of legalistic religion. He earlier describes it as:

> Formerly, when you did not know God, you were enslaved to those who by nature are not gods. But now that you have come to know God, or rather to be known by God, how can you turn back again to the weak and worthless elementary principles of the world, whose slaves you want to be once more? You observe days and months and seasons and years! I am afraid I may have laboured over you in vain. (Gal 4:8–11)

In this area the atheists' mistake, as the Christian sees it, is that in seeking to escape from oppressive, legalistic, superstitious and opiate religion, they reject God who himself denounces such religion.

In this area the atheists' mistake, as the Christian sees it, is that in seeking to escape from oppressive, legalistic, superstitious and opiate religion, they reject God who himself denounces such religion.

The sins and crimes of Christendom

There is no doubt that these have led many people to reject all religion in favour of atheism. The Christian response is to confess them without reserve. They have been inexcusably wrong. Christendom's use of the sword to protect and further Christianity; its torture and burning of Jews and so-called heretics; its fostering of the Crusades, its sack of Byzantium, and slaughter of the Turks supposedly in the name of Christ; its frequent connivance at the oppression of the poor—all these have been wrong and sinful. Nor is it any mitigation of Christendom's offences, to point out that atheistic governments have frequently been guilty of similar oppression. Christendom has less excuse. Its behaviour has been in open, flagrant disobedience to the plain teaching of Christ. It has not been Christian behaviour at all; for Christ himself strictly forbade his disciples to use the sword for either the protection or the furtherance of his kingdom (John 18:10–11, 33–37; 2 Cor 10:4–5).

On the other hand, it would not be fair to blame God or Christ or his apostles for the disobedience and sins of Christendom any more than it would be fair to blame Stalin's purges on the teaching of Marx.

And as for Marx's compassion for, and championing of, the proletariat, true Christianity is no less outspoken in its denunciation of capitalists who oppress their workers:

> Come now, you rich, weep and howl for the miseries that are coming upon you. Your riches have rotted and your garments are moth-eaten. Your gold and silver have corroded, and their corrosion will be evidence against you and will eat your flesh like fire. You have laid up treasure in the last days. Behold, the wages of the labourers who mowed your fields, which you kept back by fraud, are crying out against you, and the cries of the

> harvesters have reached the ears of the Lord of hosts. You have lived on the earth in luxury and in self-indulgence. You have fattened your hearts in a day of slaughter. You have condemned and murdered the righteous person. He does not resist you. (Jas 5:1–6)

And, incidentally, it was a Christian, William Wilberforce, that campaigned for, and achieved, the abolition of slavery throughout the British Empire.

The atheists' claim regarding human freedom

The claim is that the way to human freedom is to reject all man-made gods. Let's return to the statement by Blanche Sanders:

> A Humanist has cast off the ancient yoke of supernaturalism, with its burden of fear and servitude, and he moves on earth a free man, a child of nature and not of any man-made gods.[20]

Jews, Christians and Muslims would unitedly applaud the getting rid of all man-made gods. The worship and service of such man-made gods demeans man and always tends towards his enslavement. But to confuse the true and living, self-existent God, Creator of heaven and earth, with man-made gods, is a category-mistake of the first order. Jews, Christians and Muslims would point out that it is precisely the rejection of the One True God that has consistently, and indeed inevitably, led mankind throughout history to adopt man-made gods, be they physical, metaphysical, philosophical or political, gods that in the end rob human beings of both their dignity and freedom.

FREEDOM AND THE DANGER OF ITS DEVALUATION

Introduction

So far we have listened to a number of atheists telling us in their own words what the motivation was, or is, behind their adoption of athe-

---

[20] See p. 67.

ism. It turned out to be a profound and powerful desire for freedom that would, as they saw it, establish man as independent of any higher power, and thus completely autonomous. To assert and enjoy such freedom, they argued, it was necessary to banish all belief in God.

Now we shall let a theist speak and give his analysis of the human situation. He will argue that rejection of God, far from increasing human freedom, actually diminishes it; leads to an anthropocentric ideology that is pseudo-religious; and implies that each individual man and woman is a prisoner of non-rational forces which will eventually destroy them in complete disregard of their rationality.

The analysis comes from the pen of Paul, the Christian apostle. Paul was a Jew, and in addition had inherited the civic honour of being 'a citizen of Rome'. He was fluent in both Aramaic and Greek, had studied theology in Tarsus and Jerusalem, and had travelled widely throughout the Roman Empire. He thus had first-hand knowledge of the hundred and one different kinds of religion that populated the world of that day.

He had also debated with both Stoic and Epicurean philosophers (see Acts 17). Stoics believed that a creative and controlling Intelligence lay at the heart and centre of the universe and pervaded every aspect of it. This Intelligence, however, was, according to them, part of the stuff of the universe and impersonal. Stoics thus were what we should call pantheists; but they are significant for us today in that they were an early example of the attempt to explain the systematic nature of the world and to develop a thoroughgoing system of ethics without postulating the existence of an other-worldly reality.

Epicureans, on the other hand, were thoroughgoing materialists. According to them there was nothing in the universe but matter and space. Man's body, brain, mind and soul were composed entirely of atoms. At death man disintegrated. There was no afterlife, and therefore, no final judgment (at which thought the famous Roman Epicurean, Lucretius, rejoiced exceedingly).[21] What gods there were—and Epicureans did not deny there were some—were utterly unconcerned with man, his world, and his behaviour. Man was completely free and autonomous. His *summum bonum* was pleasure.

[21] *De Rerum Natura*, Book 1.

From this we may observe that the philosophical materialism that most atheists have adopted in recent centuries is actually no new idea. Some philosophers had in fact advocated it for centuries before Paul was born.[22]

Paul was aware that some philosophers understandably adopted atheism in intellectual and moral disgust at the absurdities and immoralities of the polytheistic idolatry of their contemporary world.

Paul, then, was aware of the highly diverse elements in his contemporary society; and he was far from thinking that all men and women are exactly the same in their particular beliefs, in their particular unbeliefs and in the motivation that lies behind either or both.

He held that mankind's movement away from God began at the very beginning of the human race. He even thought, which may well surprise us when we first meet it, that a great deal of religion with its professed belief in gods and the supernatural had its deep-seated roots in that original movement. He was aware, moreover, that some philosophers understandably adopted atheism in intellectual and moral disgust at the absurdities and immoralities of the polytheistic idolatry of their contemporary world.

On the other hand he recognised that amidst all the welter of contemporary worldviews there were people who were doing their best to discover the truth about God, whether he existed or not, and what he might be like if he existed. This he remarked on to the Stoic and Epicurean philosophers in the Areopagus at Athens, quoting with approval two of Greece's poets, Epimenides the Cretan and Aratus (Acts 17:28).[23]

In his analysis Paul begins with a description of mankind's original flight from God and with the ongoing and increasing effects that it had had on subsequent generations, setting their fundamental pattern of thinking. He was challenging his own contemporaries to examine themselves to see whether they too were pursuing this same flight

[22] Likely in the first decade of the first century AD.

[23] The words 'for in him we live and move and have our being' form the fourth line of a quatrain preserved from a poem attributed to Epimenides the Cretan (around 600 BC, but actually from much later). The phrase 'for we are also his offspring' is part of the fifth line of a poem 'Phainomena' by the Cilician poet Aratus (born 310 BC).

from God that had marked their ancestors and doing so from the same motives. In that challenge he includes us, his modern-day readers.

His analysis forms the first part of a longish letter that he wrote to the Christian community in Rome around the year AD 57. In what follows we shall not attempt to cover the whole analysis; we shall study those of its salient points that are immediately relevant to our present discussion. But here, for the sake of reference, is the text of the whole passage.

> For the wrath of God is revealed from heaven against all ungodliness and unrighteousness of men, who by their unrighteousness suppress the truth. For what can be known about God is plain to them, because God has shown it to them. For his invisible attributes, namely, his eternal power and divine nature, have been clearly perceived, ever since the creation of the world, in the things that have been made. So they are without excuse. For although they knew God, they did not honour him as God or give thanks to him, but they became futile in their thinking, and their foolish hearts were darkened. Claiming to be wise, they became fools, and exchanged the glory of the immortal God for images resembling mortal man and birds and animals and creeping things.
>
> Therefore God gave them up in the lusts of their hearts to impurity, to the dishonouring of their bodies among themselves, because they exchanged the truth about God for a lie and worshipped and served the creature rather than the Creator, who is blessed for ever! Amen.
>
> For this reason God gave them up to dishonourable passions. For their women exchanged natural relations for those that are contrary to nature; and the men likewise gave up natural relations with women and were consumed with passion for one another, men committing shameless acts with men and receiving in themselves the due penalty for their error.
>
> And since they did not see fit to acknowledge God, God gave them up to a debased mind to do what ought not to be done. They were filled with all manner of unrighteousness, evil, covetousness, malice. They are full of envy, murder, strife, deceit, maliciousness. They are gossips, slanderers, haters of God,

> insolent, haughty, boastful, inventors of evil, disobedient to parents, foolish, faithless, heartless, ruthless. Though they know God's decree that those who practise such things deserve to die, they not only do them but give approval to those who practise them. (Rom 1:18–32)

The human race's progressive loss of freedom

Historically, humanity originally knew God and recognised that the truth about the universe and about themselves was that both it and they owed their existence to a Creator God (1:18–21). But humanity deliberately repressed, or stifled, this knowledge of God (1:18); they did not care to have, or retain, God in their knowledge; they did not regard it fitting, they refused, to acknowledge God (1:25). And the next step on this flight from the true and living God was the deification of humans, animals and the forces of nature (1:23, 25), with its resultant polytheism, and devaluing of humanity both spiritually and morally.

It will immediately be objected that the assertion that originally humanity knew the One True God and only later descended into polytheism and animism reverses commonly accepted ideas on the historical development of religion. Before we proceed, therefore, we must turn aside to consider a theory that has been widely influential.

The theory of the evolution of religion

This theory was, of course, widely accepted from Darwin's time up until the middle of the twentieth century, and perhaps still is in some places. It is easy to see how plausible it seemed at first. If humankind had evolved from the lower primates, as Darwin suggested, then it followed logically that humankind's religion must have evolved as well. As Julian Huxley remarked:

> In the evolutionary pattern of thought there is no longer either need or room for the supernatural. The earth was not created: it evolved. So did all the animals and plants that inhabit it, including our human selves, mind and soul as well as brain and body. So did religion.[24]

[24] *Essays of a Humanist*, 82–3.

Indeed, there would, according to the theory, have been a time when early humankind had no religion at all, other than the basic fear of anything strange and threatening such as animals are said to have.[25] After that, so the theory claimed, religion evolved progressively from magic and animism (the idea that there are spirits, or a spiritual force, or *mana*, in everything, that must be treated with religious respect), to polytheism, to henotheism (i.e. one major god per family, tribe or nation) to monotheism.[26] Eventually, many people predicted, monotheism would itself be left behind as evolution carried humankind forward to scientific atheism and to freedom from all religion and irrational beliefs.

> The trouble with the theory is that it was based on insufficient and inadequate fieldwork and was largely speculative and untrue to the facts.

This evolutionary theory became widely popularised by scholars like the famous Sir J. G. Frazer (1854–1941), whose book, *The Golden Bough*, is still in vogue in some quarters even today. The trouble with the theory, however, is that it was based on insufficient and inadequate fieldwork and was largely speculative and untrue to the facts. To take two examples of this:

> When Charles Darwin came to Tierra del Fuego in 1833 he believed that he had discovered an aboriginal people with no religion at all. The tremendous impact that his news had on the British people is still being felt today. And this in spite of the fact that fifty years ago a scholar who took the time to live with the Fuegians and to learn their language and customs reported that the idea of God is well developed, and that there is no evidence that there ever was a time when he was not known to them. His name is Watauinaiwa which means Eternal One.[27]

> An explorer . . . addressing the Royal Geographical Society about his safari up the Nile through southern Sudan in 1861,

[25] What A. C. Bouquet called 'Animatism', i.e., 'belief in a vague, potent, terrifying inscrutable force' (*Comparative Religion*, 42).

[26] The term 'monism' (as distinct from 'monotheism') is used to denote the religio-philosophical idea that all true being is one. This idea pervades much of Buddhism, Hinduism and New Age thinking. 'One thing really exists—Brahman, and there is no second. Like salt in water Brahman pervades the wide universe. The Atman—the principle of life in man—is the same as Brahman' (Eastwood, *Life and Thought in the Ancient World*, 62).

[27] Cited from Newing, 'Religions of pre-literary societies', 14–15.

> said: 'Like all other tribes of the White Nile they have no idea of a Deity, nor even a vestige of superstition; they are mere brutes, whose only idea of earthly happiness is an unlimited supply of wives, cattle and . . . Beer.[28]

Yet perhaps the greatest book written on the religion of a pre-literary society has one of these tribes as its subject matter—*Nuer Religion*, by Professor E. E. Evans-Pritchard (formerly Head of the Institute of Social Anthropology, Oxford). He writes, 'The Nuer are undoubtedly a primitive people by the usual standards of reckoning, but their religious thought is remarkably sensitive, refined, and intelligent. It is also highly complex.'[29]

Equally thorough and patient fieldwork among other pre-literary societies has consistently come up with similar findings. As a result, the idea that primitive tribes had been discovered who had no religion, and that this confirmed the theory of the evolution of religion, has been discredited.

But not only so. The sequence through which, according to the theory, the evolution of religion was supposed to go, from magic all the way up to monotheism, has likewise been discredited. For religion and magic recur to this present day side by side even in highly advanced civilisations; witness, for example, Japan. It is impossible, therefore, says E. O. James 'to maintain evolutionary sequences along the lines adopted by Tylor, Frazer and their contemporaries'.[30]

Moreover, as for the idea that religion eventually evolved from polytheism to monotheism, fieldwork by anthropologists among numerous pre-literary societies has frequently shown that the actual development was the other way round: from monotheism, to monotheism compromised by the addition of lesser gods, to polytheism.

Samples of the worldviews of pre-literary societies

Wilhelm Schmidt (1868–1954) reported that he found among the Pygmies of Central Africa a clear sense of the existence of one Supreme Being to whom all other existences, natural or supernatural,

---

28 Baker, 'Albert Nyanza'.

29 p. 311.

30 *Christianity and Other Religions*, 22.

are subject.[31] He and his collaborators went on to claim that a belief in some supreme being is of almost universal occurrence. It can be found in ancient Egypt, Mesopotamia, Iran and China, but has in each case been combined with, or overlaid by, polytheistic beliefs and practices.[32]

Dr E. K. Victor Pearce reports Evans-Pritchard as remarking:

> Whereas before the 1930s an evolutionary concept of religion was that it developed from animism and magic to polytheism and then finally to monotheism, fieldwork reversed this, and anthropologists now realise that belief in one Creator God preceded all other religious concepts. This gradually corrupted to polytheism, and finally to the placating of an extensive array of nature spirits.[33]

In 1954–55 Dr Leo Pospisil began to study the Papuans of New Guinea. Living in a high mountainous area, cut off from all contact with surrounding tribes, they were unaware of the rest of the world. Theirs was a New Stone Age culture, still in its aboriginal state. In his book *The Kapauku Papuans*, Dr Pospisil gives the following account of their beliefs:

> The universe itself and all existence was *ebijate*, 'designed by *Ugatame*', the Creator. *Ugatame* has a dual nature: he is supposed to be masculine and feminine at the same time, is referred to as the two entities, and is manifested to the people by the duality of the sun and the moon. To my inquiry whether *Ugatame was* the sun and the moon I received as an answer a firm denial. . . . Sun and moon are only manifestations of *Ugatame* who thus makes his presence known to the people. . . . *Ugatame* is omniscient, omnipotent, and omnipresent, credited with the creation of all things and with having determined all events.[34]

---

[31] *Origin and Growth of Religion*, 88, 191 f. and elsewhere.

[32] Schmidt, *Origin and Growth of Religion*, 251 ff.; James, *Christianity and Other Religions*, 51–4, 60–2.

[33] *Evidence for Truth*, 191.

[34] p. 84.

Edward G. Newing gives it as his view, after some years of experience in Africa:

> Most, if not all, pre-literary people have a belief in a Supreme Being which most scholars call a High God to distinguish him from the lesser divinities. It has been argued that 'Pagan peoples have a clear notion of a high god *now*, as fulfilment of a hazy idea *before*' because of the impact of Christian missions. This may be true in certain cases, but on the whole most pre-literary societies' concept of God was quite clear and well-formed before the arrival of the missionaries. True, in the majority of instances he takes very little interest in the affairs of men, contenting himself to play the part of a disinterested observer; yet it is interesting to note that among some of the most backward peoples of the world clear and high ideas of God are to be found. . . . In general the Supreme Being is a sky-divinity. He is the Creator, or Originator of the creation. He is not often worshipped and shrines to him are rare. When all else fails, however, he is appealed to since he possesses power more than any other spirit or man. To trouble him too much, most Africans believe, is only to ask for trouble. For ordinary everyday matters the living dead, nature-gods and manipulation of the *mana* are of far greater importance.[35]

Now these and many other examples of the worldviews of preliterary societies do not by themselves afford cast-iron proof that monotheism was the primitive belief of all such societies. But as Robert Brow remarks: 'original Monotheism gives an explanation of many historical facts which are very intractable on the evolution of religion hypothesis.'[36]

So much then for the evidence gathered from pre-literary societies by trained anthropologists to the effect that an original monotheism was subsequently overlaid by polytheism and animism.

But we have two much more powerful and accessible witnesses to the fact that the ever present tendency of mankind is to fall away from faith in God and yield to idolatry of one kind or another.

---

35 'Religions of pre-literary societies', 38.

36 *Religion, Origins and Ideas*, 13. Here is an example of an abductive inference to the best explanation (see Appendix, p. 253), used here in the field of social anthropology.

The religious history of Judaism and Christianity

Judaism's monotheism, according to their own sacred records, had its roots in God's revelation of himself as the One True God to their progenitor, Abraham, who was called out of his homeland as a protest against polytheism, which in his time had become universal. Yet Judaism, on its own confession, frequently compromised this original monotheism, as not only the people but also their priests lapsed into the idolatry, superstition and polytheism that prevailed among the surrounding nations. Again and again their prophets, like Elijah, Isaiah, Ezekiel and Jeremiah, had to call them back to the worship of the One True God because of their repeated compromises with idolatry, which were eventually brought to an end only by their exile to Babylon.

Christianity in its turn was born in strictly monotheistic Judaism; but in later centuries it exhibited this same tendency to lapse into pagan idolatry (to the great and understandable revulsion of Islam). Among pagan Greeks, men who had been outstanding in their lifetime were after death elevated to the status of being 'heroes'. Cultic ritual was performed at their shrines, prayer was offered to them and miracles were thought to happen in their name from time to time. Christendom eventually adopted a similar practice: outstanding men and women were elevated to the status of sainthood after death; statues were made to them, their shrines and relics were venerated; prayer was made to them, and benefits, if not miracles, expected from them. In some countries to this day one can even find congregations of people who add to their Christian traditions a good deal of outright pagan ritual and practice.

Christianity in its turn was born in strictly monotheistic Judaism; but in later centuries it exhibited this same tendency to lapse into pagan idolatry (to the great and understandable revulsion of Islam).

The theory of the evolution of religion, then, with its idea of the straight ascent from animism through polytheism to monotheism, has not survived the results of rigorous fieldwork and research; and it goes against the trend which we see exhibited by the human heart throughout history. It is now discredited. We can, therefore, leave discussion of it and return to our main theme.

The human race's progressive loss of freedom and its underlying cause

The human race's flight from God, Paul argues, was deliberate. It did not happen through inadvertence or carelessness. They repressed, they stifled, the truth (Rom 1:18). They did not see fit, they refused, to retain God in their knowledge (1:28). Knowing God, they did not glorify him as God, or give thanks to him (1:21).

Those last words in particular, 'or give thanks to him', are a key to understanding their motivation. To thank someone for a helping hand, or for a gift, great or small; to thank a surgeon for saving one's life even; such gratitude can be expressed without surrendering one's sense of independence. With God it is different. Start thanking him, and you will never be done with it. For to glorify him as God is to acknowledge that we are dependent on him for everything, from the planet we live on to the elements necessary for the building of our bodies; for the sunlight and for the ozone which filters out the sun's harmful rays; for the breath in our bodies, the food for our mouths, the circuits in our brains and the intelligence of our minds; for the coding in our cells, and for the moral laws written on our hearts; in short, for life and for everything. To glorify God as God and to render him thanks is to confess, cheerfully and gratefully, our utter dependence on God. And that, says Paul's analysis, is what men have found distasteful and have refused to do.

How true is the analysis? And how far is it applicable to modern humanity? Let's remember what, a few pages ago, we heard Marx say:

> A man does not regard himself as independent unless he is his own master, and he is only his own master when he owes his existence to himself. A man who lives by the favour of another considers himself a dependent being. But I live completely by another person's favour when I owe to him not only the continuance of my life but also its *creation*, when he is its source.[37]

Marx was not willing to acknowledge such dependence on God. Remember, too, how we heard Sartre speak of his determination to stand resolutely over against God in radical independence.

[37] 'Difference between the Natural Philosophy of Democritus and the Natural Philosophy of Epicurus', 5.

But the desire to be independent of God, so Paul held, goes back a long way in human history. It is an essential part of man's fallenness. According to the Bible the initial sin was not something lurid like murder; it came about when man listened to the tempter's voice suggesting that the way to a full realisation of human potential was to grasp independence of God and take the forbidden fruit in defiance of God's warning of its deadly consequences: 'You shall not surely die,' said the serpent, 'For God knows that when you eat of it . . . you will be like God, knowing good and evil' and thus not have to depend on God to lay down what is wrong and what is right (see Gen 3:1–5).

Man succumbed to the temptation, says the story, though still in full awareness of God's existence. It was not that he had come to doubt that there was sufficient evidence to justify continuing to believe in God, and so decided he must take his destiny into his own hands. Even when he grasped at independence of God, he still believed in him—and fled from him, trying to hide from him among the trees of the garden (Gen 3:9–10).

So, in the Bible's account, began man's flight from God. It was the prototype of what would be the behaviour of subsequent generations. Still today many think that if they immerse themselves in the affairs of life, or in the scientific study of the universe, they will be able to escape their innate awareness that there is a God.

> Still today many think that if they immerse themselves in the affairs of life, or in the scientific study of the universe, they will be able to escape their innate awareness that there is a God.

But for a creature to attempt to live in independence of the Creator, is to live at cross-purposes with reality. Which is why Paul's analysis, 'For although they knew God, they did not honour him as God or give thanks to him', follows on with a description of the logical consequence: 'they became futile in their thinking, and their foolish hearts were darkened'. Or as another, vigorous translation puts it: 'hence all their thinking has ended in futility, and their misguided minds are plunged in darkness' (1:21 NEB). That does not mean to say that atheists are not intelligent. They are—many of them brilliantly so. It does mean that their atheism leads to a worldview which, in existentialist terminology, is ultimately absurd, as we shall later see.

The human race's flight from God, says Paul's analysis, was not only deliberate and motivated; it was culpable. 'They are without excuse' (1:20), there is no possible defence for their conduct. How so? Because men and women have shut their eyes and refused to see the evidence of God's everlasting power and deity which lies plain before their eyes, because God himself has made it plain to them. The text runs:

> For since the creation of the world God's invisible attributes, that is, his eternal power and deity, have been clearly seen, being perceived from the things he has made. (1:20 our trans.)

Now the assertion that, by looking at creation around us, everyone can see clear evidence of God's power and deity, is hotly disputed by many. '*We* can't see it,' they protest. 'We would believe it, if you could prove it. But you can't prove it.'

The analysis, however, is very carefully worded. It does not say you can prove God's existence from nature by the abstract reasoning of philosophical argument. It is, indeed, a very sensible thing that it does not say that. Many of God's human creatures are not blessed with highly developed powers of abstract thinking such as philosophy demands. If, then, knowledge of God could be arrived at only by people who possessed such powers of logic, multitudes would be permanently—and highly unfairly—barred from it. In any case, things like the beauty of music or poetry, love and loyalty, are not perceived, grasped and enjoyed only by means of abstract philosophical reasoning. Neither is God's existence.

Things like the beauty of music or poetry, love and loyalty, are not perceived, grasped and enjoyed only by means of abstract philosophical reasoning. Neither is God's existence.

Paul uses two Greek words. One is *kathoraō*, which means 'to observe something attentively with one's eyes'. The second one is *noeō*, and means both 'to see something with one's eyes' and then 'to perceive something with one's mind'.

Thus one could observe a painting attentively with one's eyes, and then perceive with one's mind how magnificent it is, and what a genius the artist must have been to conceive such a grand design in his mind and then execute it with such brilliant success on his canvas.

It is so with the world and the universe around us. The more closely and attentively we look at it, the more clearly we perceive that it is clearly designed. That means it must have had a designer, and that designer not only had vast power, he must have been supernatural, that is, divine. All can see it if they will. It does not take outstanding skill in philosophical logic to perceive it.

But Paul is about to argue that many people do not want to see it. It is not that they can't or don't; it is that, seeing it and then its implications, they deliberately suppress it. Is this analysis fair? Let's recall some modern examples.

Sir Francis Crick, discoverer of the DNA double helix, gives it as his opinion that 'the origin of life seems almost a miracle, so many are the difficulties of its occurring'. Yet he remains a determined atheist and, rather than admit a creator, pushes the problem of life's origin into outer space and suggests life must have originated there and subsequently have been transported to earth.

Professor Richard Dawkins remarks: 'Biology is the study of complicated things that give the appearance of having been designed for a purpose.'[38] So he can see what every human being sees and knows in his heart to be true. But then he rejects the 'Conscious Designer' theory in favour of the bleak theory of natural selection, which he describes as 'the blind, unconscious, automatic process which Darwin discovered . . . which . . . has no purpose in mind. It has no mind and no mind's eye. It does not plan for the future. It has no vision, no foresight, no sight at all.'[39]

Why then, we might ask, does Dawkins prefer the Darwinian to the Conscious Designer theory? For he himself admits that 'it is almost as if the human brain were specifically designed to misunderstand Darwinism, and to find it hard to believe'.[40]

The motivation seems to peek through when Dawkins describes what he thinks might have been the feeling of a pre-Darwinian atheist:

> An atheist before Darwin could have said, following Hume: 'I have no explanation for complex biological design. All I know is that God isn't a good explanation, so we must wait and hope

---

[38] *Blind Watchmaker*, 1.

[39] *Blind Watchmaker*, 5.

[40] *Blind Watchmaker*, xv.

> that somebody comes up with a better one.' I can't help feeling that such a position, though logically sound, would have left one feeling pretty unsatisfied, and that although atheism might have been *logically* tenable before Darwin, Darwin made it possible to be an intellectually fulfilled atheist.[41]

In other words, atheism was the prior, preferred stance. Hume's philosophical argument might have made the position of an atheist logically possible; but it remained a pretty unsatisfying one, until Darwin came to the rescue and made it possible not only to continue to be an atheist, but now to feel oneself an intellectually fulfilled atheist. Atheism, obviously, had all the way along been the a priori preference, in spite of the overwhelming testimony of highly complex design in nature to a Conscious Designer.

We may quote Francis Crick again: 'Biologists must constantly keep in mind that what they see was not designed, but rather evolved.'[42] The evidence for design is apparently so strong that biologists have constantly to make a conscious effort to resist it.

Biologists must constantly keep in mind that what they see was not designed, but rather evolved.
—Francis Crick, 'Lessons from Biology'

The SETI programme, which we discussed earlier[43] sets its radio telescopes searching for any signals from outer space that might be coming from some intelligent source. Their hypothesis is that any signal which could be analysed as a code (and not just noise) would thereby be shown to be coming from an intelligent source. How? Because we know it as a basic fact that blind impersonal matter does not speak intelligent language; only persons do that. All scientists agree with the hypothesis.

But then the DNA double-helix has been shown to be a code conveying complex information. It, too, then, according to the same hypothesis, must have its origin in an Intelligent Source. Ah, but no! This time many people reject the hypothesis. Why? Because this time the Intelligent Source could only be God the Creator.

---

41 *Blind Watchmaker*, 6 (emphasis in original).

42 'Lessons from Biology', 36.

43 Introduction, p. 28.

The famous Marxist geneticist Richard Lewontin explains his position as a philosophical materialist: 'materialism is absolute, for we cannot allow a Divine Foot in the door'.[44]

'They did not see fit', says Paul's analysis, 'to retain God in their knowledge'; and it adds that such an attitude is morally and spiritually culpable: people will be accountable to God for it. In saying so Paul is clearly talking not only about what happened to the early human race, but also about what happens to the modern human race as well.

The human race's progressive loss of freedom and its consequences

We now have ample evidence that the human race's flight from God has in all ages been motivated by a desire for moral and spiritual independence and freedom. But Paul's analysis is about to argue that humankind's flight from God, far from securing them independence and freedom, first devalues them, and then lands them ultimately and inevitably in a spiritual prison. It always has done; it still does.

Paul first shows this was so for early humankind. They grasped at independence of the One True God their Creator, only to find themselves now subject to a whole array of false gods. They had 'bartered away the truth of God for the lie', and now felt themselves compelled to offer reverence and worship to created things rather than to the Creator (cf. Rom 1:25).

At first sight it might seem strange that humankind should so demean themselves; and yet on second thoughts such behaviour is readily understandable. When man was still loyally dependent on God, he knew himself to be made in the image of God. He lived in fellowship with his creator; and since that fellowship was with the eternal God, it had an eternal dimension that even physical death could not destroy (see Matt 22:31–32).

In virtue of this, man knew himself to be superior in rank, dignity and significance to all the mere matter and forces of the universe. It wasn't, of course, that he could control them; he was, scientifically and technologically, still a child. But living in trustful dependence

[44] 'Billions and Billions of Demons'.

on their creator, he knew these forces to be his servants under the control of his Father, God.

But now, having chosen to go his own way independent of the Creator, he found himself increasingly alienated from him. Lacking trustful faith in him, he felt he was now on his own having to cope by himself with these powerful (and to him mysterious) forces on which his life depended and which could so easily destroy him. He must respect them: they were his masters. They controlled him, not he them.

What freedom is it for a rational human being to bow down like a slave to mindless, non-rational matter and forces?

So he deified them. He bowed down to the sun and the moon and the stars, to the mysterious powers of fertility, to the storm, to man's own physical powers of sex or aggressiveness, to blind Fate and Chance. He treated them all like gods. So much for freedom and independence! What freedom is it for a rational human being to bow down like a slave to mindless, non-rational matter and forces?

But he felt he had to. He could not control these forces. The best he could do was to reverence, worship, and sacrifice to the powers of Nature in the hope of persuading, cajoling, manipulating them to be favourable to him. He lived a life, not of freedom as a creature in the image of the Creator, but of servility to the non-rational powers of the universe.

But someone may well ask, 'What has that got to do with us. We don't bow down to, and worship, the non-rational powers of the universe. Thanks to science and technology we understand them. Indeed, we can harness some of them for our own use and betterment, thus lifting ourselves out of the ignorance, fear and superstition of pre-scientific humankind.'

Quite so; and a wonderful epic of human scientific effort and discovery it has been! In spite of all this progress, however, realism reminds us that humankind in the ultimate sense is no nearer controlling the great forces of the universe than ever they were. Take the first essential for the maintenance of human life on earth: light and heat. The source on which we are helplessly dependent for these necessities is not under our control, and never will be, let alone all the other forces and conditions that have been fine tuned to make life on our planet possible. Science itself, moreover, tells us that eventually our sun will explode and in that instant earth will evaporate. It does not matter how far off into the future that event may be: logically, it makes no difference to the fact that human life on this planet as we have known it is a temporary phenomenon; one day it will be a thing of the past. Humankind is only a temporary tenant of earth.

But let's come nearer home: to our own lives here and now as individuals. Ask an atheist what ultimate powers were responsible for bringing him into the world, and what ultimate powers will cause his eventual demise, and the atheist will say (though in much more sophisticated language) exactly the same as the ancient idolater. He will say it was, and will be, the fundamental forces and processes of nature: energy, the weak atomic power, the strong atomic power, electro-magnetism, gravity, the laws of physics, chemistry, biochemistry, physiology and so forth. As Professor George Gaylord Simpson remarks, 'Man is the result of a purposeless and natural process that did not have him in mind. He was not planned.'[45] The atheist will not call these forces and processes gods, nor bow down and worship them. But it makes no difference: in the end, as at the beginning, they control him, not he them.

And the striking, but melancholy, fact is this: the atheist is a warm, feeling, purposeful, intelligent human being. But these forces which produced, and one day will destroy, him, his feelings, loves, purposes and intelligence are, all of them, by the atheist's own definition, non-rational, non-sentient, mindless and purposeless.

The atheist will claim that, in him, matter has evolved intelligence so that he can understand how these powers and processes work—though the powers and processes themselves don't know how they work. They had no purpose in mind—they don't have a mind[46]—when they gave him birth. His existence, therefore, serves no ultimate purpose, and has no ultimate meaning. One day these same mindless forces will begin to destroy him. He will have the intelligence to see what they are going to do to him, but no power to stop them. The final irony will be that when these mindless forces have destroyed him and his

The final irony will be that when these mindless forces have destroyed him and his intelligence, they won't even know they've done it.

[45] *Meaning of Evolution*, 345.

[46] See the quotation from Dawkins, p. 139.

intelligence, they won't even know they've done it. Mindless, non-rationality will have triumphed over human conscious rationality and intelligence.

To a theist, then, the atheist's position cannot but seem self-defeating. He began his flight from God in order, among other things, to be able to give his rationality free rein without being curbed or restricted in any way by having to acknowledge a creator. He then uses his rationality to the full—only to discover that mindless matter and forces will eventually make a mock of his rationality and destroy both him and it without knowing they've done it. To the theist this use of rationality bears out what Paul's analysis says: 'knowing God, they have refused to honour him as God, or to render him thanks. Hence all their thinking has ended in futility.' (Rom 1:21 NEB).

The atheist may well reply that theists die just the same as atheists do. Mindless forces and processes destroy their bodies and brains too.

Yes, but with this difference. The theist knows that she was not the product of blind matter and forces in the first place, but a creature of God, made in God's image. Secondly, she is not just matter, but spirit as well, able to form a spiritual relationship with God that, like God himself, is eternal. And as far as the forces of nature are concerned, Paul who wrote the analysis which we have been considering concludes by saying:

> I am convinced that there is nothing in death or life, in the realm of spirits or superhuman powers, in the world as it is or the world as it shall be, in the forces of the universe, in height or depths—nothing in all creation that can separate us from the love of God in Christ Jesus our Lord. (Rom 8:38–39 NEB)

This the atheist cannot—perhaps does not want to—say. But it leaves him, so to speak, a prisoner in a materialistic universe in the certain expectation that mindless forces will eventually triumph over, and destroy, him, his mind, rationality and intelligence. It doesn't sound much like freedom. Professor William Provine of Cornell University, a leading historian of science, confesses it:

> Finally, free will as it is traditionally conceived—the freedom to make uncoerced and unpredictable choices among alternative

> possible courses of action—simply does not exist. . . . There is no way that the evolutionary process as currently conceived can produce a being that is truly free to make choices.[47]

The human race's progressive loss of freedom and its degradation

According to Paul, man's original flight from God led him into perverse forms of religion: they 'exchanged the glory of the immortal God for images resembling mortal man and birds and animals and creeping things' (Rom 1:23).

At this the atheist may well retort—somewhat triumphantly, perhaps—that this is typical of all religion: it demeans human beings and alienates them from their true dignity with its absurd, degrading superstitions and rituals; and that is why atheism is implacably opposed to religion.

Did not Lenin say:

> Every religious idea of a god, even flirting with the idea of a god, is unutterable vileness of the most dangerous kind, 'contagion' of the most abominable kind. Millions of sins, filthy deeds, acts of violence, and physical contagions are far less dangerous than the subtle spiritual idea of a god.[48]

Other atheists will use milder language; but they will still criticise faith in God and religion as being at best a crutch for weak and inadequate people, a crutch which atheists pride themselves on not needing.

But things are not necessarily quite so simple. Secular humanists (humanist, as we recall, in the philosophical sense) are by definition atheists. Yet in America the 1980 preface to the *Humanist Manifestos I & II* itself announced 'Humanism is a philosophical, religious and moral point of view.'[49]

In 1934 the notable humanist John Dewey, who rejected the supernatural in general and the supernatural God in particular, wrote a book entitled *A Common Faith* in which he stated:

---

[47] 'Evolution and the Foundation of Ethics.'

[48] *Complete Collected Works*, 35:122.

[49] Kurtz (ed.), 3.

> Here are all the elements for a religious faith that shall not be confined to sect, class, or race. . . . It remains to make it explicit and militant.[50]

At the centennial celebration of the publication of *On the Origin of Species* held by the University of Chicago in 1959, Sir Julian Huxley announced in his lecture:

> Finally, the evolutionary vision is enabling us to discern, however incompletely, the lineaments of the new religion that we can be sure will arise to serve the needs of the coming era.[51]

Even Marxism—shocking though that might seem to Marxists—often appeared in the past to outsiders to have the characteristics of a religion. It had a basic creed that one had to take on faith, namely that there is nothing but matter in the universe, which, of course, cannot be proved. It had its gospel for the salvation of mankind: the irresistible law of historical dialectic.[52] Marxism had its Mediator: the dictatorship of the Party. It had its promised land: the eventual advent of full communism, when all oppression, all strife, all alienation, all government would be gone forever; and it had its vigorous missionaries devoted to the spread of the Marxist gospel throughout the world. It also vigorously suppressed its 'heretics', or revisionists as they were called.[53]

Be that as it may. The important thing is not whether it is or is not valid to attach the label 'religion' to some forms of atheism; it is that we should understand why, according to the Bible, suppression of belief in God inevitably results in idolatry.

The reason is this. It is in practice very difficult for a man or woman to place his or her ultimate faith and confidence in nothing

---

[50] p. 87. In more recent years American humanists for various practical and political reasons have dropped the terms 'religious' and 'religion' from their manifestos.

[51] *Essays of a Humanist*, 91.

[52] Cf. N. Berdyaev's remark: 'the dialectical materialist attribution of "dialectic" to matter confers on it, not mental attributes only, but even divine ones'. Cited from Wetter, *Dialectical Materialism*, 558.

[53] Cf. the estimate given by the famous humanist atheist, Bertrand Russell:

> To call these religions [*scil.* Communism and Nazism] may perhaps be objectionable both to their friends and to their enemies, but in fact they have all the characteristics of religions. They advocate a way of life on the basis of irrational dogmas; they have a sacred history, a Messiah, and a priesthood. I do not see what more could be demanded to qualify a doctrine as a religion. (*Understanding History*, 95).

at all, as G. K. Chesterton long ago observed.[54] If they decline to put their ultimate faith in God, they will inevitably put it in something or someone else—or risk becoming thoroughgoing sceptics with regard to life's purpose and meaning and prosperity.

An idol, then, according to biblical definition, is something or someone in whom a man puts his ultimate faith, instead of putting it in God. If then Feuerbach's dictum, 'MAN is man's god' (Feuerbach's emphasis), rightly sums up the essential principle of his philosophy, his philosophy is straight idolatry.

This point was already perceived by ancient writers centuries ago. In the eighth to seventh century BC, for instance, the prophet Isaiah in a series of vivid vignettes describes what was going on in the minds of his contemporaries when they made idols:

> To whom then will you liken God,
> or what likeness compare with him?
> An idol! A craftsman casts it,
> and a goldsmith overlays it with gold
> and casts for it silver chains.
> He who is too impoverished for an offering
> chooses wood that will not rot;
> he seeks out a skilful craftsman
> to set up an idol that will not move.
> (Isa 40:18–20)

> He shapes it into the figure of a man, with the beauty of a man, . . . And the rest of it [*scil.* the tree which he has cut down] he makes into a god, his idol, and falls down to it and worships it. He prays to it and says, 'Deliver me, for you are my god!' (44:13, 17)

Like all people everywhere in all ages, these ancient men and women felt the need for salvation in the broadest sense of that term—in the regular difficulties and crises of life. So they needed a god to save them, and they set about making one. Now, of course, they had their concepts of the qualities that their god would need to have, in

[54] The quote that is commonly attributed to Chesterton: 'When a man stops believing in God he doesn't then believe in nothing, he believes anything,' is drawn from two separate Chesterton quotes. The precise history of the quote and its various versions has been helpfully summarized in an article by The American Chesterton Society (https://www.chesterton.org/ceases-to-worship/).

order to save them. The first was durability. So they looked either for metal or for wood that would not easily rot. It would not be good to have a god that was liable to decay and go rotten!

The second quality they looked for in their concept of a god was stability. A god that was liable to wobble or topple over would be useless! So they stabilised their god with chains or nails so that it wouldn't fall over.

The third requirement was that their god should be rich in majesty and resources. So they decorated it with their silver and gold.

They made this god in the form of a man; and then they bowed down to it and prayed to it to save them. But what actually was this god of theirs? It was not, of course, the living God, Creator of heaven and earth such as Isaiah believed in. It was but the objectivisation of their own concepts projected on to the form of a man.[55]

But now listen to the basic thesis of Feuerbach's philosophy: 'We have reduced', he says, 'the supermundane, supernatural, and superhuman nature of God to the elements of human nature as its fundamental elements. . . . The beginning, middle and end of religion is MAN.'[56]

What he means by that is well summed up by M. J. Inwood of Trinity College, Oxford:

> God is in fact the essence of man himself, abstracted from individual, embodied men, and objectified and worshipped as a distinct entity. . . . We need to heal the fissure between heaven and earth, to replace love of God by love of man, and faith in God by faith in man, to recognise that man's fate depends on man alone and not on supernatural forces.[57]

So then, to say that God is love, means, according to Feuerbach, not that there is a self-existent God, independent of man, who loves man; it means simply, that love, human love, is an absolute. Similarly, according to Feuerbach, to say that God saves us, means that the in-

[55] In this, one suspects, Isaiah would have agreed with Freud's view of man-made religion; though, of course, he would have criticised Freud severely for confusing man-made religion with faith in the living God.

[56] Essence of Christianity, 184.

[57] Inwood, 'Feuerbach, Ludwig Andreas', 276b.

dividual man is weak and needs salvation; but that the god who saves him, is not God, but humanity as a whole:

> All divine attributes, all the attributes that make God God, are attributes of the species—attributes which in the individual are limited, but the limits of which are abolished in the essence of the species, and even in its existence, in so far as it has its complete existence only in all men taken together. My knowledge, my will, is limited; but my limit is not the limit of another man, to say nothing of mankind; what is difficult to me is easy to another; what is impossible, inconceivable, to one age, is to the coming age conceivable and possible. My life is bound to a limited time; not so the life of humanity.[58]

On this principle, then, to say that God is almighty must mean that humanity as a whole is almighty. Not any one generation of humanity, of course; for each generation proves flawed, grows old, decays, dies. But somehow all generations put together as a whole are almighty.

Two comments are in order. For humans to put their ultimate faith in humanity like this is clearly beyond all doubt the exercise of religious faith. Secondly, humanity as a god would seem to suffer from the same disadvantages as the ancient wooden and metal idols: it is apt to go rotten and topple over. History suggests that so far from humanity being able to save us, it is humanity itself that needs to be saved.

[58] *Essence of Christianity*, 152.

CHAPTER 3

THE NATURE AND BASIS OF MORALITY

It is clear, then . . . that it is not possible to be good in the strict sense . . . without moral virtue. . . . The choice will not be right without practical wisdom any more than without virtue; for the one determines the end and the other makes us do the things that lead to the end.

—Aristotle, *Nicomachean Ethics*

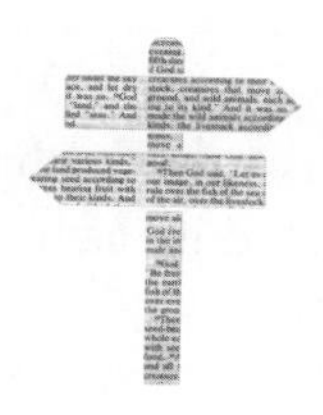

SOME GENERAL CONSIDERATIONS CONCERNING HUMAN BEHAVIOUR

Our topic in this chapter is to be 'human behaviour'. Let's begin by explaining our terms. By 'human behaviour' we do not mean simply 'how we human beings behave' but 'how we as human beings ought to behave'. Understood in this way, our book's title suggests that there is such a thing as truly human behaviour, different, for instance, from sub-human or mere animal behaviour; and that to be truly human, we must behave in a truly human way.

We have, of course, a lot in common with animals, and to some extent we behave in the same way. When animals get hungry, they eat; so do we. When they get thirsty, they drink; so do we. They mate and produce offspring; so do humans. Nature, or instinct, call it what you please, dictates this behaviour.

But very soon we discover that there is a whole dimension to human behaviour that is lacking in animals: we have a moral sense, animals, as far as we can observe, do not. You can train your dog, if you have one, not to go into your neighbour's house and steal meat off the table. You can train it by whacking it every time it attempts to enter the house. Thereafter, entering the house will be associated in its memory with the pain of the whacking and it will desist. But while you can train a dog not to steal the neighbour's meat, you will never get it to understand why it is morally wrong to steal. It is no good plying it with reasons.

But reasons are precisely what human beings will demand if you tell them they ought to do this, or ought not to do that. Tell some teenager, 'You should obey your parents', and you are likely to get the reply 'Why should I?' Tell someone else, 'You shouldn't tell lies', and he or she is liable to retort, 'Why shouldn't I, if it suits me?' And if you should insist: 'It is morally wrong to tell lies, that's why you shouldn't', the retort is likely to be 'Who are you to impose your moral standards on me?'

Reasons, reasons, reasons—that's what we all demand to be given when we are told that it is our duty as human beings to behave morally in this way or that.

Ethics and Morality

Two of the technical terms customarily used in connection with the topic of human behaviour are 'ethics' and 'morality' (or 'moral philosophy'). Before we proceed, let us explain how we shall be using these terms. At one level 'Ethics' is the name of a subject as, for instance, 'mathematics' or 'physics'; and in that case its subject matter is moral philosophy. So, for instance, we refer to Aristotle's treatise on morality as his *Nicomachean Ethics*.[1] At this level 'ethics' and 'moral philosophy' are interchangeable terms.

At another level it is helpful to make a distinction between them. We do so, for instance, when we speak of 'medical ethics'. By 'medical ethics' we mean a code of behaviour for physicians, surgeons and psychiatrists, based, of course, on general moral principles, but indicating how those general moral principles should be applied to specific situations and decisions that doctors have to face in their day-to-day treatment of patients. 'Would it be ethical', we ask, 'when a woman dies, for a surgeon to remove the deceased's kidneys, and implant them in some other patient, without first asking the permission of the dead woman's next of kin, or of the woman herself before she died? Or would it be ethical for the surgeon to sell the kidneys secretly to some wealthy person and keep the money for himself?'

In this usage, then, 'ethics' refers to right, practical behaviour, while 'morality' is concerned with the basic principles that guide and control that behaviour. The latter is concerned more with the theory of morality; the former with putting the theory into practice.

Why is it important and helpful to make this distinction? Let's take a few practical cases.

Sometimes the same basic moral principle can be applied in practice in different, indeed in opposite, ways

Take the general moral principle that we are to love our neighbours

[1] Nicomachus was the name of Aristotle's son. This book is called after him either because Aristotle dedicated it to him, or because he edited it.

as ourselves, and therefore not harm them in any way. Among the ten thousand other ways this principle will affect our behaviour is that it will control the way we drive our cars. We must do everything to avoid accidents. To that end the government, sensibly enough, lays down a regulation as to which side of the road we should drive on. In some countries it is the right-hand side. In other countries it is the very opposite, the left-hand side. In and of itself it does not matter on which side we drive, so long as everyone in any one country obeys the same regulation. Whether it is right or left is morally neutral. Both regulations equally satisfy the basic moral directive: avoid accidents that harm your neighbour.

But now take a more serious example:

A morally good end may not be achieved by morally bad means

Take the basic moral principle that a man must love his wife and children. In practice that will mean working to support them. Suppose that finding employment is difficult; but then the man is offered the chance to become a drug dealer. That would solve his problem of maintaining his family, for he could earn a lot of money by selling drugs. But should he? The end in view in making the money is morally good: maintaining his family. But the proposed means of achieving that end is morally evil. Drugs can, and often do, lead to addiction, brain damage, a life of crime to maintain the drug habit and physical and moral ruin.

Such a situation is an example of the importance of the ethical rule: the end does not justify the means. It is not morally acceptable to use morally evil means on the pretext that they are being used to achieve a morally good end. Means must be able to justify themselves as morally right without depending for their justification on the ends they serve.

Sometimes it is necessary to break the letter of a moral law in order to keep its spirit

An example commonly cited by the moral philosophers in the ancient world would run as follows. Moral principle says that it is morally wrong to break solemnly given promises.

A man borrows a very sharp knife from his friend, solemnly promising to give it back the moment the friend asks for it. But when the friend comes asking for it back, it is at once evident that the friend has gone mad. He insists on the knife being returned at once because he needs it to murder his wife!

What shall the borrower do? Should he keep the letter of his promise and forthwith hand the knife back to its owner? But that would facilitate the madman's intended crime and be the means of his wife's death. That would not be fulfilling the moral law that forbids harming our neighbour.

Should he then refuse to give the knife back there and then? Yes, for though he would appear to be breaking the letter of his original promise, he would be keeping its spirit. For the intention of the law that prescribes promise keeping, is to prevent the harm that promise breaking normally does to the one to whom the promise was made. But in this abnormal circumstance keeping the promise literally would do him harm and not prevent it.

Where it is impossible to carry out two moral laws simultaneously, precedence must be given to the higher of the two laws

For example, in saying that lying is morally wrong we do not condemn people who during the Second World War deceived the Gestapo rather than betray the places where Jews were hiding. To have told the truth, or even to have kept silent, would have led to certain death for those Jews. They had a moral duty to do good and show mercy to the Jews. They had a moral duty to tell the truth. But in their situation they could not do both. They had to choose between them. They rightly gave precedence to the higher moral law. And, incidentally, deceiving the Gestapo did them no harm, it did them good: it saved them from committing a foul crime.

Lessons so far

From these few examples, then, we can see that basic moral principles can be clear enough; the right way of carrying them out can sometimes be somewhat complicated. But from these examples we can also see that carrying out the basic moral principles can involve complicated questions and differing solutions; but that does not mean that such complications invalidate the moral principles themselves.

There are, incidentally, many parallels to this at the scientific and technological level. For instance, the basic principle at the heart of aircraft flight is that of the aerofoil, that is, the aerodynamic shape of the wing, which gives the aircraft the necessary lift. This principle is exceedingly simple, but putting it into practice in the design of aircraft is enormously complicated. At the same time none of the complications compromises the validity of the basic principle.

Certainly, theoretical moral principles are not enough by themselves; they need to be implemented by right ethical practice. The famous Roman Stoic philosopher and plutocrat Seneca (first century AD) wrote treatises on moral philosophy, telling people how they ought to behave. Yet when the Roman Emperor Nero murdered his own mother, Agrippina, Seneca helped him to write a letter to the Roman Senate, covering up his crime and falsely attributing Agrippina's death to another cause![2]

On the other hand, if we are to act virtuously, practice alone will not be enough; our practice will need to be informed and directed by correct moral theory and principles. As Aristotle said:

> It is clear, then . . . that it is not possible to be good in the strict sense . . . without moral virtue. . . . The choice will not be right without practical wisdom any more than without virtue; for the one determines the end and the other makes us do the things that lead to the end.[3]

A further requirement

We have talked so far of theoretical morality and of practical morality (that is, ethics), and of how both are necessary. But there is a further necessity. If we are going to behave virtuously we shall not only need an intellectual grasp of the moral laws: we shall need a properly adjusted emotional response to the values for which those laws stand. Not mere emotionalism or sentimentality, of course; but deeply felt emotions, appropriate to those moral values.

In a very real and practical way our sense of value determines our behaviour. If a man found his house on fire, he would not brave the flames and go in to rescue a bar of chocolate. If he had a bar of gold

[2] Tacitus, *Annals*, XIV.11.

[3] *Nicomachean Ethics*, Ross trans, VI.13 (1144b29, 1145a11).

> If we are going to behave virtuously we shall not only need an intellectual grasp of the moral laws: we shall need a properly adjusted emotional response to the values for which those laws stand.

hidden in the house, he might dare to go in to get it. But if two of his little children were trapped by the flames in their bedroom, he might well risk his own life to save them.

In times of danger, or in the face of loss, or temptation, a mere intellectual grasp of the basic principles and laws of morality is often not sufficient to keep a man from compromising those principles. During the reigns of some of the despotic, tyrannical and cruel Roman emperors, like Nero or Domitian, many of the members of the Senate buckled down under them, not because they had no clear intellectual understanding of moral principles, but because they did not have strong enough emotional attachment to those principles. They valued life more than integrity.

Having made these preliminary observations and explanations we must now concentrate the rest of this chapter on the major question concerning morality. We shall not discuss the details of ethical practice, vastly important though they are. This is not the place to do so. We must rather discuss the question that lies at the heart of all systems of morality, namely: What is the source and nature of moral law and moral values?

THE SOURCE AND NATURE OF MORAL LAW

This, as we all know, is a hotly disputed subject, and many widely different views are held. Whatever view we ourselves hold, it is an important part of our education to inform ourselves about these different views and especially to try to understand the reasons why people hold them. Perhaps the best, and certainly the easiest, place to start is with our own personal experience of ourselves and of other people.

Our innate sense of fairness

All of us have within us an innate sense of fairness. It is found already in quite small children. Two brothers can be playing when the older snatches the younger's toy and refuses to give it back. A row ensues, with much shouting and screaming. Presently Mother, hearing the rumpus, comes into the room just at the moment when the younger boy is slapping his brother across the face. Now Mother was not there when the quarrel began, and so she did not see that it was the older brother who caused it. But the older boy is her favourite; and to see him slapped across the face by the younger brother rouses her ire. She punishes the younger brother, tells both to be quiet, removes the toy, and departs. And when she has gone the younger brother protests through his tears 'It isn't fair! It wasn't my fault! I didn't start it', and so forth.

We might ask where this disappointed young child got the idea from in the first place that the world ought to be, and would be, fair. But leaving that aside, we should ask, where did the child get his concept of fairness from, which enabled him to see, with a minimum of thinking, that this whole incident was grossly unfair? Doubtless his mother's smack caused him physical pain and emotional shock. But if our own memories of childhood and our experience as adults are any true guide to what children feel, we may surmise that the sharpest pain was the internal one which the younger child felt at the wounding of his sense of fairness.

That sense of fairness and of justice remains with us as adults, though long experience of the world's injustices tends to harden our sensibility and make us cynical. We sometimes feel as if our sense of fairness is not worth having, since it is so frequently mocked by events. The question is: What authority or significance shall we attribute to this sense of fairness? We didn't invent it ourselves. Where did it come from? Is it valid?

What authority or significance shall we attribute to this sense of fairness? We didn't invent it ourselves. Where did it come from? Is it valid?

In this connection it could be helpful to think of some of our other senses.

Our aesthetic sense

We did not invent this sense either. We were born with it. We value it immensely for all the beauty of form and colour that it allows us to perceive and enjoy; and at the same time we notice that it is offended and pained by ugliness. Indeed, we often find that our aesthetic sense moves us to defend beauty and oppose, and if possible remove, ugliness.

Moreover, as we reminded ourselves in the Introduction, perceiving, say, that a rose is beautiful is a highly subjective experience, something that we see and feel at a deep level inside ourselves. Nevertheless, when we show a rose to other people, we expect them too to agree that it is beautiful; and they normally have no difficulty in doing so. From this two things seem to follow: (1) that though the appreciation of beauty is a highly subjective experience, yet there are some objective criteria for deciding what is beautiful and what is not; and (2) we assume that everybody has these inborn criteria for perceiving beauty. If some people haven't, or even prefer ugliness, we feel they must suffer from some defect, or other, like colour-blindness, or brain damage that does not allow them to perceive shape or colour properly.

Our innate language faculty

The second innate sense is our inborn language faculty. It used to be thought that human language evolved out of animal cries. When some primitive pig, say, encountered a lion, the shock of it drew a startled grunt from the pig. When this happening was repeated many times (presumably by different lions and different pigs), all other pigs hearing this particular type of grunt associated it with 'lion!'; and so this special grunt came to *mean* 'lion'. From such primitive beginnings, then, and from thousands of other nuanced grunts, it was supposed that human language gradually evolved over millions of years. To support this theory long experiments have been performed with the great apes in an attempt to prove that they can be taught language. Up to the present they have all failed. The evolutionist Professor George Gaylord Simpson expresses himself decisively on this topic:

> Human language is absolutely distinct from any system of communication in other animals. That is made most clear by comparison with other animal utterances, which most nearly resemble human speech and are most often called 'speech'.

> Non-human vocables are, in effect, interjections. . . . The difference between animal interjection and human language is the difference between saying 'Ouch!' and saying 'Fire is hot'.[4]

> Darwin's study and many later studies sought to trace the evolutionary origin of language from a prehuman source. They have not been successful. As a recent expert in the field has said, 'The more that is known about it [that is, communication in monkeys and apes], the less these systems seem to help in the understanding of human language.'[5]

> Moreover at the present time no languages are primitive in the sense of being significantly close to the origin of language. Even the peoples with least complex cultures have highly sophisticated languages, with complex grammar and large vocabularies, capable of naming and discussing anything that occurs in the sphere occupied by their speakers. . . . The oldest language that can reasonably be reconstructed is already modern, sophisticated, complete from an evolutionary point of view.[6]

Moreover, Noam Chomsky, the American linguist and philosopher, in his pioneering work on language[7] has pointed to the fact that the genius of human language consists, not merely in the use of arbitrary sounds (and thus, words) to represent things and ideas, but even more in the ability to conceive, grasp and then express in syntax the logical relationships between ideas.

The astonishing thing is how early in life a child gives evidence of this ability. It is not a question of which language a child first heard spoken and then learned to speak: she could have learned Russian or Japanese or Amharic or any other language with equal ease. The remarkable thing is that, whatever language it is that she first hears and learns, from early childhood onwards she can begin to understand the inner logical relationships between her phrases and sentences expressed through the syntax of the language.

---

[4] 'Biological Nature of Man', 476.

[5] 'Biological Nature of Man', 477, quotation from J. B. Lancaster in *Origin of Man*, P. L. DeVore, ed. Transcript of a symposium, New York: Wenner-Gren Foundation, 1965.

[6] 'Biological Nature of Man', 477.

[7] *Syntactic Structures*; 'Review of B. F. Skinner's Verbal Behaviour, Language'; *Knowledge of Language*.

A child can for instance understand quite sophisticated logical connections of thought such as hypothetical conditions. When a mother says to her four-year old: 'If you are good today, I will buy you an ice-cream this evening', the child can perceive the logical relationship between the subordinate clause and the main clause, and so understands quite well that the future enjoyment of the promised ice-cream is conditional upon his intervening good behaviour.

> The remarkable thing is that, whatever language it is that she first hears and learns, from early childhood onwards she can begin to understand the inner logical relationships between her phrases and sentences expressed through the syntax of the language.

Dogs or apes could not do that, however many words, sounds, colours or gestures they can learn to recognise. The logic behind the intricate syntax of spoken language remains beyond their intellectual grasp: they have no inborn language faculty comparable to that of a human being. We must conclude that the young human has this ability because it was born with it. On it depends his ability to learn and to express himself in any language he may choose to learn.[8]

The implications for our sense of fairness

Now a child's aesthetic sense can be enhanced by training and experience, but only because it was already there to start with. The same is true of a child's innate language faculty. It certainly can be developed and strengthened by experience, study and analysis, but only because, unlike mere animals, the child had this language-faculty born in him to start with.

With that we come back to the sense of fairness. In adults it has been developed, perhaps also challenged, tested and questioned by life's experiences. But, as we saw, children already have it from their earliest years. It does look as if the sense of fairness, like the aesthetic sense and the language faculty, is inborn, part of our human nature.

[8] Research into the possibility of teaching animals language has, of course, moved on since George Gaylord Simpson and Noam Chomsky; and opinions are still divided. But human language continues to be an embarrassment to evolutionary theory.

Our inborn sense of particular moral virtues and vices

We now observe that, not only do we have an innate sense of fairness and unfairness, we also have an innate awareness that certain actions and attitudes are morally wrong, while others are morally right. And with that comes a sense of duty that we ought to do the right and not the wrong.

Take lying as an example. Observe the way people react to it, not simply when they are thinking about it philosophically, but more especially in the heat of practical living. Person A has been having business negotiations with Person B for some time, when A discovers that B has been deceiving him. Full of indignation A confronts B with the undeniable evidence of deceit and vehemently accuses him: 'You've been lying to me!'

From this, certain things are at once evident. First, A expects B to acknowledge the force of the accusation and to feel guilty for his despicable breach of the moral law. A does not embark on a detailed philosophical argument to teach B, as if he didn't know it, that lying is wrong. In A's thinking, B, like everyone else, knows that lying is wrong.

A is, of course, realist enough to know that multitudes of people do, from time to time, tell lies, large or small; but A simultaneously holds that every individual in each of those multitudes, including B, knows in his or her heart that lying is wrong—which is often shown by the unease and embarrassment they evince when their lying is found out.[9]

So A, then, accuses B of lying and expects B, and anyone else who hears of their dispute, to agree to the universal objective standard which A's accusation presupposes, that lying is morally wrong. Then how do we imagine that Person B will in fact respond to A's accusation? At first he may argue that he was not actually lying. Failing that, he may just shrug his shoulders and walk away. More likely, he will try to excuse his lies: his circumstances or his fears forced him to lie. But the very fact he tries to excuse his lying shows that he does admit that lying is wrong. He admits the existence and validity of the universal moral law and then tries to excuse himself for breaking it.

9 We note also in passing that the theory behind the use of lie detectors is that the act of lying produces measurable, telltale, physical reactions in the one lying.

But then, how could he deny that universal moral law? How could he say, 'Of course I have constantly lied to you. I see nothing wrong with it. I always lie.'?

Lying is a parasite on truth. Lying relies for its effectiveness on the expectation that people will speak the truth. If everybody always lied, nobody would ever believe anything that anybody ever said. All relationships would be undermined, and domestic, social, business and political life would become impossible. Insecurity would be endemic.

Lying is untrue to reality; that is, it does not correspond to what really is the fact. Lying destroys reliability. A liar does not merely convey unreliable information: he shows himself to be an unreliable person. He takes advantage of the other person's trust in him, in order to betray that trust and do him harm.

Lying is untrue to reality; that is, it does not correspond to what really is the fact. Lying destroys reliability. . . . A liar simultaneously diminishes himself and increases the unreality and treacherous insecurity in the world.

He is like a main beam in a house that looks solid and invites trust, but is eaten through with dry rot. Should you trust it and lean your weight on it, it lets you down. A liar simultaneously diminishes himself and increases the unreality and treacherous insecurity in the world.

This very human habit, then, of accusing other people when they lie, and of excusing one's own lying, shows that the moral law against lying is, so to speak, written on the human heart. And this is true not only of the law against lying but of many other basic moral laws as well. They are innate.

The universal awareness of the natural law

Now the fact that certain moral laws are written on the human heart and are thus common to all mankind, does not mean that all men and women everywhere at all times throughout all the centuries have either kept them or even been reluctant to break them. When people develop the habit of breaking these moral laws, conscience becomes deadened and no longer protests. They can in fact come to regard cheating as clever and adult, an acceptable way to achieve success in examinations or sport. Unscrupulous businessmen come to think that lying is an essential part of business. Politicians think that lying is an inevitable part of politics and misuse the fair name of diplomacy in order to justify it.

In spite of such attitudes and practices, the evidence of history right down to our present time is of a universal persistence of the awareness of the basic moral laws. In *The Abolition of Man*,[10] C. S. Lewis collected a list of moral principles common to all the world's major civilisations. He called them 'Illustrations of the Natural Law' and grouped them under eight headings: (1) The Law of General Beneficence; (2) The Law of Special Beneficence; (3) Duties to Parents, Elders and Ancestors; (4) Duties to Children and Posterity; (5) The Law of Justice; (6) The Law of Good Faith and Veracity; (7) The Law of Mercy; (8) The Law of Magnanimity.[11]

But perhaps the temptation assails us to think that the moral laws which people of past centuries observed are now in our modern world obsolete. So let us perform a thought experiment. We shall first listen to an ancient Egyptian listing what for him were the important moral laws; and then we can examine our own conscience to see whether and to what extent our moral sense agrees with his.

Here is a list of claimed virtues compiled from the Egyptian *Book of the Dead* by John A. Wilson.[12] The *Book of the Dead* was a kind of document that was attached to a person's body when he or she was buried. The idea was that after death a person had to face the final judgment, which would decide, so they thought, whether he or she would be admitted to eternal life or not. The document, therefore, contained the person's 'defence statement', so to speak, claiming that he or she had not done wrong and broken the moral laws. Here, then, are some items from the deceased's list of claims:

---

[10] pp. 49–59.

[11] Under (1), he lists such things as not murdering, not inflicting misery; not being grasping, oppressive, cruel or calumnious; not slandering, not giving false witness, not doing to others what you would not like them to do to you; and the positive counterparts. (2) is concerned with special love to one's wife, family, kin and country. (5) comprises sexual justice, honesty, and justice in the courts. (8) covers things like courage, the willingness to suffer to protect others; counting death to be better than a life with shame; doing or thinking nothing uncomely, effeminate or lascivious. The contents of (3), (4), (6) and (7) are self-evident.

[12] *Ancient Near Eastern Texts*, 35.

I have not committed evil
I have not stolen
I have not been covetous
I have not robbed
I have not killed men
I have not damaged the grain measure
I have not caused crookedness
I have not told lies
I have not been contentious
I have not practised usury
I have not committed adultery

Now the point of our thought-experiment is not to decide whether this ancient Egyptian lived up to the claims which he is making here. Rather we should now ask three questions:

1. What according to the ancient Egyptian were the important moral laws binding upon mankind?
2. Would you say that any of these moral laws were not laws at all, and that it would not matter if you or anybody else in our modern world broke them?
3. Or would you conclude that there are certain moral laws inborn in the human heart throughout all races and all centuries?

But if there are moral laws, not invented by humans, but inborn in them, written on their hearts, so to speak, we shall presently have to ask how they came to be there. Who or what put them there? But before we do that, we should first consider two more of our inborn senses.

Conscience and shame

All of us will be aware from our own personal experience that we human beings are equipped with two internal mechanisms designed to restrain us from breaking these laws, or, if we break them, to act as internal witnesses against us. The first of these is conscience, and the second is a sense of shame. It is certain that we did not invent either of them; for both of them can be highly troublesome, embarrassing and unwelcome, so much so that people often try to silence or suppress them.

Conscience sits like an arbiter over our proposed actions and either consents that they shall be carried out or else protests and fills us with unease at the very thought of carrying them out. And if in spite of it we persist in going against some moral law, conscience will rise up against us, nagging us with its insistent accusation of having done wrong, and filling us with a sense of guilt.

The other mechanism is a sense of shame, and like conscience it is equipped with foresight to warn us of the disgrace we could suffer if we proceeded with our proposed wrong action. And if, in spite of it, we persist, and are found out in our misdeed, then not only does it fill us with a sense of shame, but the shame can often express itself through the physical phenomenon of blushing. Moreover, even if our misdeed is not found out and exposed, this shame mechanism can make us feel internally ashamed of ourselves, though no one else knows about it.

Conscience sits like an arbiter over our proposed actions and either consents that they shall be carried out or else protests and fills us with unease at the very thought of carrying them out.

Both of these mechanisms, then, bear their witness to the universal moral law. They can, of course, be so constantly and forcefully overridden that they virtually cease to function. One ancient writer complained of people whose consciences had been 'seared as with a hot iron' (the Apostle Paul in 1 Tim 4:2 NIV) and so no longer functioned; while another berated his extremely corrupt commercial and religious contemporaries in these terms: 'Are they ashamed of their detestable conduct? No, they have no shame at all; they do not even know how to blush' (the prophet Jeremiah in Jer 6:15 NIV).

A reasonable conclusion

What shall we say, then, of all these inborn senses and mechanisms: our sense of fairness, our aesthetic sense, our language faculty, our awareness of certain basic moral laws, our conscience and our sense of shame?

If only we were aeroplanes, we should know immediately what to say. The cockpit of a modern aircraft is equipped with a vast array of dials, lights, radar and klaxons to help the pilot in flying the aircraft, to warn him what to avoid, and to sound alarm if danger threatens, to let him know his height, direction, speed, fuel and other necessities. While he himself must take the decisions, all these mechanisms have been deliberately designed and built into the cockpit to guide and help him in making those decisions.

The natural thing, therefore, to say about the inborn senses and mechanisms that we find inbuilt into our human make-up would be that they too were deliberately designed and implanted within us for the purpose of guiding us in our decision making.

This is in fact what the Bible says about them:

> Indeed, when Gentiles, who do not have the law, by nature do what the law requires, they are a law to themselves, even though they do not have the law. They show that the work of the law is written on their hearts, while their conscience also bears witness, and their conflicting thoughts accuse or even excuse them. (Rom 2:14–15)

This passage is saying that God has used two ways of making known his moral law. One way has been through the progressively ever more detailed revelation of the requirements of that law through the Ten Commandments given through Moses and expounded by the Old Testament prophets, and then through the teachings of Christ—such as the Sermon on the Mount—and the ethical instruction of his apostles.

When as Creator he made man in his image, he wrote the basic principles and requirements of his moral law on the human heart. Hence its universality, but hence also its authority.

But the fact that this detailed teaching had not by that time percolated through to the Gentile nations at large (which is what is meant by the phrase 'even though they do not have the law', i.e. the law of Moses, v. 14), did not mean that God had left the Gentile nations in complete ignorance of his moral law. When as Creator he made man in his image, he wrote the basic principles and requirements of his moral law on the human heart. Hence its universality, but hence also its authority.

If a pilot disregarded the instructions and warnings of his dials, and as a result the plane crashed but he survived, he would have to give account for his deliberate rejection of these warnings. Moreover, he would have to give it, not to the dials, nor to himself, but to the aviation authority that polices the airways, and to the airline owners at whose orders the maker of the aircraft put these warning devices in the cockpit. If then it was God the Creator who wrote the basic principles and requirements of his moral law on our hearts, it will be to him that we will have to answer for it, if we disregard or reject those principles.

This writing of God's law on the human heart was not, of course, like programming a computer, so that the computer automatically, and machine-like, carries out its fixed programme. It was more like building into the airline pilot's cockpit the screens, dials, radar and klaxons to help him take the right decisions and fly the aircraft properly. Human beings, like the pilot, were left with free will: they could decide to carry out the requirements of God's moral law—which in fact they often did; but they were also free to neglect, ignore, distort, pervert or reject that law—which all of us have done all too often.

Now, if it is true that these moral laws are written on our hearts by God, this fact carries a highly significant implication to which we must return in more detail later on. Briefly put, it is this: as moral persons we are related not simply to an impersonal code of laws but to a person. And if that relationship is one of mutual respect, friendship and love, as it should be, then the keeping of the moral laws will be a matter not of mere legality, but of a truly personal relationship.

But as we all know, this account of the source and authority of the moral laws is for many people unacceptable. In the first place they do not believe in God; and in the second place they hold that regarding God as the authority behind the moral laws has been the cause of endless suffering and misery to the human race. In our next section, therefore, we must turn to consider what their understanding of morality is, and what are its implications.

MORALITY: OBJECTIVE OR SUBJECTIVE?

We have considered the view that the universality and authority of the moral laws derive from mankind's creator, God. Now we must begin to study the opposite, atheistic, concept of morality and its source.

There is a certain difficulty in doing so, particularly in a brief survey such as this must necessarily be. The difficulty is this: there is not just one atheistic concept of morality but many, since the various kinds of atheist (humanist, Marxist, existentialist, and so forth) hold widely different views on the topic. Moreover, in saying this we are not thinking about details of ethical practice, that is, their different views on how the same basic moral principles should be applied in particular, practical situations; we are thinking about their differing views on the basic principles of morality themselves, and on the sources of those principles.

It is impossible, then, in this short survey to cover all these different views fairly and in equal proportion. Students, therefore, should be reminded of their need to read widely in the original sources or in the large-scale histories and encyclopaedias of philosophy. That said, there are two fundamental questions that any theist will want to put to any atheistic morality. The first is: does the atheistic morality, whatever it is, provide any absolute standard, or standards, by which to judge and assess the validity of its moral principles? This question is important because atheists generally object to the theistic view that God is the source of all moral law, for that view invests the moral law with divine, absolute authority; and such authority, they feel, is an affront to man's dignity and moral autonomy, and reduces him in the end to a kind of moral serfdom.

Are there any objective moral values? Or, are all moral values *subjective*?

So, a theist will want to ask: does the atheistic morality, of whichever sort it is, incorporate any absolute, objective, authoritative standard into its system? If so, what is it? And if it does, how does this authoritative standard better interact with human freedom than God's authoritative standard does? And if it does not incorporate any absolute, objective, authoritative standard into its system, is that system altogether subjective and therefore arbitrary?

The second fundamental question is only a slightly different way of expressing the first question, but the difference will, if nothing more, explain more fully a couple of technical terms. This second question is: Are there any objective moral values? Or, are all moral values *subjective*?

The meaning of the terms 'objective' and 'subjective'

Our first task here is to understand what the terms 'objective' and 'subjective' mean in this context; and then to ask why it is important to decide whether moral values are objective or subjective.

To say that there are objective moral values is to say that there are things that are always right, independent of anyone's personal feelings, likes or dislikes; things which impose a corresponding duty on everybody universally and at all times. Similarly, it says that there are certain things that are always wrong, whether individuals, groups or nations agree they are wrong or not: things from which it is the duty of everybody everywhere to refrain.

To say, on the other hand, that moral values are subjective is to say that moral values depend on people's likes and dislikes. One person approves of certain moral values because they appeal to him or her; another person rejects these same values, because they don't appeal to him or her; and there is no ultimate, independent standard by which to judge which set of moral values is right or wrong.

Or let's put it another way. To say that the moral laws are objective is to say that they resemble the laws of arithmetic. We human beings did not invent them: we discovered them. At different times in history different nations have invented different number-systems (e.g. the ancient Babylonians used a sexagesimal system, whereas we today use the decimal system); but all these invented number-systems express the same laws of arithmetic: no one invented the laws.

Suppose, then, a child at school does his sums and comes up with the result that $\sqrt{9} = 4\frac{1}{2}$. The teacher will point out that this is wrong: the right answer is $\sqrt{9} = 3$. But the teacher is not imposing her views on the child. She is as much subject to the laws of arithmetic as the child is. Those laws do not depend for their validity on her views of the matter. It is merely that with her longer experience she has come to realise what, according to the laws of arithmetic, is objectively right and what is objectively wrong; and in her wisdom she is teaching the child to submit his thinking to arithmetic's objective laws.

On the other hand those who deny that moral values are objective, and likewise deny that there is any absolute standard by which to decide which moral values are true and universally binding and which are not true and not universally binding, tend to think that moral laws were invented by different people or groups of people at different times in history, in order to meet different contemporary situations. Therefore they were never, and should never be regarded as, universally applicable; and they are always open to revision as time, place and circumstances change.

Such subjective moral values would be like fashions in clothing, which differ from nation to nation, from climate to climate, and from generation to generation.

The implications of subjectivism in morality

A matter of taste?

One implication to note is that subjectivism in morality would ultimately reduce moral values to a matter of taste. We have already touched on this issue in Chapter 1, but let us elaborate on it a little further here.

In matters of taste no one can be said to be right and no one wrong. Taste is a matter of subjective preference. If Natasha says, 'I adore spinach,' and Alex says, 'I loathe spinach,' we obviously have statements of two diametrically opposite preferences. But we could not say that either of them was untrue. Unless Natasha is being a hypocrite and saying she likes spinach when she doesn't, her statement 'I like spinach' is true: she likes it; none can deny it; and that's the end of the matter. The same is true of Alex's statement of his preference.

Moreover, it would not make sense for Alex to claim that Natasha ought not to like spinach; she ought to like beetroot as he does. 'Ought' does not come into it. No one has a duty to like beetroot, or not to like spinach. It is simply a question of each person's subjective taste.

Natasha might, of course, say: 'You ought to like spinach because it is better for you than beetroot is.' But in that case Alex has the right to reply: 'By what standard are you judging that spinach is better for me than beetroot is?' It would not then be enough for Natasha to answer, 'Dr A says it is'; for Alex might well reply 'But Dr B says that spinach isn't; beetroot is'. And when two expert opinions differ (as they often do on all sorts of topics), the only way of deciding which is right, is somehow to prove that one of them is right and the other wrong. And to do that you would need some objective standard by which to assess both views, and judge which was objectively the better. It would no longer be a matter of subjective judgment.

The conclusion so far, then, would be that if moral laws and values were simply a matter of subjective taste or preference, then we could never say that one preference was morally wrong and the other morally right; or that we ought to embrace one preference and reject the other.

But see what that would mean: we could never, for example, condemn Hitler for genocide. All Hitler would need to say is: 'You don't like murdering Jews? Don't murder them then. But I do like murdering Jews. It's simply a matter of taste. Who are you to impose your taste on me?'

> If moral laws and values were simply a matter of subjective taste or preference, then we could never say that one preference was morally wrong and the other morally right.

For now notice another thing. If someone says simply 'I think genocide is appalling', and someone else says 'I think genocide is perfectly acceptable', neither is actually telling you anything about genocide; both are simply telling you something about themselves, that they either approve, or disapprove, of genocide.

If, on the other hand, one of them said 'I think genocide is appalling because it is a crime against humanity', then she is beginning to tell you something about genocide (or rather what she thinks genocide is). But then, of course, the other person might reply 'I think genocide is perfectly acceptable. It is not a crime: it rids humanity of a deadly cancer'; and this too would be saying something about genocide itself, and would convey his moral estimate of it. But which of them would be morally right? You could not settle that on subjective grounds. You would need some objective moral standard by which to judge it.

But if there are no absolute, objective moral standards, how shall the matter be decided?

A question of agreeing the rules?

Could we regard moral laws like the rules of a game? Take football (soccer), for instance. The rules are not a question of individual taste or preference. All the players on both sides in a match have to agree to play according to the rules of the game; and they have an independent referee to decide if and when any player breaks the rules, and to adjudicate when any dispute arises between the teams. What is more, in international contests, an international body sets the rules and football teams from all over the world agree to keep the rules set by this body. It is not, therefore, a question of merely personal subjective taste, or of any national or cultural preference. Here are objective rules and standards; yet they have been arrived at by common consent, not imposed by some arbitrary, outside authority.

But in this case, so the argument continues, though the rules of football are in that sense objective, that does not mean that the rules have always been the same and must never change. They can, and do change from time to time, so that what was allowed fifty years ago is not allowed now, and vice-versa. That can happen because the rules are laid down not by divine authority but by a consensus of all the football authorities around the world; and if all agree to change the rules so as to make the game more interesting and enjoyable, they can be changed; and what was wrong before, is now right, and properly so.

So, then, why can we not have objective moral values on those same terms: made up by a consensus of all mankind, but open to change and adaptation as conditions change?

Superficially the argument sounds attractive; but the analogy that it is built on is defective, and that for a number of reasons.

1. The rules for a game of football are largely mere regulations. It is not for the sake of morality that players are forbidden to handle the ball.

2. The rules of football cannot by themselves tell a player whether he should or should not present false tax returns to the government; whether he should love his children, honour his parents, be true to his wife and so forth. For these are moral principles, and lie quite outside the remit of the rules of football to decide. Some players and officials have been accused of corruption and 'fixing' a number of games in collusion with betting syndicates in different parts of the world. These are criminal charges, and they will have to be decided by an authority outside the game of football, namely the law courts.

3. The next weakness in the analogy that suggests that moral laws

can be settled by consensus like the rules of football is this: football is not the only game that people like to play. There are others, and each one of them has a different set of rules; so that what is allowable in, say, handball, is forbidden in football. A footballer cannot say that the rules of handball are wrong just because they are different from the rules of football. Nor can anyone say that you ought to play, say, cricket and not hockey. Everyone must be left free to play any game he likes, and thus to choose what set of rules he will follow.

But how could that be true of the moral laws? For if it were, on what grounds could cannibalism be condemned? The cannibal could simply say that he was playing a different game, and who were you to say his game was not so good as yours?

4. Yet maybe we are being unfair to the analogy. Those who put forward the analogy may intend only to argue that the game of football has evolved to the point where universally accepted rules have been arrived at by universal consensus; and that as far as each individual player and team is concerned, the rules, though created by humans, are absolute (for the time being) and perfectly objective. Then, if humankind has been able to do this for the rules of football, why should it be thought impossible that one day humanity may evolve to the point where all the people of the world will be able by consensus to appoint a worldwide moral authority which will be able to do for morality what has been done for football, i.e. to set objective universally accepted, absolute, moral laws?

The idea is intriguing. Suppose—though it is a very big suppose—that it did actually happen, and this worldwide authority laid down the absolute law that, say, rape was always and absolutely wrong for human beings. The evolutionist, Michael Ruse has pointed out that if intelligent beings on the Andromeda galaxy (if there were any) visited earth, we might discover that they did not consider rape wrong at all, since according to Ruse their evolutionary history might have been different from ours.[13]

In that case, presumably, it would be necessary to appoint—by consensus of course—an intergalactic moral authority to settle by a supra-galactic standard what the moral laws should be for all the inhabitants of all the worlds that might exist throughout the universe.

[13] 'Is Rape Wrong on Andromeda?'

It is not facetious to remark here, as an aside, that there is such a supra-galactic authority: he is called God. The point is, however, that atheists apparently would not object to a universal authority that could impose and enforce a universal law, so long as that universal authority, unlike God, was established by human consent.

But Michael Ruse's evolutionary speculations about the morality of hypothetical inhabitants of Andromeda have clearly led this discussion off into realms of fantasy. What we need is an adequate morality to guide our lives here and now.

We cannot wait for some speculative worldwide moral authority to evolve. We need an objective morality now in this real everyday world.

Moreover, all of us surely applaud the sincere efforts of the United Nations to produce a worldwide consensus on the need to end aggression and violence, to urge restraint in political ambition, the maintenance and extension of human rights, an end to the exploitation of the Majority World, the relief of poverty, the banning of weapons of terror and of torture, a more just distribution of the world's wealth and so forth. No one of good will would wish to minimise the successes which have been achieved.

But it is painfully obvious how difficult it often is for the UN as a representative body to reach a consensus in theory, let alone in practice, in its field of things political, social and economic, without having also to shoulder the responsibility for deciding and enforcing a worldwide objective morality.

Moreover, and in any case, it is highly questionable whether it would even be desirable to have a semi-political world authority, however appointed, as the final authority and enforcer of the world's moral laws. The history of totalitarian governments that have enforced their moral beliefs on their own countries and have then aspired to implant them on the whole world, has often been one of oppression and cruelty and the denial of freedom of conscience. At the other extreme democratic majority vote is hardly the way to decide questions of morality. Have majorities always been right? Or minorities for that matter? And how would you be able to judge whether the majority or the minority was right, if there did not exist a higher moral authority above both of them by which to settle the question?

But it is time to let atheists tell us how they deal with this problem.

COMPARATIVE MORALITIES

An ancient parable tells of two men, each of whom built a house. One built his house on a rock, the other on the sand. When the storms and floods came, the house on the sand collapsed; the house on the rock stood firm. Within the parable no criticism is made of the superstructure of the house that collapsed. Its superstructure may have been virtually the same, at least externally, as the other one. But its superstructure had no adequate foundation.

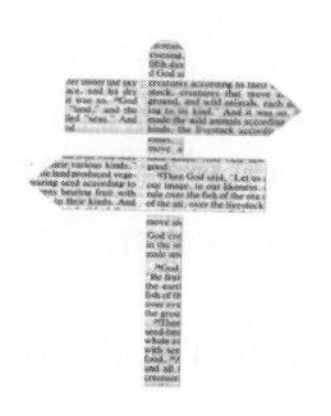

We begin with moralities based on an evolutionary account of human origin and development. First comes a widespread view.

SCIENCE HAS DESTROYED THE TRADITIONAL BASIS OF MORALITY

As representatives of this view we may quote, at the scientific level, Professor William Provine, once again:

> The implications of modern science, however, are clearly inconsistent with most religious traditions.
>
> No purposive principles exist in nature. Organic evolution has occurred by various combinations of random genetic drift, natural selection, Mendelian heredity, and many other purposeless mechanisms. Humans are complex organic machines that die completely with no survival of soul or psyche. . . . No inherent moral or ethical laws exist, nor are there absolute guiding principles for human society. The universe cares nothing for us and we have no ultimate meaning in life.[1]

> There are no gods and no designing forces that are rationally detectable.
>
> The individual human becomes an ethical person by means of two primary mechanisms: heredity and environmental influences. That is all there is . . .
>
> Fourth, we must conclude that when we die, we die and that is the end of us . . .
>
> Finally, free-will as it is traditionally conceived—the freedom to make uncoerced and unpredictable choices among alternative possible courses of action—simply does not exist . . .

[1] 'Scientists, Face it! Science and Religion are Incompatible', 10.

> There is no way that the evolutionary process can produce a being that is truly free to make choices.[2]

At the popular level, we may quote Alasdair Palmer, Scientific Correspondent of the *Sunday Telegraph*:

> But it is not just the religious explanation of the world that is contradicted by scientific explanations of our origins. So, too, are most of our ethical values, since most of them have been shaped by our religious heritage. A scientific account of mankind has no more place for free-will or the equal capacity of each individual to be good and act justly than it has for the soul.[3]

The idea that science has destroyed the basis of religion and morality

The 'logic' of this view, whether at the professional scientific, or at the popular, level is easy to follow.

1. Science, so people assume, often as a result of what they have been taught, has proved that there is no God.

2. That means that the universe is one huge, impersonal system, or machine, mindless and purposeless.

3. That means also that we human beings are the products of purposeless processes. We are biological machines without free will and therefore without moral responsibility. There is no designed goal for us to aim at in life; and when we die, we perish completely, nothing survives; there is no final judgment after death (there is no one to do the judging), and, therefore, in the end it will make no difference whether we have behaved well or badly. After all, the universe contains no inherent moral or ethical laws nor any absolute guiding principles for human society any more than the engine of a bus carries within it moral guidance for the way its passengers should run their lives. And so ethics is merely a question of fitting into one's contemporary culture as best as one can on a pragmatic basis.

4. Science has thus destroyed the basis of religion, and of the morality which religion taught. What's left is mere superstition.

---

2 Provine, 'Evolution and the Foundation of Ethics'.

3 'Must Knowledge Gained Mean Paradise Lost?'

This, then, is a very widespread—though often poorly thought out—view; yet it rests on a false assumption: science has not in fact proved that there is no God, nor anything like it.[4]

Of course, when people imbibe this view that the basis of morality has been destroyed, they do not start behaving like criminals right away—or even at all. They may well lead exemplary lives at the moral level. For the fact is that people find it virtually impossible to live as if there were no such thing as morality. Let someone steal an atheist's money, slander his reputation, bear false witness against him, run off with his wife, be cruel to his children, and the atheist, even if he intellectually holds the views expressed by Professor Provine above, will be full of moral indignation! He will protest vigorously against these outrages and will show clearly that he does in fact believe that there is, or should be, such a thing as justice, truthfulness, etc., and that society has a moral duty to do something about the person that has treated him so evilly. The righteous requirements of the Creator's moral law remain quite clearly written on his heart, even if intellectually he denies the Creator's existence.

Outwardly, then, any atheist may well live a good and honourable life, little different from someone who believes in a God-given moral law. But there is a profound difference. As Provine implies, the basis of his morality has been destroyed.

Any atheist may well live a good and honourable life, little different from someone who believes in a God-given moral law. But there is a profound difference.

An ancient parable tells of two men, each of whom built a house. One built his house on a rock, the other on the sand. When the storms and floods came, the house on the sand collapsed; the house on the rock stood firm. Within the parable no criticism is made of the superstructure of the house that collapsed. Its superstructure may have been virtually the same, at least externally, as the other one. But its superstructure had no adequate foundation. Provine's observations are true to life in the sense that the erroneous impression that science has made belief in God impossible, has for many people destroyed the moral foundation of their lives. The inevitable result is that when temptations, storms and ultimate

[4] See the Appendix: 'The Scientific Endeavour'.

crises come, they discover they have no adequate underlying strength to maintain their stand against them. The moral underpinning of life collapses. Morality becomes unstable shifting sand.

Now certainly all scientists must be free to teach what they believe to be the truth. Truth must not be watered down or distorted for the sake of any metaphysical belief. But by that same token all science teachers, like any other teachers, need to distinguish their metaphysical presuppositions and their theories from the actually proven facts of science.

But Provine's view that the physical universe gives us no moral guidance as to our behaviour has not always been shared even by atheistic scientists like himself. Since the advent of Darwin and his evolutionary theories, there have been at least two major schools of thought that have insisted that an adequate human morality can be, and should be, based on the physical processes that evolution, according to them, has used to engineer the human race.

The first of these was the theory that just as evolution had used the principle of 'the survival of the fittest' to get us from protoplasm to full humanity, so that same principle of 'the survival of the fittest', if allowed to apply to man's moral and ethical practice in his social, commercial, ethnic and international relationships, would bring mankind to the pinnacle of his moral achievement.

The second theory is more modern: in its present form it dates from the 1960s and is still gaining ground today. It teaches that an adequate morality can be, and must be, built on the workings and strategies of the genes in the cells of our bodies.

So let us look at each of these theories in turn.

'SURVIVAL OF THE FITTEST' AS THE BASIS OF MORALITY

The theory that came to be known as 'Social Darwinism' says that the biological evolutionary law 'the survival of the fittest' is, and should be, the basis of human social ethics. It has long since been discredited; but at the first its founders did not perceive it to be the potentially evil thing that it actually became when Hitler took it over and used it to justify his extermination of six million Jews (see pp. 47–48).

The inventor of the term 'Social Darwinism' was Herbert Spencer (1820–1903).[5] Spencer,[6] like Darwin, took the optimistic view that evolution always leads to progress, that evolutionary adaptations always bring about improvement, provided only that people's freedom was not restricted.

In his theorising, moreover, he followed Lamarck (rather than Darwin) who taught that characteristics acquired by parents can be passed on to their offspring. Thus Spencer did not think that the main goal of evolution was reproductive success, but the development of moral character. Maladaptation of character to surrounding social and economic conditions caused pain. Adaptation of character led to pleasure or at least to 'the good'. So, if each person was left to experience the good and evil results of his own nature and its resultant conduct, adaptation would take place, and the prosperity of the species would be achieved automatically.

Moreover, according to Lamarckian principle, the evolution of good character would have a snowball effect. As each generation developed the habit of exercising the social virtues of sympathy, benevolence, honesty, altruism, self-discipline and so forth, their offspring would inherit these improved characteristics.

According to Lamarckian principle, the evolution of good character would have a snowball effect. As each generation developed the habit of exercising the social virtues of sympathy, benevolence, honesty, altruism, self-discipline and so forth, their offspring would inherit these improved characteristics.

But Spencer's optimistic theory just did not work out. Class conflict and militarism increased; the hoped-for individual harmony and moral progress did not.

Secondly, Spencer's Lamarckian view of evolution was dealt a seemingly mortal blow by the work of German biologist August Weismann (1834–1914), published in the 1880s and 1890s. This denied inheritance of acquired characteristics, and postulated a stable germ plasm unaffected by the environment. Now the mindless, ruthless process of natural selection would alone control what evolutionary

[5] Information taken from Miller et al., *Blackwell Encyclopaedia of Political Thought*, 500–1; and from Kaye, *Social Meaning of Modern Biology*. See especially his Ch. 1, 'Social Darwinism—the Failure of the Darwinian Revolution', which argues cogently that the label 'Social Darwinism' has been unfairly attached to both Spencer and Darwin; it should rather be attached to those who took over their theories, perverted and misapplied them.

[6] *Social Statics*.

development there was; and that development would be biological not moral.

It was not Spencer's fault, nor Darwin's either, as Professor Kaye has shown,[7] that the label 'Social Darwinism' was misappropriated by others and used to justify brutal capitalism and racism on the ground that the evolutionary law of the survival of the fittest should apply to unrestrained, ruthless competition in business and to racism in international relations. It was simply the law of nature that the weakest should be trampled down and the strongest survive, a theory which eventually fuelled the infamous genocidal policies of Hitler's Germany.

On the other hand, the result of allowing evolutionary biology to affect moral thinking can be seen all too clearly in statements like these by Charles Darwin:

> At some future period, not very distant as measured by the centuries, the civilized races of man will almost certainly exterminate and replace the savage races throughout the world.[8]

> The more civilised so-called Caucasian races have beaten the Turkish hollow in the struggle for existence. Looking to the world at no very distant date, what an endless number of the lower races will have been eliminated by the higher civilized races throughout the world.[9]

It is to be pointed out at once, and emphasised, that many contemporary evolutionists found these ideas abhorrent, and resisted them on Christian or humanist grounds. In particular they wanted to confine evolution to man's biological development; morality they felt belonged to the higher level of man's culture (if they were atheists) or to man's spirit (if they were theists).

This kind of Social Darwinism, as we said earlier, has long since been discredited. But it still stands as a warning of what can happen when people, in their enthusiasm for materialistic evolution, attempt to base human morality not on God, nor even on human culture, but on mere biological processes.

---

[7] *Social Meaning of Modern Biology,* see note 5.

[8] *Descent of Man,* 178.

[9] Francis Darwin, *Life and Letters,* Letter to W. Graham, July 3, 1881, 1:316.

GENES ARE THE BASIC MORAL AUTHORITY[10]

The theory that we are now to consider has come to be known as 'sociobiology'. It says that since genes control the human body, brain and mind; genes therefore are the basic moral authority, and true morality lies in cooperating with their strategies. It is to be distinguished from the older 'Social Darwinism'. The latter taught, as we have seen, that the ruthless, compassionless law of biological Darwinian evolution, 'the survival of the fittest', rightly applied also to man's social, commercial and international relationships. The newer theory, sociobiology, teaches that the genes form and control the mechanisms of our bodies, brains and minds, and programme our behaviour, whether we are conscious of that fact or not. True ethics, therefore, means bringing ourselves to understand the programme laid down by our genes, and consciously conforming ourselves and our behaviour to that programme.

The theory, in its modern form at least, goes back to the discovery of the double helix structure of DNA by Watson and Crick in 1953. By 1959 two French scientists, Jacques Monod and François Jacob, were able to explain, in part, how DNA regulated and co-ordinated the chemical activity within living organisms. In 1961 Marshall Nirenberg and Johann Matthaei were able to decipher the first 'word' of the genetic 'code'; and that same year Jacques Monod announced he had discovered the second secret of life: his theory of allosteric proteins and the stereo-chemical means by which organisms organised their activities.

These were brilliant, epoch-making discoveries. They rightly command our admiration and gratitude for the benefits, particularly in the field of medicine, which they confer upon us—though the genetic engineering that these discoveries have made possible is increasingly facing us with profound problems in medical ethics (more of that in Ch. 6).

But it is not the medical benefits that concern us here; it is the implications which these discoveries had—or rather which their discoverers and many sociobiologists since have thought they had—for

[10] We are here indebted to the very helpful account and critique by Kaye, *Social Meaning of Modern Biology*. For detailed references see note 5.

culture in general and ethics in particular. Let's consider some of their statements.

Francis Crick

> The development of biology is going to destroy to some extent, our traditional grounds for ethical beliefs.[11]

This remark was made at a CIBA Foundation Symposium in 1963, at which the evolutionary biological humanists Julian Huxley and Jacob Bronowski, among others, were present.[12] Now humanists of this kind, being atheists as was Crick, have traditionally sought an objective ground for the values of justice, tolerance, freedom, independence, love, tenderness, altruism, self-fulfilment, either in the practice of science itself or in the course of organic and cultural evolution.[13] But Crick made it clear that his above quoted remark was aimed not simply at Christians and 'their particular prejudice about the sanctity of the individual', but at the 'biological humanists' as well. The humanists' attempt to find an objective base for human values in man's cultural (as distinct from biological) evolution was, according to Crick, no longer possible.

Crick joined with other Nobel Laureates in advocating large-scale eugenics programmes: the reversible sterilization of the citizenry by placing 'something into our food' and licensing 'the people with the qualities we like' to bear children

And as far as Crick's sensitivity to the dignity of the human individual is concerned, Wolstenholme reports[14] that at that symposium Crick joined with other Nobel Laureates in advocating large-scale eugenics programmes: the reversible sterilization of the citizenry by placing 'something into our food' and licensing 'the people with the qualities we like' to bear children. (We may add as an aside, that people who vigorously protest against belief in God are not always averse to playing God themselves.)

11 Reported in Wolstenholme, *Man and His Future*, 364.

12 The CIBA Foundation, as it was called at the time of this symposium, is now known as the Novartis Foundation.

13 Kaye, *Social Meaning of Modern Biology*, 49.

14 *Man and His Future*, 275–6, 294–5; Kaye, *Social Meaning of Modern Biology*, 48.

Crick said, 'Science in general, and natural selection in particular, should become the basis on which we are to build the new culture'—and as for those who thought that science, as such, was value-free and had little to do with 'what concerns them most deeply', Crick added: 'tomorrow's science is going to knock their culture right out from under them.'[15]

It can be said at once that this centring of human significance, purpose and morality on the gene has led to the grossest of reductionism.

François Jacob and Jacques Monod

Here, for instance, is a statement by François Jacob of the main purpose and function of what he calls the organism. To understand it, you need to keep in mind that 'organism' here can refer to a human being as much as to the lowliest fungus:

> The organism thus becomes the realisation of a programme prescribed by its heredity. . . . An organism is merely a transition, a stage between what was and what will be. Reproduction [of the organism's molecules] represents both the beginning and the end, the cause and the aim.[16]

In the light of his new-found knowledge of the gene and of DNA's insatiable determination to duplicate itself Jacques Monod also sets out in similar reductionist vein to explain the true significance of human love and love poetry: it is simply DNA using human beings as agents to replicate itself. In his book *Chance and Necessity: An Essay on the Natural Philosophy of Modern Biology*, he envisages the situation where a shy poet's poems dedicated to the woman he loves bring about her surrender, and thus the poet achieves success in his 'essential project', which is the replication of his DNA, and his poems are thereby made meaningful.[17]

The discovery of DNA seems to have launched Monod, as it did Crick, on a campaign to cure the world's moral sickness, by

[15] In his 1966 Jessie and John Danz Lectures at the University of Washington, published under the title *Of Molecules and Men*, xii, 7, 93–5.

[16] *Logic of Life*, 263–4.

[17] p. 48.

persuading mankind to abandon all other bases for morality, and to found their morality on the biological impulses of the gene. Howard Kaye sums up Monod's crusade well:

> In the name of the 'molecular theory of the genetic code' and its 'scientifically warranted conclusions', Monod diagnoses the modern 'mal de l'âme' as a kind of individual and collective schizophrenia: we live in a society and a world ordered and shaped by science, yet we still desperately cling to values based on religious beliefs and myths utterly destroyed by the findings of modern science. Molecular biology, by closing the last loopholes in Darwinian theory . . . has delivered the death blow to all religious beliefs and their philosophical substitutes (for example, dialectical materialism and the 'scientistic progressism' of Spencer, Teilhard de Cardin, and the biological humanists), by destroying the 'anthropocentric illusion' upon which all 'animisms' are based.[18]

But Monod's zealous determination to found human morality and significance on the gene, its strategies and workings, leads him not only into a grievous reduction of human dignity but also subsequently into mythological, instead of scientific, explanations, and finally into incoherence.

Since his thesis is that our genes and their workings (as discovered by Crick and himself) are our true guide to morality and not religions or scientisms like dialectical materialism, he is logically obliged to explain how and under what constraints we developed these religious illusions and scientisms in the first place. His explanation is that it was those very genes which are now urging us away from religion, that originally constrained us to seek religion!

First he assures us that there was a time in our evolutionary past when it was necessary for evolution to build into our minds strong emotional support for the law, social structures and cultural traditions. Using the genes as its agent to supply this need, evolution 'created and inscribed somewhere in the genetic code' a feeling of anxiety 'which goads us to search out the meaning of existence'; and it is this

[18] *Social Meaning of Modern Biology*, 84, and citing Monod, *Chance and Necessity*, 43–4, 180.

search that has created 'all religions, all the philosophies and science itself'.[19]

We should pause to ask some questions. How does Monod know this? Did he discover this in the course of his examination of modern genes? Or is this Monod's own mythological reconstruction of the past history of genes?

> Monod's zealous determination to found human morality and significance on the gene, its strategies and workings, leads him not only into a grievous reduction of human dignity but also subsequently into mythological, instead of scientific, explanations, and finally into incoherence.

If this account is true, and religion is written in to the genes, and it is the genes that drive us to seek religion, then one would logically expect atheist Monod to urge us now to take no notice of genes whatever. But this is not what the modern sociobiologists advise us to do. In fact they urge us to do the very opposite: we are to recognise that true morality consists in understanding the strategies of the genes and cooperating with them.

If we ask how we can do this, for it is very difficult for a non-scientist to study his own genes, the answer given is two-fold. First, it is the genes that prescribe the wiring of the brain. It is a set of biological processes that determine the structure of the mind—how it perceives, how it processes information, how it makes decisions, how it evaluates courses of action, and how it motivates action.

If this is so, we must conclude that whatever anyone thinks about morality at any one time must be what his genes are making him think. But the plain fact is that, at least up until the present, genes do not make everyone think the same thing about morality. How then shall we know what advice from what set of genes to follow?

Second, the answer to this question seems to be, according to Monod, that scientists like himself must meet our need for moral understanding and guidance by offering us the 'humanly significant ideas arising from their area of special concern'. These ideas will then act as a 'substitute for the various belief systems upon which the social values and structures were traditionally founded'.[20]

---

[19] *Chance and Necessity*, 160–9.

[20] *Chance and Necessity*, xii-xiii; *From Biology to Ethics*, 2; 'On the Logical Relationship between Knowledge and Values', 15; see Kaye, *Social Meaning of Modern Biology*, 84–5.

But that raises further questions. Why should we set up a scientist like Monod as our expert in morality? According to his own theory, is not his mind largely biased by his genes just like everyone else's is? Monod was an atheist and anti-religious before he made his discoveries regarding cellular biology. How could we be sure that the atheism which he says the genes now favour, has not been read into the genes by himself? After all, according to him, in the past they favoured religion and not atheism. But of course, Monod is not the only geneticist to advocate the founding of morality on the gene. The topic is gathering ever-widening interest.[21]

E. O. Wilson

So perhaps at this stage we ought to consider some excerpts from the writings of Professor Edward O. Wilson. Renowned for his work on entomology, he published, in 1975, a book entitled *Sociobiology: The New Synthesis* which has done more than any other to promote the idea that morality can, and should be, based on our genes.[22] Here then is his description of what he calls 'the morality of the gene':

> In a Darwinist sense the organism does not live for itself. Its primary function is not even to reproduce other organisms; it reproduces genes, and it serves as their temporary carrier. . . . The individual organism is only their vehicle, part of an elaborate device to preserve and spread them. . . . The organism is only DNA's way of making more DNA.[23]

The extreme reductionism of this statement becomes clear when one realises that in contexts like this man is an organism. If the primary purpose of a human being is simply to produce another human being, and the primary purpose of that human being is to produce another human being and so on ad infinitum, then human beings are nothing but links in a chain that is going nowhere: the chain itself has no ultimate purpose or goal. But if the primary purpose of the human being is simply to act as 'the temporary carrier for the

21 See, for instance, Avise, *Genetic Gods*; Rose, *Lifelines*.

22 See his book, *Consilience*.

23 *Sociobiology*, 3.

genes', 'part of an elaborate device to preserve and spread them', 'only DNA's way of making more DNA'—then humanity is degraded indeed. From being, as traditionally understood, a being made in the image of God to love and serve God and to enjoy him for ever, each individual human becomes no more than a temporary vehicle and device to serve the purpose of a few biochemicals. Even at the biological level the idea would seem to be absurd. It would bid us view the fully grown oak tree, not as a thing of majestic glory in its own right, a very worthy end for an acorn to develop into, but merely as a temporary device for the sole purpose of producing ever more acorns.

Then as to the sense in which Wilson regards morality as based on the gene, let us consider a further statement:

> Morality, or more strictly our belief in morality, is merely an adaptation put in place to further our reproductive ends. Hence the basis of ethics does not lie in God's will. . . . In an important sense, ethics as we understand it is an illusion fobbed off on us by our genes to get us to cooperate.[24]

This is very odd. One might have thought that the moral commandment 'Thou shalt not commit adultery' might considerably restrict, rather than further, our reproductive ends. Genes are obviously a very *unethical* bunch of biochemicals if they cheat us with an illusion in order to get us to cooperate with them. Clearly they hold that the end justifies the means. But why should we cooperate with them? Because, according to Wilson, true morality is to cooperate with the strategies of one's genes:

> Ethical codes work because they drive us to go against our selfish day-to-day impulses in favour of long-term group survival and harmony. . . . Furthermore, the way our biology enforces its ends is by making us think that there is an objective higher code, to which we are all subject.[25]

Once more it is to be noted that as with the older Social Darwinism so with Darwinism's latest offspring, sociobiology, many atheistic humanists reject its reductionism and its attempt to found

[24] Ruse and Wilson, 'Evolution of Ethics', 51–2.

[25] 'Evolution of Ethics', 52.

morality on biology instead of on man's social and cultural relationships. Theodosius Dobzhansky, one of the twentieth century's leading exponents of the modern biological theory of evolution, is a notable example of this.[26]

But, in fact, Wilson, reductionist though he is, neither forgets nor ignores the development of human culture and social organisation. On the contrary he emphasises its importance. In his *Sociobiology: The New Synthesis* he admits that 'the genes have given away most of their sovereignty'[27] and in his *On Human Nature* he further admits that 'human social evolution is obviously more cultural than genetic'.[28] But that does not mean that culture has now evolved to the point where it is all-powerful: the genes still hold culture on the leash.[29] And necessarily so, because, according to Wilson, the genes prescribe the wiring of the brain, a set of biological processes that determine the structure of the mind—how it perceives, how it processes information, how it makes decisions, how it evaluates courses of action, and how it motivates action.[30] On the other hand, the genes do not determine our choices, they merely bias them. That therefore accounts for the chance variations between societies: it does not mean that the genes have lost control. But it does mean that natural selection eventually leads to cultural adaptation.

If all this is true, we naturally ask how the bias which our genes give to our choices led during the twentieth century alone to such vast variations as provoked world wars and caused the destruction of multi-millions of human beings. Were not our genes supposed, according to Wilson, to keep our cultures on a leash?

The answer is, yes, that is what our genes were supposed to do. But our cultural evolution is largely an elaboration of underlying biological imperatives, most of which were originally designed for our ancestors' hunter-gatherer existence.[31]

---

26 See his 'Chance and Creativity in Evolution'.

27 *Sociobiology*, 550.

28 *On Human Nature*, 153.

29 See generally his *Genes, Mind and Culture* (1981) and Lumsden and Wilson, *Promethean Fire* (1983).

30 Kaye, *Social Meaning of Modern Biology*, 118.

31 Must we not ask, Who designed these biological imperatives for this purpose? See Wilson, *On Human Nature*, 88–95; 'Ethical Implications of Human Sociobiology', 28; Kaye, *Social Meaning of Modern Biology*, 120.

From this, then, we might deduce that our genes are hopelessly out of date and should not be listened to on matters of morality. But apparently not so. For Wilson goes on to explain that the monstrous destructive forms that culture has developed in advanced societies—racism, wars, massacre, genocide—are what he calls *hypertrophies*—grotesquely exaggerated growths of a basically healthy attitude to kinship preservation produced by the genes. They are, so to speak, cancerous growths in human cultures; and the cure would be to get back to our genes, understand their original healthy intentions and live according to them.

So, in the end, the genes are still to be our guides, our ultimate moral authority.

There is, then, a fundamental flaw in this atheistic attempt to base human morality on our genes. If there is no creator, and if humans are nothing but matter and have no spirit-element, then certainly the human body, brain and mind are altogether the product of our genes. But then how could humans ever turn round on their genes and question them as to whether they were healthy or not? What part of a human could it be that was not produced by his or her genes and so could think independently of them?

We are built as gene machines . . . but we have the power to turn against our creators. We, alone on earth, can rebel against the tyranny of the selfish replicators.
–Richard Dawkins, *The Selfish Gene*

Richard Dawkins, author of the famous book *The Selfish Gene*, holds a similar view to that of Wilson on the genetic basis of human morality. Our genes are concerned, so he says, solely with using human bodies for the purpose of replicating themselves. This then is their strategy, and it this strategy that is written into the genetic code in every cell in our bodies and brains. And yet Dawkins assures us that somehow—he does not explain how—we are free to rebel against our genes:

> We are built as gene machines . . . but we have the power to turn against our creators. We, alone on earth, can rebel against the tyranny of the selfish replicators.[32]

[32] *Selfish Gene*, 215. For a more recent expression of this view, see Dennett, *Darwin's Dangerous Idea*, 471.

Could it be that our genes are themselves in rebellion one against the other? In that case it would be very difficult, surely, to found a morality on them; and how, and by what criterion, would we decide between them? And what non-genetic, non-aligned part of us would we have that would be capable of adjudicating between the rival genes?

On the other hand, as Professor Steven Rose acutely observes:

> If on the other hand it is not our genes that are rebellious, what other options are available? Dawkins never says, but implicit in his argument is that somewhere there is some non-material, non-genetic force moulding our behaviour.[33]

And Professor Kaye asks a similar question of E. O. Wilson:

> How can will and sociobiological knowledge so effortlessly transcend the 'machinery' of the mind, 'programmed' by its 'hidden masters', the genes, and by natural selection?[34]

APPROPRIATE RESPONSE TO ECONOMIC CHANGES IS THE ONLY MORALITY

We come now to Marxism/Leninism. So let us just remind ourselves what we are looking for in this survey of various moralities. We are not setting out to study the many details of these moralities' related ethical practices. We are looking rather at each morality to see whether it is based on any absolute moral principle that, because it is an absolute principle, every thinking person everywhere could rightly be expected to accept it or be faulted for rejecting it; or whether its basic principle is a matter of arbitrary choice.

Now Marxism is different from the various atheistic moralities that we have hitherto been discussing in that it does not attempt to found morality on the raw facts and processes of biology. Instead it holds that true morality consists in the right practical response to the social and economic conditions brought about by the workings of historical materialism in the flow of human history.

---

33 *Lifelines*, 214.

34 *Social Meaning of Modern Biology*, 131.

Marx accepted, of course, the Darwinian doctrine of evolution, and the special Marxist doctrine of dialectical materialism is itself an evolutionary doctrine. But dialectics, which Marxists see at work at all levels in the universe, and particularly in history, can scarcely be regarded as a moral value: it is rather a force, a process: it provides the necessary conditions for the exercise of true Marxist morality—perhaps also the impulse for it and the guarantee that this morality is sure to prevail in the end. But it can scarcely be regarded as a moral value itself.

The basis of Marxist morality

On what value then is Marxist morality based? Well not, on any absolute moral value, regarded as something absolutely true and valid at all times and in all places and circumstances, like, say, the laws of arithmetic. Consider the statements of some of its early proponents.

Friedrich Engels, co-founder with Marx of Marxism said,

> We . . . reject every attempt to impose on us any moral dogma whatsoever as an eternal, ultimate, and forever immutable moral law on the pretext that the moral world too has its permanent principles which transcend history and the differences between nations. We maintain on the contrary that all former moral theories are the product, in the last analysis, of the economic stage which society had reached at their particular epoch.[35]

On the other hand, in spite of what Engels says, from time to time in the vast amount of theoretical literature that Marxism has produced, we find some Marxists writing as if Marxism does recognise one 'highest' and presumably eternal and unchanging good, by which all other things and activities must be judged, namely freedom, as the American Marxist philosopher Howard Selsam makes clear:

> the struggle for freedom . . . itself is moral or right because freedom is the highest good and that alone by which all acts and institutions can be judged.[36]

[35] Cited in Hunt, *Theory and Practice of Communism*, 113.
[36] *Socialism and Ethics*, 214.

Again, Professor T. M. Jaroszewski states that in socialist thought 'man, each real, specific individual, is the main social value';[37] and he goes on to explain 'this does not refer to any select groups of classes, but to the mass of working people. The source of moral values is not the individual withdrawn into himself; moral values are produced by men in concrete work communities.'

Now Judaism, Christianity and Islam all regard human beings, of whatever nation, and of whatever class within a nation as being of infinite value, as being made in the image of God; and it is this intrinsic value of each and every human being that governs the ethical code in relation to man.

Marxism, by contrast, rejects this basis for the value of man. Vladimir Lenin wrote:

> In what sense do we reject ethics, reject morality? In the sense given to it by the bourgeoisie, who based ethics on God's commandments. On this point we . . . say that we do not believe in God, and that we know perfectly well that the clergy, the landowners and the bourgeoisie invoked the name of God so as to further their own interests as exploiters. Or, instead of basing ethics . . . on the commandments of God, they based it on idealist or semi-idealist phrases, which always amounted to something very similar to God's commandments.[38]

It is altogether possible and, if so, completely inexcusable, that some of the landowners and clergy in Lenin's day may have invoked the name of God to further their own interests. Christ himself found it necessary to expose some of the religious Pharisees and Sadducees of his own day for similar behaviour (Luke 11:37–46). He was especially severe on certain hypocritical theologians 'who like to walk around in long robes, and love greetings in the market-places and the best seats in the synagogues and the places of honour at feasts, who devour widows' houses and for a pretence make long prayers. They will receive the greater condemnation' (Luke 20:46–47). Christ's apostle, James, likewise denounced the unscrupulous landowners of his day:

[37] *Socialism as a Social System*, 249–50.

[38] *Collected Works*, 31:291.

> Come now, you rich, weep and howl for the miseries that are coming upon you. Your riches have rotted and your garments are moth-eaten. Your gold and silver have corroded, and their corrosion will be evidence against you and will eat your flesh like fire. You have laid up treasure in the last days. Behold, the wages of the labourers who mowed your fields, which you kept back by fraud, are crying out against you, and the cries of the harvesters have reached the ears of the Lord of hosts. You have lived on the earth in luxury and in self-indulgence. You have fattened your hearts in a day of slaughter. (Jas 5:1–5)

And the Hebrew prophets, (such as Isaiah, Jeremiah, Ezekiel and Amos) were equally loud and equally persistent in denouncing those who oppressed the proletariat of their day.

In the light of this, the following statement by G. L. Andreyev seems somewhat strange:

> In the reigning morality under capitalism that act is considered moral which promotes the preservation and strengthening of the system of exploitation and the acquirements of profits. Religion merely justifies this unjust and oppressive, bloody, and inhuman system in the name of God.[39]

One cannot help thinking that had not Marx and Lenin and their followers in the twentieth century rejected belief in God to start with, they might even have approved of a God who inspired his prophets thus to champion the cause of the oppressed. But as it was, they explicitly rejected the idea that each individual human being has an absolute intrinsic worth as created in the image of God, as Lenin makes clear:

> We reject any morality based on extra-human and extra-class concepts. We say that this is deception, dupery, stultification of the workers and peasants in the interests of the landowners and capitalists.[40]

On what then is Marxist morality based? From what does it spring, if all these other bases are rejected? Let Lenin, once more, tell us:

[39] *What Kind of Morality Does Religion Teach?* Cited in Raymond S. Sleeper, *A Lexicon of Marxist-Leninist Semantics*, Alexandria, VA: Western Goals, 1983, 174.

[40] *Collected Works*, 31:291.

> We say that morality is entirely subordinated to the interests of the proletariat's class struggle. Our morality stems from the interests of the class struggle of the proletariat. The old society was based on the oppression of all the workers and peasants by the landowners and capitalists. We had to destroy all that, and overthrow them but to do that we had to create unity. That is something God cannot create. . . . That is why we say that to us there is no such thing as a morality that stands outside human society; that is a fraud. To us morality is subordinated to the interests of the proletariat's class struggle.[41]

Perhaps Lenin is speaking here with the freedom of an orator rather than in the precise terminology of a philosopher, for in most people's minds justice is an integral part of morality. To say therefore, that 'morality is entirely subordinate to the interests of the proletariat's class struggle', sounds strange to any outsider; for it appears to imply that the proletariat's interests must override any considerations of justice. Similarly, to say that 'our morality *stems from* the interests of the class struggle of the proletariat' sounds perilously like saying that justice is whatever the interests of the proletariat's class struggle dictate it shall be.

Indeed, this is how V. N. Kolbanovskiy appears to define communist morality:

> From the viewpoint of communist morality that is moral which promotes the destruction of the old, exploiting society, and the construction of the new, communist society. Everything that hinders this development is immoral or amoral. To be a moral man, in our understanding, means to devote all his forces and energy to the cause of the struggle for a new communist society.[42]

It would seem, then, that here Marxism is declaring that it does have an absolute basis for its morality: whatever the interests of the proletariat's class struggle dictates as necessary to its cause is by definition moral. And this being so, it is understandable that communist

---

[41] *Collected Works*, 31:291–2.

[42] *Communist Morality*, 20.

leaders felt free—perhaps felt duty bound—to use any methods, fair or foul, in order to establish the classless society and the earthly paradise; for whatever the methods were, the simple fact that they were being used to bring about the classless society conferred on them the quality of true morality. The end justified the means, whatever the cost in terms of the destruction of millions of 'individual specific men'.

Here is Joseph Stalin:

> To put it briefly: the dictatorship of the proletariat is the domination of the proletariat over the bourgeoisie, untrammelled by the law and based on violence and enjoying the sympathy and support of the toiling and exploited masses.[43]

Nikita Khrushchev carries the theme forward:

> Our cause is sacred. He whose hand will tremble, who will stop midway, whose knees will shake before he destroys tens and hundreds of his enemies, he will lead the revolution into danger. Whoever will spare a few lives of enemies, will pay for it with hundreds and thousands of lives of the better sons of our fathers.[44]

Final comments

If what Engels said is true, that there are no permanent principles which transcend history and the differences between nations, communist morality must, at least to those outside it, seem to be arbitrary, a matter simply of taste, inclination and preference. To campaign for justice for all human beings, qua human beings, on the ground that all are equal, and all have a right to freedom, would certainly have universal appeal. To define justice and morality as the interests of one particular class cannot but seem arbitrary to the rest of mankind.

Marx and Hitler both accepted Darwinian evolution, rather than creation by God as the origin of man. Hitler used it to justify the *Übermensch*; Marx to justify (by way of historical materialism) the

[43] Speech delivered 24 April 1924 (*J. Stalin Works*, 6:118).

[44] Nikita Khrushchev, *Ukrainian Bulletin* (1–15 August 1960), 12.

proletariat class. Both Marxism and Hitlerism slaughtered millions in order to promote their particular ideal of humanity. If man has no creator outside of evolution's materialistic forces to be the ground and basis of man's intrinsic value, by what criterion shall one decide between Marx's and Hitler's evolutionary theories?

Perhaps communism would say in answer to the above question: 'historical materialism' has already declared in favour of Marx's theories, since its irresistible working in history has overturned the capitalist bourgeoisie and established the proletariat; and by that same irresistible working it will one day bring in the classless society and the earthly paradise.

Certainly the irresistible process of change, which historical materialism constantly brings about by its dialectics, does seem to be another absolute in Marxist thinking; so much of an absolute in fact, that because matter is said by Marxists to be eternal and dialectics is a property inherent in matter, change will not cease even when the communist utopia has arrived, but will irresistibly turn that utopia into something else.

How could people possibly have a moral duty to struggle, suffer and die for future generations whom they would never know, and who would never know them?

It is true, of course, that the nature of historical materialism and its relation to human endeavour in Marxist thought has been hotly and endlessly debated;[45] but what consensus there is seems to favour the idea that historical materialism is not fatalistic but rather deterministic. It does not relieve man of his need to struggle; it is effective only through the efforts of people. And yet from Marxist writers one has the impression that historical materialism not only provides the necessary enabling conditions for man's struggling, but is the underlying, ultimately irresistible, tide that will bear the communist revolution triumphantly through to the achievement of the classless society and the earthly paradise, the final victory and reward of communist morality.

It speaks volumes for the immense power of the thought and influence of Marx, Lenin, Stalin, Khrushchev and their successors that they were able to inspire millions of people of successive genera-

[45] See Ernst Fischer, *Marx in His Own Words*, 80–93.

tions to struggle, suffer and lay down their lives for the sake of their promised paradise. But the stark reality is that millions of them died; and the paradise for which they loyally suffered privation, pain, and death has not yet come. And there being, according to Marxism, no God, no resurrection, no life to come, they will not enjoy any fruits of their sacrifice ever.

How would one justify a morality which used the theory of historical materialism to entice, inspire, and compel people to sacrifice, suffer and die for a paradise they would never see? How could people possibly have a moral duty to struggle, suffer and die for future generations whom they would never know, and who would never know them? And what could possibly be the source of such a moral duty? Mere materialism?

HUMANITY ITSELF SETS THE MORAL LAW

We now examine briefly the secular humanists' view of morality. The label 'secular humanist' covers a wide range of people, and, in consequence, a great variety of detailed opinion. The one thing that unites them is their conviction that there is no God, and humans must learn to live as morally as they can in that situation.

The list of persons who have been honoured with the title 'Humanist of the Year' has included such well-known personages as Julian Huxley (1962), Erich Fromm (1966), B. F. Skinner (1972), Andrei Sakharov (1980), Carl Sagan (1981), Isaac Asimov (1984), John Kenneth Galbraith (1985), Margaret Atwood (1987), Richard Dawkins (1996), E. O. Wilson (1999), Daniel Dennet (2004), and Gloria Steinem (2012).

All humanists, as we have said, are atheists. All embrace some version of atheistic evolution. Unlike Social Darwinists, sociobiologists, or dialectical materialists, they do not necessarily found their morality on theories of biology or history. But all of them agree that when it comes to morality it is man, not God, who sets the rules.

Professor Paul Kurtz, who was a member of the faculty at the State University of New York at Buffalo and a primary writer and editor of the *Humanist Manifesto II*, made clear the distinction he saw between humanism and any belief in God:

> Humanism cannot in any fair sense of the word apply to one who still believes in God as the source and creator of the universe.[46]

And Professor Max Hocutt likewise makes clear the distinction in the source of authority behind ethical rules:

> The fundamental question of ethics is, who makes the rules? God or men? The theistic answer is that God makes them. The humanist answer is that men make them. This distinction between theism and humanism is the fundamental division in moral theory.[47]

The humanist position then is very clear; but on its own confession it runs into a number of difficulties.

The difficulty of ethical relativism

It is easy to say that humans make the rules, and at first sight it seems to promise freedom from the moral tyranny that many people feel is implied in a divine-command-morality.

How would civilised life be possible if people were free to lie, murder, and steal, or not, according to their personal set of rules which they had made up for themselves?

But what does it mean to say that 'humans make the rules'? Is each man and woman free to make his or her own set of rules?

One would have thought that this was impossible. How could you have a sensible game of football if each player was free to make up his own set of rules as the game was in progress? And how would civilised life be possible if people were free to lie, murder, and steal, or not, according to their personal set of rules which they had made up for themselves?

Nonetheless some leading humanists seem to approve of a limited, if not total, ethical relativism, and it may not be an exaggeration to say that, when it comes to practice, ethical relativism is the rule by which many humanists actually live. Here are some of them in their own words.

46 'Is Everyone a Humanist?', 177.

47 'Toward an Ethic of Mutual Accommodation', 137.

Arthur E. Gravatt

The morality or immorality of any behavior, including sexual behavior, has been put in the context of 'situation ethics'. In this approach moral behavior may differ from situation to situation. Behavior might be moral for one person and not another, or moral at one time and not another. Whether an act is moral or immoral is determined by 'the law of love', that is the extent to which love and concern for others is a factor in the relationship.[48]

Paul Kurtz

Humanists . . . are committed to free thought and to the view that ethical values are relative to human experience and needs. This means that ethics need not be derived from any theological or metaphysical propositions about the nature of ultimate reality, that it can be autonomous, and that ethical judgments to some extent may be grounded in reflective inquiry.[49]

But not all humanists are happy with this kind of ethical relativism. We quote, for instance, Professor Max Hocutt once again:

> Denying that there is an absolute right and wrong laid up in heaven does not require us to subscribe to the confused doctrine usually mislabelled 'ethical relativism'; it does not require us to believe that right and wrong are mere 'matters of opinion'. On the contrary, the latter doctrine . . . is as objectionable as theological absolutism. Thinking something true doesn't make it true, either in ethics or in anything else. Thinking the earth to be flat doesn't make the earth flat, and thinking a practice right doesn't make it right.[50]

Quite so. If one person thinks the earth is flat, and another thinks it is a cube, then in order to settle their disagreement they will need some objective facts independent of their opinions. So it is with morality: we need an independent criterion to judge between our relativistic moral opinions. Without it, how could we know which, if any, of our moral opinions was true or false?

---

[48] Cited in Genné, 'Our Moral Responsibility', 63.

[49] 'Does Humanism Have an Ethic of Responsibility?', 11.

[50] 'Toward an Ethic of Mutual Accommodation', 138–9.

Theists, of course, find such a criterion in the objective moral law laid down by God, by his transcendental will and divine imperative. But as Joseph Fletcher, a humanist and the famous proponent of 'situation ethics' says, such an objective, God-given, moral law 'does not fit a humanistic ethic in which human beings must, as moral agents, themselves choose and freely posit or assert the ideals and values and standards of mankind.'[51]

The need for a moral yardstick

So then what kind of a yardstick do humanists propose for assessing which moral opinion is right and which is wrong? Hocutt, who, as we have seen, disapproves of ethical relativism, offers us what he feels is an adequate yardstick:

> If there is no morality laid up in heaven, by what yardstick will we measure earthly moralities? The answer, of course, is that we should use the same yardstick we use to evaluate any other human artifact: satisfaction of our needs.[52]

But this surely is a very inadequate yardstick. Far from being an objective criterion that everyone would accept, 'satisfaction of our needs' is something about which people are most likely to disagree, especially when they are engaged in some dispute.

And moreover, when later he comes to discuss the problem of justice, Hocutt says:

> How should that problem be solved? I know no answer which could satisfy everybody. Having different, perhaps even incompatible, interests, we all wish to see the problem solved in the way that is best calculated to maximize the achievement of our own ends. Therefore, if I told you how the problem ought to be solved, if I laid down my ideas of 'justice', I would be doing no more than trying to get you to accept a set of principles that would maximize my interests. Instead of putting out that kind of dishonest propaganda, I prefer to engage in open and forth-

51 'Comment by Joseph Fletcher on Nielsen Article', 71.
52 'Toward an Ethic of Mutual Accommodation', 138.

> right negotiations: let me have things partly my way, and I won't stand in the way of your having them partly your way.[53]

That is fine practical common sense, if it were concerned simply with settling a case of a conflict of interests. But it is no way at all to settle the question of justice involved in deciding whether, say, theft, or murder, or rape is right or not.

And that leads another humanist, Vithal Mahadeo Tarkunde to comment:

> I cannot fully share Prof. Hocutt's statement that the yardstick for evaluating ethical rules is the 'satisfaction of our needs'. . . . This approach has led Prof. Hocutt to conclude that there is no absolute right or wrong.[54]

Moreover, humanists are concerned, and quite rightly too, to develop an ethic appropriate for the whole world. Professor Paul Kurtz writes:

> We need to draw on the best moral wisdom of the past, but we also need to develop a new, revisionary ethics that employs rational methods of inquiry appropriate to the world of the future, an ethics that respects the dignity and freedom of each person but that also expresses a larger concern for humanity as a whole.[55]

They are fine words and praiseworthy aspirations. But what realistic hope of success would this scheme have if the yardstick by which the disputes between the nations were to be settled was 'the satisfaction of our needs'? It is the determination of each nation to satisfy what it regards as its needs that lies behind the disputes.

The aim of morality

Humanists are also divided on what should be the proper goal of morality. Different ethical systems have from time to time proposed different aims. One thinks, for instance, of utilitarians who have defined

53 'Toward an Ethic of Mutual Accommodation', 143.

54 'Comment by V. M. Tarkunde on Hocutt Article', 148.

55 'A Declaration of Interdependence: A New Global Ethics', 6 in original article; also on p. 42 in *Toward a New Enlightenment.*

moral rightness to be what brings the greatest good for the greatest number of people in the long run. Jeremy Bentham (1748–1832) understood the term 'greatest good' quantitatively; John Stuart Mill (1806–73) qualitatively. The difficulty with both schemes lay in how to define 'good'. Others have defined the aim as 'pleasure' (so the ancient Epicureans) or as 'happiness' (so Aristotle).[56]

But humanists, according to one of their number, do not agree on what the aim of morality should be nor on a number of other fundamental ethical questions, as we see from the book entitled *Humanist Ethics*, edited by Morris B. Storer, who writes in the preface:

> Humanists are largely united in emphasising human fulfilment, a measured freedom, the dignity of the individual, a factor of situational relativity, and a broad spectrum of human rights as cornerstones of humanist ethics. But it is clear that, beyond these essentials, we differ widely. Is personal advantage the measure of right and wrong, or the advantage of all affected? Humanists differ. Is there truth in ethics? We differ. Are 'right' and 'wrong' expressions of heart or head? Do people have free wills? Do you measure morality by results or by principles? Do people have duties as well as rights? We have our differences on all these and more.[57]

Humanists, however, put great faith in reason and humanity for the solving of these many problems; and since many humanists are very gracious and reasonable people, it is, perhaps, natural for them to think that patient application of reason will in the end solve everything.

The British Humanist Association published the following statement regarding their beliefs:

> Humanists believe that man's conduct should be based on humanity, insight, and reason. He must face his problems with his own moral and intellectual resources, without looking for supernatural aid.[58]

---

[56] For a fuller discussion of the positions of these thinkers, see the fourth book in this series, *Doing What's Right*.

[57] *Humanist Ethics*, 3.

[58] Annual General Meeting of the British Humanist Association, July 1967.

But even among reasonable people of good will reason alone is often not sufficient. Kurt Baier, another humanist, remarks:

> Plainly, it is not easy to determine in an objective way what conduct is morally ideal. Hence even among people of good will, that is, among people perfectly willing to do what is morally ideal, there may be sincere disagreement. But if people are to have the assurance that others will by and large do what is morally ideal, it is desirable that such conduct should be publicly recognised and taught to the next generation. For that will apprise people of good will what exactly will be generally regarded as morally ideal. The problem, of course, is that if there is likely to be disagreement on this score even among people of good will, it is also likely that some will disagree with at least some of what is regarded as morally ideal, and indeed sometimes rightly so.[59]

And if this is true of people of good will, what hope is there of getting agreement when masses of people, ourselves included, can at times be far from reasonable?

The fact is that any realistic moral system must face the sobering fact that men and women are imperfect. We are not well ordered computers into which you can enter a bit of software containing moral laws and principles and the computer will carry them out to the letter without a murmur. We are selfish, and proud, and jealous and envious and greedy and impure and a great many things beside. We need, therefore, something more than mere unaided reason to prevail upon us to live as we ought.

Humanists recognise this, of course, as the following three passages from Kurtz make clear.

> Nevertheless, the humanist is faced with a crucial ethical problem: Insofar as he has defended an ethic of freedom, can he develop a basis for moral responsibility? Regretfully, merely to liberate individuals from authoritarian social institutions, whether church or state, is no guarantee that they will be aware of their moral responsibility to others. The contrary is often the case. Any number of social institutions regulate conduct by some

[59] 'Freedom, Obligation, and Responsibility', 8.

> means of norms and rules, and sanctions are imposed for enforcing them. Moral conduct is often insured because of fear of the consequences of breaking the law or of transgressing moral conventions. Once these sanctions are ignored, we may end up with [a man] concerned with his own personal lust for pleasure, ambition, and power, and impervious to moral constraints.[60]
>
> Some utopian anarchists maintain that human nature is basically beneficent: it is restrictive societal laws that corrupt human beings, and not the contrary. Their solution is to emancipate individuals from them; this they believe will untap a natural propensity for altruism. Regretfully, there is no guarantee that individual moral beneficence will reign once all institutional sanctions are removed. Moreover, even if the world were only full of people with good intentions, they might still differ in their interpretation or application of their moral convictions, and this can be a further source of conflict.[61]
>
> Professor Lorenz[62] and others . . . maintain that aggression is innate in the human species. Human vices, such as selfishness, laziness, vindictiveness, hatred, sloth, pride, jealousy are so widespread in human behaviour that we are all capable of their temptation at times. Perhaps humanists have been overly optimistic about the full reaction of human nature.[63]

Well then, what policies, we naturally ask, would humanists have us adopt to deal with this all-too-real human need?

Kurtz suggests, at least to start with, moral education; and of course that is necessary and helpful.

> As I have said, moral freedom is a central humanist value: the freeing of individuals from excessive restraints so that they may actualize their potentialities and maximize free choice. However, such a normative value is hardly sufficient unless a moral

[60] 'Does Humanism Have an Ethic of Responsibility?', 15.

[61] 'Does Humanism Have an Ethic of Responsibility?', 15.

[62] The ethologist and Nobel Prize winner Konrad Lorenz published Das sogenannte Böse zur Naturgeschichte der Aggression in 1963, which was published in English as On Aggression in 1966 (repr. London: Routledge, 2002).

[63] 'Does Humanism Have an Ethic of Responsibility?', 20.

> growth takes place. It is not enough to release individuals from authoritarian institutions, for some individuals may degenerate into hedonistic fleshpots or amoral egoists; thus we need also to nourish the conditions for moral development, in which an appreciation for the needs of others can emerge; and this is dependent upon moral education.[64]

Quite so, but on what shall this moral education be based? Simply that humans—some humans—somewhere make the rules? That there are no absolute codes? That traditional morality is passé? Or that all present moral codes are bourgeois and therefore sinister? That there is no God nor any final judgment? That kind of teaching scarcely seems calculated to capture the hearts and consciences of men and women and turn them into fine moral characters.

It is therefore interesting to see that in spite of humanism's relentless rejection of God and the supernatural, experience led the humanist Professor Hans Eysenck to give it as his opinion: 'In rejecting religion altogether, Humanism may be throwing out the ethical baby with the supernatural bathwater.'[65]

Similarly, the humanist Professor Corliss Lamont (1902–95) wrote:

> Any humane philosophy, must include such New Testament ideals as the brotherhood of man, peace on earth, and the abundant life. There is much ethical wisdom, too, in the Old Testament and its Ten Commandments. Without accepting any ethical principle as a dogmatic dictum never to be questioned, the Humanist certainly adheres in general to a biblical commandment such as 'Thou shalt not bear false witness against thy neighbour'.[66]

Any theist would, of course, applaud this; but then would point out that the morality of the Old and New Testaments is rooted in the character of the God of the Old and New Testaments. And one can't very well have the character of God without God himself, and you can't have God himself without facing his assurance that morality is

---

64 'Does Humanism Have an Ethic of Responsibility?', 17.

65 'Reason with Compassion', 92.

66 *Lifetime of Dissent*, 55.

far more important than people often care to recognise. According to God, we have not finished with morality's concerns when we die: there is to be a final judgment (Acts 17:30–31; Heb 9:27–28).

Now as we all know, it is this element, among others, in the Bible's teaching that atheistic humanists reject as being a mediaeval superstition; though it is not always clear why they think that it is better for the cause of morality that there should not be a final judgment and that outrageous sinners like Hitler should get away unscathed from all justice and punishment simply by shooting their brains out.

But sometimes some humanists seem to have second thoughts even on this topic, as apparently did the humanist agnostic Will Durant, when he confessed to a difficulty that inevitably besets humanist morality:

> We shall find it no easy task to mould a natural ethic strong enough to maintain moral restraint and social order without the support of supernatural consolations, hopes, and fears.[67]

And as for Jesus Christ and the morality which he taught, it was the world-famous humanist-atheist, Bertrand Russell, who said: 'What the world needs is Christian love and compassion.'[68]

It is to the Christian ethic and in particular to some of the objections that people raise against it that we shall turn in our next section.

GOD IS THE AUTHORITY BEHIND THE MORAL LAW

The survey of five systems of morality which we have just completed has brought to light the bases upon which they are built. Let's review them here briefly:

1. *The popular view*: Science has destroyed the traditional bases of morality. Ethics, therefore, is simply a matter of 'doing one's own thing' within the practical limits imposed by the need to get on with one's family, friends, employers and the State.

---

[67] *The Humanist* (Feb. 1977), cited in Francis A. Schaeffer. A Christian Manifesto. 1981. In The Complete Works of Francis A. Schaeffer. Vol. 5. A Christian View of the West. Carlisle, UK: Paternoster Press, 1982, 5:439.

[68] *Human Society in Ethics and Politics*, viii.

2. *Social Darwinism*: Morality is based on the evolutionary principle, 'the survival of the fittest'.

3. *Sociobiology*: Our genes dictate our behaviour: true morality means cooperating with (or sometimes rebelling against) the strategies of our genes.

4. *Marxism*: There is no absolute morality. Morality consists in responding to the economic and social conditions brought about by the workings of historical materialism. During the present phase of these workings morality stems from and is subordinate to the struggles of the proletariat.

5. *Secular Humanism*: Man himself sets the rules. Morality is not an absolute system imposed by God: it is an empirical and relativistic system worked out and constantly adjusted in the light of reason and humanity to meet life's ever changing situations.

Now to complete our study we must consider what we may call the traditional view that the authority behind the moral law is God.

General objections to this view

There is no denying that many people feel a deep and powerful antipathy to this view. Our task here therefore is twofold. First, it is to understand some, at least, of the reasons why there is such hostility to it; and secondly to ascertain, as far as we can, whether their criticisms of the theistic view of morality are based on what the theistic view actually stands for, or simply on what people imagine it stands for.

Let's begin with one of the most common objections towards the theistic view.

Objection 1: Fear of an interfering deity

The first objection is that the idea that there is an almighty God above us, always interfering in our lives and commanding us what to do and what not to do, is an insult to our human dignity and a tyrannous restriction on our freedom.

There is no doubt that this is how many people feel, but it is strange nonetheless. If a man buys a car, and receives along with it an owner's manual from the manufacturer, telling him how to treat the car, what to do and what not to do—he does not feel it to be an insult to his dignity as an autonomous human being. Nor does he find himself saying: 'I will not have the manufacturer dictating to me what I must and must not do. I will put diesel and not petrol into the tank if I please. If I don't want to, I shall not obey the direction that I must keep the engine topped up with lubricating oil.' No, the car owner accepts the idea that the manufacturers of the car know best how it should be treated; and he holds that it is in his own best interests to comply with their directions.

Why then should people think or feel that, if there were a creator, he would automatically be against them, and constantly out to destroy their enjoyment and spitefully to restrict their freedom?

That is apparently how Julian Huxley must have felt for, as we noted previously, he confesses:

> For my own part, the sense of spiritual relief which comes from rejecting the idea of God as a supernatural being is enormous.[69]

The Bible's own explanation of this state of suspicion towards God on the part of the human heart is that people are 'alienated from the life of God because of the ignorance that is in them' (Eph 4:18). This diagnosis does not mean by 'ignorance' that people are not intelligent. It means that people are actually (and one might say, strangely) ignorant of what God is actually like.

Objection 2: Resentment against the theistic view's strict sexual morality

This resentment comes frequently to expression in humanist literature. Lamont declares:

> The Humanist ethics is opposed to the puritanical prejudice against pleasure and desire that marks the Western tradition of morality. Men and women have deep-seated wants and needs of an emotional and physical character, the fulfilment of which is an essential ingredient in the good life. . . . Contempt for or suppression of normal desires results in their working themselves out in surreptitious, coarse or abnormal ways.[70]

[69] *Religion Without Revelation*, 32.

[70] 'Ethics of Humanism', 47–8.

> Anyone who thinks that the designer and creator of marriage is against the pleasure which he himself designed, cannot have read the Bible's delightful love poem, the Song of Songs.

That is perfectly true; but anyone who thinks that the designer and creator of marriage is against the pleasure which he himself designed, cannot have read the Bible's delightful love poem, the Song of Songs. But by that same token the Creator is against all distortions of his gift of married love. Yet it is freedom to engage in any form of sexual expression that many humanists demand, and it is for forbidding these things that many of them reject God as the authority behind the moral law. The *Humanist Manifesto II* declares:

> We believe that intolerant attitudes, often cultivated by orthodox religions and puritanical cultures, unduly repress sexual conduct. . . . The many varieties of sexual exploration should not in themselves be considered 'evil' . . . individuals should be permitted to express their sexual proclivities and pursue their lifestyles as they desire.[71]

The result of this sexual 'freedom' in our modern world is millions of broken families, children traumatised by the divorce of their parents and the break-up of their homes, myriads of abortions and a virtually worldwide epidemic of sexually transmitted diseases. God's law is kinder than its opponents.

Objection 3: Belief in God justifies oppression of the proletariat and neglect of the poor

The idea that belief in God justifies and encourages these evils doubtless arose from confusing formal, nominal religion with what the Bible actually teaches. But the idea was never true, as we have already seen (p. 71). The minimum of acquaintance with the Bible would quickly have shown that it was not true. God explicitly declares himself to be against the oppression of the proletariat and neglect of the poor.

---

71 p. 18.

Objection 4: Observance of rules destroys life

Many would hold that observance of endless rules and regulations supposedly imposed by God ruins the spontaneity of life, destroys life's joy, engenders a legalistic spirit and induces religious pride. Well, it certainly could! It all depends, of course, on what you mean by 'spontaneity'. Surgeons are required rigorously to scrub and disinfect their hands before every operation. If meticulous adherence to this rule ruins their spontaneity, then ruining their spontaneity would be a very good thing, as far as their patients are concerned. If spontaneity meant carelessly disregarding the rule, then spontaneity would be criminal. Since our sinning damages other people, true spontaneity will not include moral carelessness.

But that said, there is certainly a danger of turning observance of the law of God into a hard, prideful legalism. Christ himself pointed out the danger to some of his very religious contemporaries: 'Woe to you, scribes and Pharisees, hypocrites! For you tithe mint and dill and cumin, and have neglected the weightier matters of the law: justice and mercy and faithfulness' (Matt 23:23). And again, 'If you had known what this means "I [God] desire mercy, and not sacrifice", you would not have condemned the guiltless' (Matt 12:7).

According to Christ, the greatest commandment, the central heartbeat, of God's law is this: 'You shall love the Lord thy God with all your heart and with all your soul and with all your mind. This is the great and first commandment. And a second is like it: "You shall love your neighbour as yourself". On these two commandments depend all the Law and the Prophets' (Matt 22:37–40).

Of course, when people are convinced that the universe is nothing more than an impersonal machine, they tend to think of God—if he existed at all—as some kind of distant, inhuman, arbitrary dictator. They could not begin to think of spontaneously loving him any more than they would think of loving the second law of thermodynamics; and they dismiss those who do claim to love him—and that would include Christ himself—as suffering from irrational fantasies. Says Professor Kai Nielsen:

> In cultures such as ours, religion is very often an alien form of life to intellectuals. Living, as we do, in a post-Enlightenment era, it is difficult for us to take religion seriously. The very concepts seem

> fantastic to us. . . . That people in our age can believe that they have had a personal encounter with God . . . is something that attests to human irrationality and a lack of a sense of reality.[72]

But then, in Charles Dickens's immortal novel *A Christmas Carol*, the wealthy, hard-bitten, soul-shrunk miser, Scrooge, could not understand even the simple family joys of his underpaid clerk, Cratchit, and dismissed them all as humbug. A licentious man no longer understands the virgin's sense of honour; a traitor dismisses as mere sentiment the loyalty that he has long since trampled underfoot. And when spiritual atrophy has set in, the very idea of a God who is spirit, seems fantastic. As we've quoted already, men and women are 'alienated from the life of God because of the ignorance that is in them'. Just as some people are tone deaf and see nothing in music, so some people are spiritually dead: their lines of communication with God are blocked (Eph 2:1; 4:18).

The wealthy, hard-bitten, soul-shrunk miser, Scrooge, could not understand even the simple family joys of his underpaid clerk, Cratchit, and dismissed them all as humbug. A licentious man no longer understands the virgin's sense of honour; a traitor dismisses as mere sentiment the loyalty that he has long since trampled underfoot. And when spiritual atrophy has set in, the very idea of a God who is spirit, seems fantastic.

And then there is another objection to the idea that God could be the authority behind the moral law. It is so well known and so frequently discussed that it has come to be called the Euthyphro Problem.

Objection 5: The Euthyphro problem

The problem gets this name because it was first raised in European literature, as far as we know, in Plato's dialogue *The Euthyphro*. Euthyphro is discussing with Socrates the nature of holiness, and, at one point, he describes holiness as 'what the gods like'. Socrates asks, in effect, 'Is holiness liked by the gods because it is holiness? Or, is holiness holiness because the gods like it?'

People still ask the same question when God is said to be the authority behind morality. Does God command something, they

[72] 'Religiosity and Powerlessness', 46.

ask, because it is morally good? Or does something become morally good, because God commands it?

If God commands it because it is good—so the argument goes—then it must be good independently of God's command. And that would mean that goodness is a standard to which God himself is subject. And that, in turn, would mean that there is something above God, so that God is not the supreme authority.

On the other hand, if something becomes morally good just because God commands it, that would mean that God could command anything at all, however bad or shocking, and it would become good simply because of God's arbitrary command. And that would mean that God was no better than the worst of dictators.

People therefore conclude that God, even if he exists, cannot be the ultimate authority behind morality: morality must be completely autonomous. But the argument is fallacious, and springs from a failure to realise that we are here dealing with both God's will and command on the one hand and God's essential character on the other.

Let's take one of God's basic commands: 'Be holy, for I am holy' (Lev 11:44–45; 19:2; 20:7; 1 Pet 1:16). The command to us to be holy is not the arbitrary command of an unscrupulous tyrant: it is based on the essential character of God: 'I am holy'. At the same time it is not based on some standard external to God and of superior authority to him. God is in his own being the sum total and perfection of holiness. And that is why, for instance, he cannot be unfaithful, or lie, because he cannot deny himself (Titus 1:2; 2 Tim 2:13). God cannot act 'out of character' or command anything that is inconsistent with his character.

But then there is another objection.

Objection 6: Rewards for goodness

Christianity is morally defective, so some say, because it teaches people to be good for what they get out of it; and this false motivation destroys true morality.

Now those who urge this criticism against Christianity seem generally to have in mind a crude version of what they imagine the New Testament teaches: 'Be good; for if you do your best to behave well, you stand a good chance of going to heaven when you die; but if you don't, you won't.' And then they declare that if you were truly moral, you would be good just for the sake of being good, regardless of whether it earned you a place in heaven or not, regardless, indeed, of whether there was a heaven to go to, or not.[73]

The false reward motive

But in the first place the Bible rarely speaks in terms of 'going to heaven when you die'. It does teach that there is a heaven and that believers do go there when they die (Luke 23:39–43; Phil 1:23; 2 Cor 5). But it is much more concerned with people being reconciled to God and being accepted by him in the here and now. That is the beginning of salvation without which no one will get to heaven when they die. But in that connection the New Testament emphasises again and again in unmistakably categorical terms, that salvation in this sense, and assurance of acceptance with God, cannot be earned by 'being good'. On the contrary, acceptance with God is a completely free gift:

> For by grace you have been saved through faith. And this is not your own doing; it is the gift of God, not a result of works, so that no one may boast. (Eph 2:8–9)
>
> By the works of the law no human being will be justified in his sight, since through the law comes knowledge of sin . . . for all have sinned and fall short of the glory of God, and are justified by his grace as a gift, through the redemption that is in Christ Jesus. (Rom 3:20–24)
>
> To the one who does not work but believes in him who justifies the ungodly, his faith is counted as righteousness. (Rom 4:5)
>
> Since we have been justified by faith, we have peace with God through our Lord Jesus Christ. (Rom 5:1)
>
> He saved us, not because of works done by us in righteousness, but according to his own mercy, by the washing of regeneration and renewal of the Holy Spirit. (Titus 3:5)

One might think that the New Testament returns to this scheme excessively often. However, the idea that acceptance with God now

[73] This idea owes a lot to Kant, and nothing to the New Testament.

and a place in his heaven hereafter have to be earned by man's good works is so ingrained in the human psyche that constant repetition of the opposite is scarce enough to dislodge it.

This lesson was the topic of Christ's most famous parable of the Prodigal Son. The returning, repentant, prodigal certainly did not earn acceptance with his father by his good deeds. He returned bankrupt, ragged, starving and filthy and was forgiven, reconciled, welcomed, accepted and re-installed as his father's son, altogether by his father's grace and not on the ground of his merit, for he had none (Luke 15:11–32). It was the elder brother in the parable that suffered from the false idea that his father's love had to be earned by his good works, and so complained bitterly: 'Look, these many years I have served you, and I never disobeyed your command, yet you never gave me a young goat, that I might celebrate with my friends. But when this son of yours came, who has devoured your property with prostitutes, you killed the fatted calf for him!' (15:29–30).

By the works of the law no human being will be justified in his sight, since through the law comes knowledge of sin . . . for all have sinned and fall short of the glory of God, and are justified by his grace as a gift, through the redemption that is in Christ Jesus.

As for the proper motivation for moral living: it is the fact that initial salvation and acceptance with God is altogether by God's unearned grace that puts a person's subsequent life of spiritual discipline and progress on the right motivational basis. For now Christ's follower seeks to develop a truly moral lifestyle not in order to gain salvation and heaven at last, but out of love and gratitude to God for his salvation already granted. As one of the greatest Christian saints put it: 'I live by faith in the Son of God, who loved me and gave himself for me' (Gal 2:19–21).

The true reward motive

Once reconciled to God and accepted by him on these terms, then, a follower of Christ will find that God holds out to him many rewards; not bribes, but genuine and appropriate rewards.

Parents who set a child to learn the piano will not make their love and acceptance of the child dependent on the child's success at playing the piano. Their love for the child is not a reward for piano playing, of course not. But they will hold out to the child what the true reward for learning to play the piano is: the ability to make and enjoy beautiful music, and then to delight other people by playing.

So Christ points us to the reward for praying, which is primarily an ever closer and richer knowledge of God (Matt 6:5–6). And there is a reward for work done for God and one's fellow men and women. It is twofold: creating something that will last eternally and at the same time developing one's abilities so as to be able to do more, and more significant, work.

But to return to the question of the right motive for morality: the Bible is careful to maintain the distinction between reward for work done and salvation, which is not by works, but is a gift.

> Each one's work will become manifest, for the Day will disclose it, because it will be revealed by fire, and the fire will test what sort of work each one has done. If the work that anyone has built on the foundation survives, he will receive a reward. If anyone's work is burned up, he will suffer loss, though he himself will be saved, but only as through fire. (1 Cor 3:13–15)

Objection 7: Submission to God amounts to slavery

A further objection is that the requirement always to submit to the law of an omnipotent deity alienates a man from his true autonomous self and reduces him to the status of a slave. It is this feeling that submission to a divine law imposes on human beings a burden of fear and servitude that led Blanche Sanders to say what she did:

> A Humanist has cast off the ancient yoke of supernaturalism, with its burden of fear and servitude, and he moves on the earth a free man, a child of nature and not of any man-made gods.[74]

The fact is that God himself in the Bible points out that it is a person's unaided, self-reliant attempt to achieve moral and spiritual perfection by keeping God's law which does precisely what Sanders—and many others—complain of: it reduces men and women to slavery. Worse than that, God's own very law, so God says, often provokes human fallen nature to sin yet more (see Gal 4:1–7; 4:21–5:1; Rom 7:5).

[74] See p. 67.

It is not that there is anything wrong with God's law: 'the law is holy, and the commandment is holy and righteous and good' (Rom 7:12). The trouble lies with us.

Lamont diagnoses our trouble as 'irrational impulses'. 'The irrational impulses of human beings', he says, 'have played an enormous role in bringing recurrent disasters upon humankind and remain a sinister danger in contemporary affairs. For the humanist, stupidity is just as great a sin as selfishness.'[75]

'I am unspiritual, sold as a slave to sin,' says the Christian apostle Paul. 'I do not understand what I do. For what I want to do, I do not do, but what I hate I do' (Rom 7:14–15 NIV). And all of us will recognise ourselves in this.

The fact is, we are fallen creatures, sinful, weak, ungodly, rebels at heart and enemies of God. When, with a mixture of pride and fear, we try to prove that we are morally capable of keeping God's law in order to gain acceptance with God, our determined but unavailing struggle against our shortcomings makes slaves of us. At other times, the very fact that God's law commands us to do this, or not to do that, provokes the rebel within us to defy the command. God himself recognises it and understands the cause. His Word points it out.

When, with a mixture of pride and fear, we try to prove that we are morally capable of keeping God's law in order to gain acceptance with God, our determined but unavailing struggle against our shortcomings makes slaves of us.

But God has an answer to this problem that can turn us from slaves driven by pride and fear to try to keep God's moral code into freeborn sons of God who, because they share the Spirit of their Father, have the desire and potential to live by the standards of their Father. 'For you did not receive the spirit of slavery to fall back into fear, but you have received the Spirit of adoption as sons, by whom we cry, "Abba! Father!"' (Rom 8:15–17).

God, then, is not like the ancient pharaoh of Egypt, driving his slaves to make bricks without giving them the straw to make the bricks with (Exod 5). God recognises our spiritual resourcelessness, weakness and perversities; but his scheme of redemption includes a

[75] *Philosophy of Humanism*, 271.

process called regeneration by which he infuses within us a new spiritual life that has the potential to live as a freeborn child of God and learn to fulfil the requirement of his law (Rom 8:1–4).

Objection 8: Talk of heaven is escapism

Marx in his famous aphorism likened religion to opium that dulled people's pain with false hopes of heaven, and made them submit to capitalist oppression when they should have been struggling to destroy it.

Professor Paul Kurtz declares that:

> The traditional supernaturalistic moral commandments are especially repressive of our human needs. They are immoral insofar as they foster illusions about human destiny [heaven] and suppress vital inclinations.[76]

And it is a common, widespread view that belief in heaven distracts people from making the most of their lives here on earth.

The reverse is true. Marx held that philosophy ought to start with the basic fact that man has to eat to live; and that is self-evidently true. But there is more to life than eating. Life has higher dimensions than that. And the highest of them was indicated by Christ when he said 'Man shall not live by bread alone, but by every word that comes from the mouth of God' (Matt 4:4).

When one is invited to a dinner party, the food provided by one's host is, of course, the basis and centre of the occasion. But of far more human significance is the conversation, music, poetry and friendship with one's host and hostess. So is it with life itself. Its highest and most significant dimension, here and now in this life on earth, is the friendship and spiritual fellowship that we may enjoy with God through him who is the Bread of Life (1 John 1:1–4, John 6:35). And for that we do not have to wait until we get to heaven, though, to be sure, this fellowship will there expand without limit in both depth and glory.

To fail, or refuse, to recognise that dimension to life here on earth, is to miss life's highest significance now.

And in addition, it is because there is a heaven—and a hell—beyond this life, that every day of life on earth is packed full of eternal

76 *Humanist Alternative*, 50.

significance. After all, it is not the constant awareness of the career he hopes to follow when he leaves school that stops a schoolboy from making the most of his school days. School's significance lies precisely here, that it is the necessary preparation for the career. The more he thinks of the career, the more he will take advantage of the preparation.

Objection 9: Fear of punishment makes God a monster

Many will object that a God who would threaten human beings with eternal hell in order to frighten them into keeping his commandment would himself be an immoral monster. But there is surely a difference between a threat and a warning. A doctor who impresses on a teenager that if she develops the habit of smoking she is liable to contract fatal lung cancer and heart disease is not threatening the teenager. But he is warning her; and he will make his warning as dire as he possibly can in order to save the teenager from throwing her life away prematurely.

God is the source and sum total of all goodness. It is impossible for him to construct an alternative paradise for those who knowingly persist in denying and rejecting him. When those who do thus reject him are finally and forever shut out from him, they are simply being given what they themselves have chosen.

But when they discover the horror of what they have chosen, why won't God give them another chance to repent, and so let them into his heaven?

But they won't want to repent. Anyone who can knowingly reject the love of God will not be moved to repent by the sufferings of hell, as Christ himself pointed out (Luke 16:19–31).

Moreover having given human beings genuine free will and the ability, if they should so choose, finally to say no to God, he will not remove that free will if they do in fact say no. He respects them too much for that. A human being bereft of free will would no longer be a human being but more like an animated machine. God will never degrade human beings into machines. It is atheistic evolutionary theory that does that.[77]

[77] For a discussion of the problem of pain and evil, which many people feel makes faith in a loving God impossible, see the authors' book *Christianity: Opium or Truth?*

THE ROLE AND POWER OF HUMANS OVER NATURE

You made him a little lower than the heavenly beings
 and crowned him with glory and honour.
You made him ruler over the works of your hands
 you put everything under his feet.
—Psalm 8:5–6

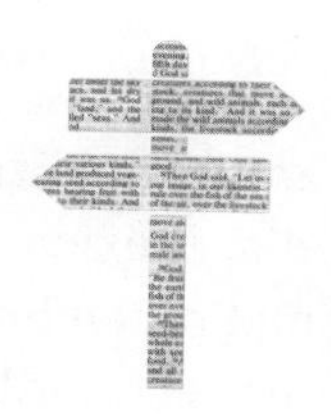

WHAT A WONDER HUMANITY IS!

It is a very healthy and stimulating thing to turn aside every now and again from the monotonous humdrum of life with its routine of little things to contemplate what an amazingly wonderful thing the human race is.

We could think in the first place of the nobility, grace and beauty, harmony and proportions of the ideal human form which sculptors and artists have so enthusiastically and tirelessly represented for our admiration, and which Leonardo da Vinci analysed so stunningly. But the wonder of humanity is seen especially in the way humans have used their intelligence, their imagination, their sense of purpose, their urge to progress, their engineering skills, their artistic flair, their power of organisation, to develop the earth, to explore and maximise its resources and potentials, to understand and then harness the forces of nature, to impose order on their environment and to create things of beauty and indeed of majesty. True, there have been periods, sometimes very long periods, when the sheer daily labour of getting enough food to live on has consumed all humanity's time and strength. But rarely, even then, have men and women been content with the mere utilitarian. Ever and again the human spirit has risen up and, transcending the merely useful, has expressed itself in poetry, music, art, drama, philosophy, sport and adventure.

The achievements of the last two hundred years have of course been stupendous. But we should not allow that to mislead us into thinking that in bygone centuries men and women were necessarily primitive and unintelligent.

The achievements of the last two hundred years have of course been stupendous. But we should not allow that to mislead us into thinking that in bygone centuries men and women were necessarily primitive and unintelligent. Early cave paintings show an astonishing vigour of line and sense of movement.

The building of the pyramids, at Giza in Egypt, as also the megalithic buildings in Cambodia, Mexico, Peru and Bolivia, required highly sophisticated mathematics, architectural and civil engineering skills, and, it now appears, extraordinarily detailed astronomical knowledge. Yet the Egyptian pyramids were built four and a half thousand years ago (during the Fourth Dynasty of the Old Kingdom *c.*2649–2519 BC).[1]

The curve of humanity's progress, admittedly, has not gone invariably upwards. Dark ages of decline and apparent stagnation have intervened as once brilliant civilisations have flowered and then faded. But looking back over the centuries from the vantage point of our modern age, we can clearly see overwhelming evidence that man has proved himself to be the king of the earth.

In size and personal strength, in range of hearing and power of smell, the human race is certainly inferior to many of the animals; and birds have power of flight that the human frame does not. A naked, unarmed human would be no match for the giant squid or the killer shark of the oceans. Yet not only have humans devised means of mastering all of them and taming many of them, but they have turned, particularly in recent times, to care for the preservation of species that they could not tame.

More significant still: lions and giraffes, elephants and crocodiles, like the rest of animals and birds, behave today as they have always behaved. Birds have astonishing ability to construct nests, and, some of them, to migrate over vast distances. Bats are equipped with a kind of radar to enable them to catch their prey. But animals and birds show no tendency to develop these highly complex techniques and abilities. Humans alone have consciously sought to develop their techniques and abilities along with their understanding of the world and universe around them.

More astonishing still, humanity has learned in the course of the centuries to harness some of the mighty forces of nature. By inventing the sail they early made the wind and wave transport them across the oceans; they subsequently harnessed the energy of fossil fuels and even of the atom, and made it do their work; they have

1 Redford, *Oxford Encyclopaedia of Ancient Egypt* (2001) s.v. Old Kingdom.

channelled multi-phased light into laser beams to perform delicate surgical eye operations, to convey a host of message-carrying signals simultaneously, or to play back their musical recordings. They have escaped the chain by which gravity kept them restricted to earth, have built aerofoils and aeroplanes, have travelled through space to the moon, built laboratories in space, and enlisted the pull of earth's gravitational field to drag their space probes round the earth and sling them out again with added momentum towards the distant planets. Standing on earth they can control a space module circling, millions of miles away, around Jupiter; and with their visual, X-ray, ultraviolet and infrared radio telescopes they can see what galaxies are doing at the edge of the universe. They have cracked the genetic code, and have begun to be able by their genetic engineering to modify humankind.

Now man's conscious awareness that he is king of the earth, is no recent development. It is not simply the product of the amazing scientific and technological progress made during the last century and a half. Take, for example, this lyric written some three thousand years ago:

> O Lord, our Lord, how majestic is your name in all the earth!
> You have set your glory above the heavens. . . .
> When I consider your heavens, the work of your fingers,
>   the moon and the stars, which you have set in place,
> what is man that you are mindful of him,
>   the son of man that you care for him?
> You made him a little lower than the heavenly beings
>   and crowned him with glory and honour.
> You made him ruler over the works of your hands,
>   you put everything under his feet:
> all flocks and herds, and the beasts of the field,
> the birds of the air, and the fish of the sea,
>   all that swim the paths of the seas.
> O Lord, our Lord, how majestic is your name in all the earth!
>
> (Psalm 8)

This lyric was obviously written by a theist, in fact by a monotheist: the poem is framed by a repeated reference to the majesty of

God reflected for all earth-dwellers to perceive in the created universe and earth. The lyricist is clearly filled with awe at the glory of God, which induces in him the awareness of his smallness: 'What is man that you are mindful of him, or the son of man that you care for him?' But he feels no craven, slavish fear. Quite the opposite. For just when one might suppose that he is about to confess that the grandeur of the heavens reduces him to feelings of utter insignificance, he expresses instead the altogether opposite emotion: the sheer wonder that the Lord Creator of such a dazzlingly great and magnificent universe should not only take notice of, and individually care for such a tiny creature as man, but crown him with glory and honour by appointing him to this majestically high office of being earth's supremo: 'You made him ruler over the works of your hands; you put everything under his feet.'

Genesis says that God planted a garden and put man in it to dress it and to keep it. The garden, like the rest of the world, was God's. Man was its steward, manager and protector, free of course to enjoy it, but responsible to look after it for its owner.

This is true to the ancient Hebrew tradition, that at the beginning God created man and woman in his own image and appointed them as his viceroys over the earth: 'Be fruitful and multiply and fill the earth and subdue it and have dominion over the fish of the sea and over the birds of the air and over every living creature that moves on the earth' (Gen 1:28).

This, then, was man's mandate in respect to the earth, as the Hebrews understood it. It was not, as some generations have misread it to be, permission to adopt an overbearing and domineering attitude towards God's creation, nor encouragement to feel that the world is somehow entirely man's to dispose of—as income, rather than a capital asset which needs managing. The context of man's commissioning in the Genesis story makes this explicitly clear. Genesis says that God planted a garden and put man in it to dress it and to keep it (2:15). The garden was not his: he did not possess the freehold. The garden, like the rest of the world, was God's. Man was its steward, manager and protector, free of course to enjoy it, but responsible to look after it for its owner. And when he disobeyed God and misused the garden he was turned out of it. This then was man's role and responsibility, according to the ancient Hebrew story.

But now let's move on five hundred years or so, and listen to another set of lyrics, this time by Sophocles, the ancient Greek playwright (*c.*496–406 BC). What is perhaps the most famous of all his odes speaks to the same theme as the Hebrew poet's lyrics:

CHORUS

Strophe 1

Many wonders there be, but naught more wondrous than man:
Over the surging sea, with a whitening south wind wan,
Through the foam of the firth, man makes his perilous way;
And the eldest of deities Earth that knows not toil nor decay
Ever he furrows and scores, as his team, year in year out,
With breed of the yokèd horse, the ploughshare turneth about.

Antistrophe 1

The light-witted birds of the air, the beasts of the weald and
the wood
He traps with his woven snare, and the brood of the briny flood.
Master of cunning he: the savage bull, and the hart
Who roams the mountains free, are tamed by his infinite art;
And the shaggy rough-maned steed is broken to bear the bit.

Strophe 2

Speech and the wind-swift speed of counsel and civic wit,
He hath learnt for himself all these; and the arrowy rain to fly
And the nipping airs that freeze, 'neath the open winter sky.
He hath provision for all: fell plague he hath learnt to endure;
Safe whate'er may befall: yet for death he hath found no cure.

Antistrophe 2

Passing the wildest flight of thought are the cunning and skill,
That guide man now to the light, but now to counsels of ill.
If he honours the laws of the land, and reveres the Gods of
the State
Proudly his city shall stand; but a cityless outcast I rate
Whoso bold in his pride from the path of right doth depart;
N'er may I sit by his side, or share the thoughts of his heart.[2]

[2] *Antigone*, ll. 332–372 (Storr, 341–2).

Sophocles was a contemporary of the great and famous Pericles, who commissioned the building of the Parthenon at Athens. He witnessed the rise of Athens and lived through the peak of her empire and the period of her supreme cultural glory. It is understandable, therefore, that he, too, in his epoch should be moved to celebrate the sheer ability and cunning by which man had by that time achieved his mastery over nature and raised himself to such dazzling heights of glory. He has, says the playwright, discovered the technique of sail by which to cross the sea. He has invented the plough to subdue earth itself and make it produce his food. He has tamed the horse and harnessed it to work for him. He has discovered how to catch fish and fowl, how to subdue brute beasts, how to protect himself from storm and bad weather. He has developed his powers of speech, and the civil and political arts, learned to survive plagues and conquered everything but death.

Sophocles, of course, unlike the Hebrew poet, was a polytheist; hence his reference to earth as 'the eldest of the deities' and to 'the Gods of the State'. But what catches our eye is the note of unease, ambivalence and misgiving which he introduces at the end of his ode:

> Passing the wildest flight of thought are the cunning and
> skill,
> That guide man now to the light but now to counsels of ill.
> If he honours the laws of the land, and reveres the Gods
> of the State,
> Proudly his city shall stand; but a cityless outcast I rate
> Whoso bold in his pride from the path of right doth
> depart.

Of course, it suited his dramatic purpose to introduce this note of unease at this point in his drama. But in doing so he calls our attention to a theme which will presently force itself uncomfortably on our attention, namely that the intelligence and ingenuity by which man has achieved his conquest of nature can be dangerous. Unless they are bounded and controlled by profound and loyal respect for divine and human values, instead of being the cure of all man's ills and the key to social and economic paradise, they can be the source of profound misery.

But meanwhile we have other things to think of first.

WHAT IS A HUMAN BEING?

The question of a human's body, brain, mind and self

Humanity's seemingly ever-increasing power over nature inevitably raises two fundamental questions:

1. What exactly is the human race's relation to nature?
2. What exactly is a human being?

The two questions are interlocked.

First, then, let's consider the question of humanity's relation to nature. Is the human race in the last analysis nothing but a part of nature? Or are humans in any sense, or in any degree, independent of nature? Let's illustrate the meaning of these questions.

A volcano has gigantic power and is able to devastate the countryside for miles around, but no one would describe the volcano as having power over nature. We understand its mechanisms; they are all part of nature. It would not make sense to talk of nature having power over nature.

But now consider an atomic bomb. It too can wreak havoc on the countryside for miles around. We understand its mechanisms too: many of them are part of nature. But is that a full and sufficient account of the matter? It was human beings who arranged the natural components of the bomb so that they would explode at the appropriate signal. And it was human beings who pushed the button that detonated the bomb. How then ought we to regard them? Certainly their bodies were made up of atoms like the bomb was; and so were their brains. Admittedly, their bodies and brains contained far more sophisticated mechanisms than either the volcano or the bomb. But would it be appropriate to describe these human beings as having *power over* nature, if they were, in the last analysis, nothing but nature themselves? A form of nature, somewhat more evolved than the volcano, but still nature and nothing more? Or were those human beings at least in some respects somewhat more than nature? Did they have some independence of

> Is the human race in the last analysis nothing but a part of nature? Or are humans in any sense, or in any degree, independent of nature?

nature, so that in the ultimate analysis to describe them as having power over nature would answer to a definite reality?

To ask these questions is to raise another: what exactly *is* a human being? Is a human just body and brain, sophisticated forms of matter and electrochemical processes, but nothing more than that, in principle simply nature just as the volcano is? Or have human beings, in addition to their brains, a mind which, though intimately associated with the brain, is different from the brain, being not material as the brain is, but non-material, spirit, and in that sense and to that extent not part of what we normally call nature? If that is so, of course, it would make sense to talk of humanity having, to some degree, power over nature.

The Monist/Dualist debate

Our questions have now brought us face-to-face with a matter that has been debated for a very long time. But recent major advances in science and technology have given new life and vigour to the debate. One such advance is the realisation of the influence of the genes over the body and brain. Another is the invention of sophisticated apparatus for scanning the brain and measuring the activity going on in different parts of it according to what the brain's owner might be thinking or doing at the time. A third new approach has come about through the development of ever more high-powered computers and robots which raise the interesting question whether it will be possible in the future to develop artificial intelligence to such a degree that a self-conscious robot can be constructed indistinguishable from a human being.

The human nervous system is, perhaps, the most complicated thing in the whole universe, with its one hundred billion neurones, each with an average of around three thousand connections, so that each human being has in the order of one hundred trillion synaptic switches.

The debate will go on for a long time yet, for the human nervous system is, perhaps, the most complicated thing in the whole universe, with its one hundred billion neurones, each with an average of around three thousand connections, so that each human being has in the order of one hundred trillion synaptic switches.

There are two main sides in this debate,

though on each side there are a number of different positions. On the one side stand the so-called materialists, or physicalists, or monists. Their basic belief is that there is only one entity, that is, the brain, and not two: brain and mind. 'Brain' and 'mind' are for them two different words for one and the same thing; or two different ways of looking at the same thing. But, they insist, there are not two entities, only one; hence the name monism given to this view.

This view is also called materialism or physicalism, indicating its belief that man's brain, and man himself, are composed simply of physical matter; there is no such thing as 'soul', or 'spirit'; consciousness is merely a certain state of the atoms and neurones in the brain.

This view is reductionist (see pp. 50–51), because it reduces all human experience to nothing but the working of electrochemical processes in the brain, so that rational thought is nothing but the firing of certain of the brain's neurones; and 'I love you' is the exact equivalent, no more nor less, of 'your presence is sparking off intense activity in the neurones of this brain'.

On the other side of the debate stand the dualists, so called because they hold that a human being is not one single entity, but two. In addition to the material of his body and brain, there is as well a non-material element, variously called soul, or spirit or self. This view is dismissed somewhat derisively by its opponents, as implying belief in 'the ghost in the machine', and is regarded by them as being self-evidently impossible: firstly, because according to them science knows nothing of any such non-material entities and therefore they don't exist; and secondly, even if they did exist, non-material entities could not affect, have any impact on, or interact with, material brains.[3]

There is no need to emphasise how utterly fundamental these questions are to our understanding of what each one of us is, as a human being, as a person. But how shall we go about reaching a decision?

The evidence of intuition

The first thing to notice is that, in regard to this question above all others, our own direct experience is of supreme importance. After all,

[3] There are some scientists who, while denying the dualist position, also vigorously deny the materialistic reductionism of strict monism. They prefer to describe their view as comprehensive realism.

what the scientists, neurologists and philosophers are intent on understanding is precisely this: what exactly is happening when you say '*I* am enjoying this book'; or, '*I* am trying to solve this problem'; or, '*I* intend to visit my aunt tomorrow'; or, '*I* am free to choose, am I not?'

The scientist could take an encephalogram of your brain, or put you through a brain scan, or insert a probe of some kind in your brain, and he could know by the measurable activity going on in the appropriate part of your brain that you were engaging in rational thought, or experiencing some pleasure, or pain, or taste; but he could never know exactly what rational thoughts you were thinking, or what exactly was the quality of the taste, or pleasure, or pain you were experiencing unless you told him.

Or take memory. A neurosurgeon operating on the brain might activate a patient's visual memory of some situation in the past, and the surgeon might know that he had done so. But he could not tell, simply by observing the brain activity, what scene it was that the patient was recalling.

Again, a scientist might hold up a picture of a woman's face in front of a patient, having first performed an operation on the patient's cranium to expose the visual cortex. The scientist could then observe the electrochemical activity in that part of the brain as the signals from the optic nerves registered there. But the scientist would not herself see a miniature version of the picture of the woman's face projected onto that part of the brain. She therefore could not tell what exactly the patient was actually seeing unless the patient told her 'I am seeing a picture of a woman's face'; or, if that part of the brain was damaged, 'I see what looks like a monkey.'

A neurosurgeon operating on the brain might activate a patient's visual memory of some situation in the past, and the surgeon might know that he had done so. But he could not tell, simply by observing the brain activity, what scene it was that the patient was recalling.

All of us, then, have a constant stream of experiences of sensations, of making decisions, of thinking, of working out a problem logically, of imagining visual images, of comparing one thing with another in our minds, of perceiving interrelationships and discerning other people's intentions and motives (correctly or not!). In all these experiences each of us is conscious that it is 'I' that is having the experience, doing the thinking, working out the problem, making the decision, entertaining abstract ideas, exercising the freedom to choose to do one thing when 'I' could have done another.

Moreover, if asked, each one of us would say 'I am conscious of myself'. If we knock on a door and someone inside says 'Who's there?' we reply 'It's I'. We recognise our bodies as part of ourselves (unless that part of our brains that recognises our bodily parts as belonging to us is damaged). But a child born without legs, or arms, or eyes, is still aware of itself. And an adult who suffers an amputation will say 'My leg, or arm, has been amputated', but not 'I have been amputated,' or 'My self has been amputated.'

So then, we must, certainly to start with, take the evidence of intuition seriously. Professor J. Searle is a monist-materialist; yet in spite of that he states:

> For if it seems to me that I'm conscious, I am conscious. We could discover all kinds of startling things about ourselves and our behaviour; but we cannot discover that we do not have minds, that they do not contain conscious, subjective, intentionalistic mental states; nor could we discover that we do not at least try to engage in voluntary, free, intentional actions.[4]

Why and how he (and scientists of the same persuasion as himself) remain monist-materialists after having expressed such apparently dualistic views, is for the moment beside the point. What Searle's statement assures us of is this: we must take our intuitive consciousness of mind and self seriously. It is fundamental.

Let the reductionists say what they will, the human spirit will never accept, or believe, their reductionist explanation of the human self-conscious self. One wonders whether the reductionists themselves believe it. They don't always talk as if they did.

David Hume (1711–76) was one of first among many subsequent philosophers who have doubted, and still do doubt, the existence of their own self. Roy Weatherford, Professor Emeritus at the University of South Florida, for instance, speaks of 'awareness of a metaphysical

[4] *Minds, Brains and Science*, 99.

self—universally accepted among philosophers until Hume said, in short, "I can't find it", and seemed to be right'.[5]

Hume, a thoroughgoing empiricist, held that we can know nothing but our sense impressions and the 'ideas' derived from sense impressions. And since, according to him, we cannot have anything like an idea of self, he argued that there cannot *be* such a thing as the self. And so in his *A Treatise of Human Nature* (published in 1739–40) in the section 'Of Personal Identity' he refers to 'some philosophers, who imagine we are every moment intimately conscious of what we call our SELF', and he comments: 'Unluckily all these positive assertions are contrary to that very experience, which is pleaded for them, nor have we any idea of *self*. . . For from what impression could this idea be derived? This question 'tis impossible to answer without a manifest contradiction and absurdity.'[6]

> It is evident, that the idea, or rather impression of ourselves is always intimately present with us, and that our consciousness gives us so lively a conception of our own person, that it is not possible to imagine, that any thing can in this particular go beyond it.
> —David Hume, *A Treatise of Human Nature*

Yet elsewhere in that same treatise he says, unwittingly perhaps, the very reverse: 'It is evident, that the idea, or rather impression of ourselves is always intimately present with us, and that our consciousness gives us so lively a conception of our own person, that it is not possible to imagine, that any thing can in this particular go beyond it.'[7]

It arises from the very nature of the self, both as a topic and as an experienced entity, that it is impossible to be a consistent reductionist in regard to the self.

Thus far, then, we have listened to the voice of intuition; let us now hear what the scientists say.

The voice of science

As we said earlier, the scientists are strongly divided on the topic; we can at best, in our limited space, indicate the two main sides in the

[5] 'Freedom and Determinism', 293.
[6] THN 1.4.6.2 'Of Personal Identity', (Selby-Bigge, 251).
[7] THN 2.1.11.4 'Of the Love of Fame', (Selby-Bigge, 317).

debate, and give a few representative examples from each of the two sides.

Some monist explanations

Some theories on this side are expressed in extremely crude terms. Take for instance this statement of the Nobel Laureate, Francis Crick:

> 'You', your joys and your sorrows, your memories and your ambitions, your sense of personal identity and free will, are in fact no more than the behaviour of a vast assembly of nerve cells and their associated molecules.[8]

Notice the phrase 'no more than'. This is the telltale sign of reductionism. Take, by way of example, a wedding ring. As far as its constituent material is concerned, it is no more than a piece of gold. If one chose, one could reduce the description further, and say that the ring was no more than a piece of metal. That would be perfectly true but quite inadequate. For at that level a ring made of copper or iron could likewise be described as 'no more than' a piece of metal. But gold is not 'no more than' copper. Gold has an intrinsic value that copper does not have: a gold ring would certainly have cost the bridegroom much more than a copper ring.

But the significance of the ring goes far beyond what metal it is made of. To the bride the ring would not be precious simply because it was made of gold rather than copper, but because it was a *wedding* ring. As such it would be a lifelong expression and pledge of love and loyalty between two persons. The metal ring would be tangible, and scientists could measure it, and reduce it to its constituent molecules, atoms, nuclei and quarks. But science could not measure its significance and the meaning it carried for the bride and bridegroom. And yet that meaning would be the most important thing about it, such that, if later on in life, the husband was unfaithful to his wife, the gold wedding ring would lose its chief value, and to the wife it would become a mockery.

Now no one denies that our joys and sorrows register themselves at a physical level in our brains. But what Crick's extreme form of reductionism is saying is that—to continue our analogy—not only

[8] *Astonishing Hypothesis*, 3.

is the gold wedding ring no more than a vast assembly of atoms and molecules, and not only is the woman's joy when she first puts the ring on her finger no more than the behaviour of a vast assembly of atoms and molecules and their associated nerve cells in her brain, but that's what the woman herself is; that's what her identity is: no more than a vast assembly of nerve cells and their associated molecules. In other words what the bridegroom thought was a human self with a self-conscious mind that could appreciate the meaning of the ring was in fact no more than a bunch of physical nerve cells.

Now, of course, not all monists accept such extreme reductionism, and it would be unfair to attribute it to them all; but some do, as presently we shall see.

Behaviourism

Behaviourism gets its name from the idea that in order to understand mental processes it is necessary to study actual behaviour, since mental processes are not fully real or distinguishable from actual or possible behaviour. Prominent among behaviourists are the names of Ivan Petrovich Pavlov (1849–1936), who held the chair of physiology at the Imperial Institute of Experimental Medicine in St Petersburg from 1895 to 1925 (he discovered the secretory nerves of the pancreas in 1888 and received the Nobel Prize in 1904); and of B. F. Skinner, Humanist of the Year in 1972.

Skinner's views are extreme:

> A scientific analysis of behaviour dispossesses autonomous man and turns the control he has been said to exert over to the environment. The individual . . . is henceforth to be controlled by the world around him, and in large part by other men.[9]

> The hypothesis that man is not free is essential to the application of scientific method to the study of human behaviour.[10]

According to Skinner's view human behaviour follows definite physical laws and is determined:

[9] *Beyond Freedom and Dignity*, 200–1.

[10] *Science and Human Behaviour*, 447.

> We must expect to discover that what a man does is the result of specifiable conditions and that once these conditions have been discovered, we can anticipate and to some extent determine his actions.[11]

Of course, if the brain is nothing but matter and runs according to strict invariable laws; and if mind and brain are simply two terms for exactly the same thing, then man is not free, his thoughts are determined and his actions are predictable.

But if that is so, there is an end of all morality. Man is a mere machine. And in that case you would not blame or punish a man for murdering your wife any more than you would punish a car for bursting into flames and burning her to death.

Pavlov's research was conducted mostly on animals and demonstrated the possibility of creating what he called conditioned reflexes: dogs who were 'conditioned' by being given food at the same time as a bell was rung, could thereafter be induced to salivate at the mere ringing of a bell. These conditioned reflexes, he held, were determined, and therefore inevitable, and so belonged, like the unconditioned reflexes which are there from birth, entirely to the domain of physiology.[12]

> If the brain is nothing but matter and runs according to strict invariable laws; and if mind and brain are simply two terms for exactly the same thing, then man is not free, his thoughts are determined and his actions are predictable.

This sounds as if the activities of animals, at least, could be explained totally in terms of behaviourism. Moreover, elsewhere he remarks: 'I trust that I shall not be thought rash if I express a belief that experiments on the higher nervous activities of animals will yield not a few directional indications for education and self-education in man.'[13] One might suppose, therefore, that in regard to human beings he espoused the same rigid behaviourism as Skinner.

But that is not so; for Pavlov also held that man evolved the art of language as a second signal system, and Marxist psychologists urge that this development of language sets men free both to be shaped by

[11] *Science and Human Behaviour*, 6.

[12] See his *Lectures on Conditioned Reflexes*, 267.

[13] *Lectures on Conditioned Reflexes*, 391.

society and to shape it. Behaviourism, therefore, is not inconsistent with free will; and Skinner's rigid determinism is thereby refuted. Says Joseph Nahem:

> A . . . devastating refutation of Skinner is Pavlov's profound contribution to psychology by his analysis of speech and language as a second signal system.[14]

What is not so clear, however, is how this freedom of man's mind relates to Lenin's view that the mind is completely dependent on the physical matter of the brain:

> The existence of the mind is shown to be dependent upon that of the body, in that the mind is declared to be secondary, a function of the brain, or a reflection of the outer world.[15]

> Matter is primary nature. Sensation, thought, consciousness, are the highest products of matter organized in a certain way. This is the doctrine of materialism, in general, and Marx and Engels, in particular.[16]

But without any doubt a form of absolutely radical behaviourism is propounded by the famous philosopher Professor Willard Van Orman Quine (1908–2000), formerly of Harvard University, and by a number of other scientists, who hold that conscious processes and mental processes do not exist: their existence can be eliminated.

To illustrate what this radical behaviourism means in practice, Sir Karl R. Popper, the renowned professor of the history and philosophy of science, uses the example of a toothache. We here expand his example a little.

He supposes that you develop a bad toothache. That is a physico-chemical process in the world of matter, which automatically causes sensations in your brain that tell you that there is something wrong with a tooth.

The sensation of pain then leads you to look at the tooth and you discover that part of it has broken off and the rest has gone bad. You now are not only aware that your tooth is painful, but you also

---

14 *Psychology and Psychiatry Today: A Marxist View*, 9.

15 Lenin, *Materialism and Empirico-Criticism*, 66.

16 Lenin, *Materialism and Empirico-Criticism*, 34.

understand why it is painful. So pain at the physical level has led to understanding at the mental, cognitive level.

Next, mental understanding of what is wrong with your tooth, prompts you to remember that there is such a profession as dentistry; and dentistry is not a simple, automatic product—like the toothache is—of the physico-chemical world: it is the creation of another world completely: the world of human intellect, science, art, invention, institutions, etc.

Your own mental knowledge of that world then leads you to decide to visit a dentist. Notice what happens next. Your mental decision has a causal effect on your material brain and body; for you get up, consult a telephone directory, make an appointment, visit the dentist and have the tooth extracted.

So here, according to Popper, is an experience that has involved you in three closely related, but qualitatively distinct, worlds: first, the world of physico-chemical material things, your diseased tooth, a dentist's chair, anaesthetic, and dental instruments; second, the world not only of your sensation of pain, but of knowledge and understanding of the cause of the pain, and rational deliberation and decision what to do about it; and third, the world of science, theorising, and invention, medical and dental textbooks, etc.

The radical materialist, Popper points out, reduces both you and your experience of these three qualitatively different worlds to one simplistic level: physical processes in a tooth leading to physical processes in a nervous system.[17]

It cannot but seem strange when philosophers and scientists use their massive powers of intellect to argue that the processes involved in logical, intellectual thinking are not essentially, or in principle, different from those going on in a bad tooth!

But now let us look at another monist explanation.

Epiphenomenalism

This view holds that mental phenomena are side products of the brain and have no effect on actions. Thomas Hurley was an epiphenomenalist, and he expresses the view very well:

---

[17] Karl R. Popper, in Popper and Eccles, *Self and Its Brain,* 1998 repr., 51–3.

> Consciousness . . . would appear to be related to the mechanism of [the] body, simply as a . . . [side] product of its working, and to be as completely without any power of modifying that working as the [sound of a] steam-whistle which accompanies the work of a locomotive . . . is without influence upon its machinery.[18]

Popper, after a long and detailed argument, makes a final, brief, trenchant commentary on this view.

> An important but separate criticism is this. If applied to arguments, and our weighing of reasons, the epiphenomenalist view is suicidal. For the epiphenomenalist is committed to arguing that arguments or reasons do not really matter. They cannot really influence our dispositions to act—for example, to speak or to write—nor the actions themselves. These are all due to mechanical, physico-chemical, acoustical, optical and electrical effects.
>
> Thus the epiphenomenalist argument leads to the recognition of its own irrelevance. This does not refute epiphenomenalism. It merely means that if epiphenomenalism is true, we cannot take seriously as a reason or argument whatever is said in its support.[19]

In a more recent book[20] Professor David J. Chalmers sets out to take consciousness seriously and to disprove the idea, which for many scientists is unquestionable dogma, that consciousness can be fully explained by reducing it to the workings and effects of the physical, electrochemical systems of the nervous system. He argues strongly that consciousness, like mass, momentum and energy, must be regarded, by any adequate scientific system, as a fundamental irreducible property of the universe, that cannot be explained in terms of something else.

At the same time he hopes that science will discover the 'psychophysical' laws which relate the fundamental property of consciousness to the rest of the system.

At this point, however, he meets a difficulty, because he adheres to the view that science demands a belief in the absolute causal de-

[18] *Method and Results*, 1:240.

[19] *Self and Its Brain*, 74–5.

[20] *Conscious Mind*.

terminacy of the physical world. Science, he believes, has proved that the physical world is causally closed. This presupposition, therefore, obliges him to hold that our conscious minds are causally influenced by our physical brains, but cannot themselves exert any causal influence on our brains or on our behaviour.

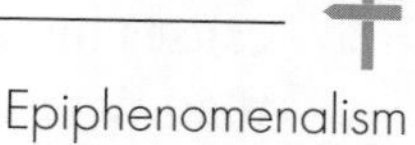

Epiphenomenalism goes clean counter to our intuitive perception that our conscious minds can and do have causal effects on our brains and behaviour.

This is epiphenomenalism, and goes clean counter to our intuitive perception that our conscious minds can and do have causal effects on our brains and behaviour.

Suppose a woman feels ill, but does not know what is wrong with her. She goes to a doctor who diagnoses diabetes, and tells her that from now on she must keep off sweet things. So now her conscious mind understands what her illness is and that sweet things will aggravate the illness. But she loves cakes and chocolates and jam. She has therefore to think through in her mind what she is going to do: will she continue eating sweet things or cut them out? She must come to a conscious decision in her mind; and she does so. Are we really to think that her mental decision cannot causally affect her physical brain and behaviour, and has nothing to do with the fact that her hands never put sweet things into her mouth again?

When the a priori dogma, that science demands belief in the absolute causal determinacy of the physical world as a system closed to any non-material influence from the outside, leads to such counter-intuitive and obviously wrong conclusions, one might think that it is time to question the a priori dogma. We should remember Popper's observation, mentioned above, that epiphenomenalism itself teaches us that any reason or argument put forward in its favour cannot be taken seriously.[21]

Identity Theory

Professor J. J. C. Smart, an identity-theorist, states categorically: 'I assert that beliefs and desires are physical states of the brain.'[22]

[21] For a lengthy, helpful review of Chalmer's book, see Larson, in *Origins & Design*.
[22] In Warner and Szubka, *Mind-Body Problem*, 21.

In this manner, then, they claim that each mental intention is identical with a pattern of neurones in my brain, so that my mental desire and intention to raise my arm is identical with a certain pattern of neurones in my brain and it is this pattern of neurones that causes my arm to rise. This solves, to their satisfaction, the problem that materialist scientists have: 'how could a non-material intention in my mind cause my material brain to raise my arm?' The answer is: it doesn't. The mental desire is identical with a neurological pattern in my brain. Similarly consciousness, for them, is simply a self-scanning mechanism in the central nervous system; it does not require a non-material self to be the subject who is conscious.[23]

We must, therefore, ask how this view has been established; indeed, how it could possibly be established.

1. *By intuition?*

Obviously not. No one who happens to be working out in his mind an abstract question of moral philosophy, whether, say, loyalty to a friend would justify concealing his crime, would intuitively feel that it was actually a bunch of electrochemicals in his brain that was discussing the moral question among themselves.

2. *By rigorous scientific research?*

But how could this be done? For let us consider some of the things that the theory would have to do to establish itself.

(*a*) If, as Smart declares, 'beliefs and desires are physical states of the brain', then in principle it ought to be possible to discover what a man believes by examining his brain cells. This would be no small task. Everyone knows that when we think, activity can be detected in certain parts of the brain. But hitherto it has never been possible sim-

---

[23] There is a certain difficulty in ascertaining exactly what identity theorists are saying (see the long discussion in Karl Popper, *Self and Its Brain*, 81–93). Popper says 'I very much doubt whether a formulation like "mental processes are identical with a certain kind of (physico-chemical) brain processes" can be taken at its face value, in view of the fact that we understand, since Leibniz, "*a* is identical with *b*" to imply that any property of the object *a* is also a property of the object *b*. Some identity theorists certainly seem to assert identity in this sense; but it seems to me more than doubtful whether they can really mean it' (p. 82).

Perhaps, then, when they assert identity, we should not take them to mean that, for instance, when I say 'I am imagining in my mind a beautiful sunset' *I mean* the same thing as 'certain of the neurological processes in my brain are in such-and-such a condition'; nor that 'if you could see a certain neurological process in my brain you would see, in miniature a beautiful sunset'. We should take the identity-theorists to mean simply that a mind-event, of whatever kind, always occurs at the same time and place as a brain-event, and therefore it may be assumed that the mind-event and the brain-event are one and the same event.

ply by examining this activity in the brain to discover what exactly the person is thinking in his mind. To correlate the brain-activity with the mental thought would be possible only if the person whose brain it was first told the experimenter what he was thinking. Scientifically to establish that a particular pattern of brain-events always necessarily accompanied, and was the equivalent of, such and such a mind-event, would involve examining large numbers of cases in large numbers of human beings in order by induction to establish the probability that it was so. (And it would also require a large number of people who on having their brain-patterns examined would be prepared honestly to confess what they were thinking at that moment.)

> No one who happens to be working out in his mind an abstract question of moral philosophy, whether, say, loyalty to a friend would justify concealing his crime, would intuitively feel that it was actually a bunch of electrochemicals in his brain that was discussing the moral question among themselves.

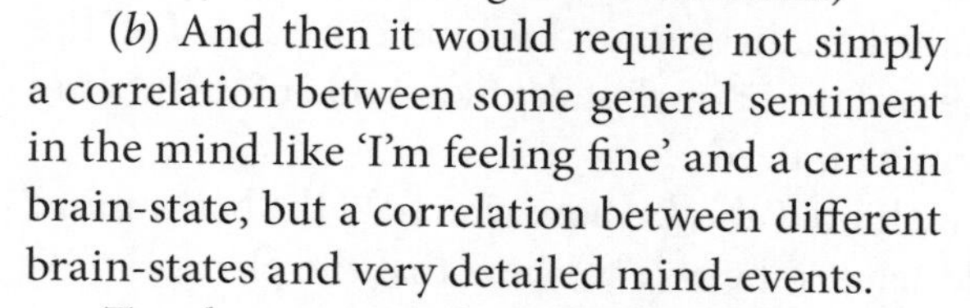

(*b*) And then it would require not simply a correlation between some general sentiment in the mind like 'I'm feeling fine' and a certain brain-state, but a correlation between different brain-states and very detailed mind-events.

To take an example from the discussion of this problem by the Oxford philosopher Richard Swinburne: 'Certainly there are general correlations between certain patterns of brain-states and certain kinds of mental activity, e.g. the occurrence of dreams; but the occurrence of one brain-state for my dream that I am Napoleon I, and a different brain state for my dream that I am Napoleon III, seems a bit speculative.'[24]

(*c*) And then the brain-mind identity theory would need to be able to demonstrate that the electrochemical workings of the neurones in the brain could indicate detailed intentions. Sitting in my study I decide to write out, say, the proof of Pythagoras' theorem. That will involve raising my arm and hand to pick up my pen; and it is perfectly possible that the brain prepares the physical processes necessary for raising my arm and hand. But is it plausible that if a scientist were able at that precise moment to examine the appropriate part of my brain and observe the direction of its electrochemical pro-

[24] *Existence of God*, 167.

cesses, he could, in theory at least, predict without my telling him, whether I was intending to write the proof of Pythagoras' theorem, or a poem, or a pen-and-ink sketch of the house next door, or do a crossword puzzle?

It is not enough to say that the physical processes in my brain could not be expected to indicate such detailed predictions. For in my mind I may have gone over all the above-mentioned options, and then have decided on which one I intended to perform. If mind-events are identical with brain-events, the brain-events were at one moment going through all these options, and then settled on one; and their configuration at that moment would indicate my intention to do the one I chose. If brain-events could not indicate all those options and then predict the one that I had chosen, how, according to their brain-mind identity theory, could my mind intend and predict it?

Scientists may express the hope that one day they will be able to demonstrate that detailed predictions of this kind can be read off the electrochemical process of the brain; but the likelihood of their being successful must be remote indeed.

(*d*) And then, as we hinted above, those who hold the brain-mind identity theory would have to be able to show that the physical processes of the brain have a moral sense. For if I sit pondering in my mind whether it would be truly moral (and not just pragmatically advisable) to collaborate with an enemy invading force, as the Norwegian Major Vidkun Quisling did with the Nazis, the identity theory requires that it is the physical substances of the electrochemical processes in the neurones that are weighing up and deciding this moral question. Have physical substances a moral sensibility, then?

Have the electrochemical processes in my brain a genuinely free will, so that they can come to a genuinely free, and therefore, truly moral decision?

With that comes an even more fundamentally important question. Have the electrochemical processes in my brain a genuinely free will, so that they can come to a genuinely free, and therefore, truly moral decision? Unfortunately, most brain-mind identity theorists hold that the physical world is a completely closed system of cause and effect. In other words, there is not really any such thing as free will. If that is so, how could mind-events, being identical with physical brain-events, ever genuinely discuss, let alone make, moral decisions?

Or how could they make rational decisions either? For in this connection it would be easier to agree with Professor John Polkinghorne's verdict, which we came across earlier (p. 52). He further says, 'The reductionist programme in the end subverts itself. It also destroys rationality. Thought is replaced by electro-chemical neural events. Two such events cannot confront each other in rational discourse. They are neither right nor wrong. They simply happen.'[25]

Now we asked some time back how the brain-mind identity theory has been established, or could ever be established. We quickly decided that it is not based on intuition; and we have since been considering the enormous difficulties there would be in establishing it by rigorous scientific research. So what grounds can there be for holding it?

3. *By first assuming as true what one then convinces oneself is fact?*

Perhaps few scientists do this; but some do. One example is the following. It comes from a scientist who first assumes that Darwinism is true and allows of no alternative explanation of the origin of man's mind. On that basis he argues that the inevitable implications of Darwin's theory must be acknowledged as fact:

> Can it be that if you put enough of these dumb homunculi together you make a real conscious person? The Darwinian says there could be no other way of making one. Now, it certainly does not follow from the fact that you are descended from robots that you are a robot. After all, you are also a direct descendant of some fish, and you are not a fish; you are a direct descendent of some bacteria, and you are not a bacterium. But unless dualism or vitalism is true (in which case you have some extra, secret ingredient in you), you are *made of* robots—or what comes to the same thing, a collection of trillions of macromolecular machines. And all of these are ultimately descended from the original macros. So something made of robots *can* exhibit genuine consciousness, or genuine intentionality, because you do if anything does.[26]

[25] *One World*, 92–3.

[26] Dennett, *Darwin's Dangerous Idea*, 206.

The flow of the argument is at least clear:

1. Robots do not have consciousness nor intentionality.
2. How then could it be possible to make human beings of robots?
3. But human beings are made of robots: no other explanation of their origin is possible or permissible.
4. And human beings do have consciousness and intentionality.
5. Therefore it is possible to make conscious human beings out of conscious-less robots.

Dennett thus appears to assume what he is purporting to prove.

Perspectivalism, or Dual Aspect Monism

This view suggests that mind and brain are simply two different ways of looking at the same thing. There is an inside story: the situation as it appears to the 'I' whose brain it is. This is the 'I-story'. And there is the story from the outside: the situation as it appears to the scientist who is observing the brain from the outside. This is the 'O-story'. The two stories will be somewhat different. The 'I' from the inside, for instance, will feel that he has genuine free will. The scientist from the outside will say that the brain is a closed physical system of cause and effect and is therefore determined. Free will is not possible. And somehow—it is very difficult adequately to explain how—both stories are true.

A cloud, for instance, looks different from the inside, from what it does from the outside. From the outside, at least on a summer's day, a cumulus cloud looks like a dazzlingly white mountain; from the inside it looks like a dismally grey fog! Quite so; but the analogy is not very helpful when applied to the brain-mind problem. Whatever the cloud looks like, white mountain or grey fog, it is the same substance throughout—water droplets.

No matter, then, what the brain-mind looks like—white mountain or grey fog—according to perspectivalism, it is the same substance throughout. It leaves unsolved, therefore, the big basic problems we have met with in the previous theories: how can the brain-mind, if it is composed throughout of mere physical matter, possess genuine free will and a moral sense?

Functionalism

This is a theory that has attracted many scientists and within its limits can be helpful. But it need not detain us long here; for when it comes to the basic mind-body question one of its main advocates confesses its inadequacy.

Let Professor Jerry Fodor, a functionalist, tell us what functionalism is:

> Functionalism construes the concept of causal role in such a way that a mental state can be defined by its causal relations to other mental states. In this respect functionalism is completely different from logical behaviourism . . . functionalism is not a reductionist thesis. It does not foresee, even in principle, the elimination of mentalistic concepts from the explanatory apparatus of psychological theories.[27]

Yet Fodor himself admits later on:

> Most psychologists who are inclined to accept the functionalist framework are nonetheless worried about the failure of functionalism to reveal much more about the nature of consciousness . . . the problem of qualitative content proves a serious threat to the assertion that functionalism can provide a general theory of the mental.[28]

And Professor Thomas Nagel, author of the influential paper, 'What Is It Like to Be a Bat?'[29] makes this comment on functionalism:

> Functionalism, though part of the truth, is not an adequate theory of mind . . . the complete truth is much more complicated and more resistant to understanding . . . a theory which succeeded in explaining the relation between behaviour, consciousness, and the brain would have to be of a fundamentally different kind from theories about other things: it cannot be generated by the application of already existing methods of explanation.[30]

---

[27] In Warner and Szubka, *Mind-Body Problem*, 31.

[28] *Mind-Body Problem*, 37.

[29] In his *Mortal Questions*.

[30] *Mind-Body Problem*, 64–5.

Modified monism

What this group of scientists, philosophers and psychologists have in common is that they reject any form of dualism. Professor John Polkinghorne gives his reasons for this rejection: it is because in dualism 'matter and mind fail to coalesce into the one world of our psychosomatic experience'. He then indicates what he sees as the only possible account of man: 'The only possibility appears to be a complementary world of mind/matter in which these polar opposites cohere as contrasting aspects of the world-stuff.'[31]

From his use of the phrase 'contrasting aspects of the world-stuff', Polkinghorne seems to hold a form of perspectivalism. But, as we saw earlier, perspectivalism seems in the end to exclude the possibility of free will. But elsewhere he remarks 'the denial of human freedom is incoherent'.[32] He argues rather that the brain is a complex dynamical system, and, like many such systems, precludes ultimate predictability (as described in the mathematical theory of chaos). This unpredictability, therefore, leaves the brain open to the practice of prayer and divine influence from above.

Perhaps, the best label to put on this kind of view is one that is used by an increasing number of scientists nowadays, as, for instance, by the psychologist Professor Malcolm Jeeves, namely, 'non-reductive physicalism'.[33]

Under this heading, too, one would be tempted to put the great and famous Theodosius Dobzhansky. He was certainly no dualist; yet he talked freely of his self-conscious self: 'I am not only alive but aware of being alive. Moreover, I know that I shall not remain alive for ever, that death is inevitable. I possess the attributes of self-awareness and death awareness.'[34]

But not all modern scientists, philosophers and psychologists are materialistic monists. It's true that many scientists give the impression that to embrace dualism would open themselves to the disparaging label that Gilbert Ryle put upon dualists, as being people who

---

31 *Science and Creation*, 1988 SPCK edn., 71.

32 *Science and Providence*, 14.

33 'Brain, Mind, and Behaviour', 73–98.

34 'Evolutionary Roots', 411.

believe in 'The ghost in the machine'.[35] But there is nowadays an increasing number of scientists of various persuasions who would not be altogether afraid of that label.

In their book *The Matter Myth*, Professors Paul Davies and John Gribbin remark:

> We mention these admittedly speculative ideas to illustrate the profound change in perspective that has accompanied the move towards a postmechanistic paradigm. In place of clodlike particles of matter in a lumbering Newtonian machine we have an interlocking network of information exchange—a holistic, indeterministic and open system—vibrant with potentialities and bestowed with infinite richness. . . . Descartes founded the image of the human mind as a sort of nebulous substance that exists independently of the body. Much later, in 1949, Gilbert Ryle derided this dualism in a pithy reference to the mind part as 'the ghost in the machine'. Ryle articulated his criticism during the triumphal phase of materialism and mechanism. The 'machine' he referred to was the human body and the human brain, themselves just parts of the larger cosmic machine. But already, when he coined that pithy expression, the new physics was at work, undermining the world view on which Ryle's philosophy was based. Today, on the brink of the twenty-first century, we can see that Ryle was right to dismiss the notion of the ghost in the machine—not because there is no ghost, but because there is no machine.[36]

From this it would appear that Davies and Gribbin are not monists of the old kind—'man is nothing but matter'—but are monists of a different kind—man is ultimately nothing but information.

Other scientists and philosophers however are unashamed dualists in the traditional sense of that word. Talking of Ryle and his disparagement of 'the ghost in the machine' idea, Karl Popper says:

> he also wishes no doubt to deny the (Socratic and Platonic) idea of the mind as the pilot of a ship—the body; a simile which I

---

[35] 'Man need not be degraded to a machine by being denied to be a ghost in a machine' (*Concept of Mind*, 301).

[36] pp. 308–9.

regard as in many ways excellent and adequate; so much so that I can say of myself 'I believe in the ghost in the machine'.[37]

And so we come to a third approach to the problem.

Dualistic Interactionism

This view is perhaps better known as 'Cartesian dualism', since it was René Descartes (1637) who gave it great prominence and vivid expression.[38] Descartes stressed the view that the mind was an immaterial substance which acted causally on the body, thus making the body act, and in turn was acted on by the body in receiving sensations, etc. This is called, therefore, Dualistic *Interactionism* to call attention to the fact that other views may accept that the body can act upon the mind but not that the mind can act on the body. Dualistic Interactionism holds that the mind can act on the body as well as the body on the mind.

Dualistic Interactionism holds that the mind can act on the body as well as the body on the mind.

This view did not, of course, originate with Descartes: it has had a long history, as Popper has shown in his book.[39] Not all of those who nowadays hold some form of Dualistic Interactionism would agree with all the features of Descartes' own exposition. Nor would they all agree among themselves as to what the immaterial part of the human dualism should be called, whether 'self' or 'mind' or 'spirit' or 'soul'! Neither would they all agree on how this immaterial entity came to be.

Popper, a Darwinian evolutionist, thinks it just 'emerged':

> From an evolutionary point of view, I regard the self-conscious mind as an emergent product of the brain. . . . Now I want to emphasize how little is said by saying that the mind is an emergent product of the brain. It has practically no explanatory value, and it hardly amounts to more than putting a question mark at a certain place in human evolution. Nevertheless, I think that this is all which, from a Darwinian point of view, we can say about it.[40]

---

37 Popper and Eccles, *Self and Its Brain*, 105.
38 See particularly his *Discourse on Method*, part 4.
39 Popper and Eccles, *Self and Its Brain*, 148–208.
40 Popper and Eccles, *Self and Its Brain*, 554.

At the same time Popper also says:

> Now in connection with the question: 'What is the self-conscious mind?' I might say first . . . 'It is something utterly different from anything which, to our knowledge, has previously existed in the world.' . . . There may be some sort of forerunner of the human mind in the experience of pleasure and pain by animals, but it is, of course, completely different from these animal experiences because it can be self-reflexive; that is to say, the ego can be conscious of itself. That is what we mean by the self-conscious mind.[41]

The contributor to the second half of the book *The Self and Its Brain* is John C. Eccles, a Nobel Laureate for his work on neurophysiology. A theistic evolutionist, he holds that while man's body and brain came to be by the processes of Darwinian evolution, the 'Self' or 'Soul' in each human being is a special creation of God, put by God into the foetus sometime after conception and before birth. So he entitles one of his own books *Evolution of the Brain, Creation of the Self*, and after a long exposition of the results of his own and others' neurophysiological research on the brain, he comes in his summing-up to express his own belief:

> Since materialist solutions fail to account for our experienced uniqueness, I am constrained to attribute the uniqueness of the Self or Soul to a supernatural spiritual creation. To give the explanation in theological terms: each Soul is a new Divine creation which is implanted into the growing foetus at some time between conception and birth. It is the certainty of the inner core of unique individuality . . . that necessitates the 'Divine creation'. I submit that no other explanation is tenable; neither the genetic uniqueness with its fantastically impossible lottery, nor the environmental differentiations which do not *determine* one's uniqueness, but merely modify it. This conclusion is of inestimable theological significance. It strongly reinforces our belief in the human Soul and its miraculous origin in a Divine creation—there is recognition not only of the Transcendent

[41] Popper and Eccles, *Self and Its Brain*, 553.

> God, the Creator of the Cosmos, the God in which Einstein believed, but also of the loving God to whom we owe our being.[42]

Another Nobel Laureate neuroscientist, Charles S. Sherrington was also a believer in dualism. He expressed himself: 'That our being should consist of *two* fundamental elements offers I suppose no greater inherent improbability than that it should rest on one only.'[43]

The distinguished neurosurgeon, Wilder Penfield, started as a brain-mind identity theorist, but after long experience embraced dualism.[44] He states: 'it is easier to rationalise man's being on the basis of two elements than on the basis of one'.[45]

Swinburne, as we have already seen, argues against identity theory

---

42 p. 237.

What Eccles means by saying that materialist solutions fail to account for our experienced uniqueness, he explains in the following technical passage:

> It will be my task to concentrate on the most extraordinary event in the world of our experience, namely the coming to be of each of us as a unique self-conscious being. It is a miracle for ever beyond science.
>
> It is not in doubt that each human person recognizes its own uniqueness, and this is accepted as the basis of social life and of law. When we enquire into the grounds for this belief, modern neuroscience eliminates an explanation in terms of the body. There remain two possible alternatives—the brain and the Psyche. Materialists must subscribe to the former, but . . .
>
> If one's experienced uniqueness derives directly from the uniqueness of one's brain, we have to enquire into the levels of uniqueness of human brains. It could not be the uniqueness of all the infinity of detailed connectivities of the 10,000 million cells of the human cerebral cortex. Such connectivities are constantly changing in plasticity and degeneration. The most usual materialist statement is that the experienced uniqueness derives from the genetic uniqueness.
>
> It is important to realize that the basic connectivities of the human brain are built before birth in readiness for the subtle changes in synaptic connectivities that develop throughout life in the learning processes. . . . Thus there is an immense developmental gulf between the genetic instructions provided by the zygote and the brain of the newborn baby. It will be realized that developmental noise renders chaotic and incoherent any attempt to derive our experienced uniqueness from our genetic uniqueness. And already we have seen that this attempt is confronted by the infinitely improbable genetic lottery governing the actual existence of one's unique genome.
>
> A frequent and superficially plausible answer to this enigma is the assertion that the determining factor is the uniqueness of the accumulated experiences of a Self throughout its lifetime. It is readily agreed that our behaviour and memories and in fact the whole content of our inner conscious life are dependent on the accumulated experiences of our lives; but no matter how extreme the change, at some particular decision point, which can be produced by the exigencies of circumstances, one would still be the same Self able to trace back one's continuity in memory to the earliest remembrances at the age of 1 year or so, the same Self in a quite other guise. There could be no elimination of a Self and creation of a new Self! (*Self and Its Brain*, 236–7)

43 *Integrative Action of the Nervous System*, xxiv.

44 See his book *Mystery of the Mind*, 97.

45 *Mystery of the Mind*, 113–14.

and for dualism, though he adds that for a full and satisfactory account of the correlation between mind-events and brain-events, one has to go beyond dualism to God.[46]

But our main point is not how many scientists and philosophers accept Dualistic Interactionism and how many don't. Rather we should come to what is the heart of the dispute between the monists, of whatever kind, and the various kinds of dualist.

The heart of the Monist/Dualist debate

Dualistic Interactionism implies, as the term itself declares, that the mind, or self, is not only acted upon by the brain, but itself acts on the brain. Take Popper's emphatic statement of this view.

> I intend here to suggest that the brain is owned by the self, rather than the other way round. The self is almost always active. The activity of selves is, I suggest, the only genuine activity we know. The active, psycho-physical self is the active programmer to the brain (which is the computer), it is the executant whose instrument is the brain. The mind is, as Plato said, the pilot. It is not, as David Hume and William James suggested, the sum total, or the bundle, or the stream of its experiences: this suggests passivity. It is, I suppose, a view that results from passively trying to observe oneself, instead of thinking back and reviewing one's past actions.
>
> I suggest that these considerations show that the self is not a 'pure ego' . . . that is, a mere subject. Rather, it is incredibly rich. Like a pilot, it observes and takes action at the same time. It is acting and suffering, recalling the past and planning and programming the future; expecting and disposing. It contains, in quick succession, or all at once, wishes, plans, hopes, decisions to act, and a vivid consciousness of being an active self, a centre of action. . . . And all this closely interacts with the tremendous 'activity' going on in its brain.[47]

This is, however, the idea that materialistic monists find impossible to accept or even to conceive of. 'How can an immaterial entity',

[46] *Existence of God*, 172.

[47] *Self and Its Brain*, 120.

they ask, 'call it self, mind, soul, or spirit, or what you will, act on, impinge on, affect, move, cause to act, a material entity, the brain?'

Their first difficulty, so they say, is this: science knows nothing of invisible, immaterial entities; it cannot measure them, nor conduct experiments on them. Science cannot allow that they exist; they are figments of people's imagination. 'Ghosts in the machine', and like all ghosts, non-existent.

But scientists who talk like this are not really being consistent. No scientist has ever yet seen a quark. But scientists all believe in quarks, for they infer their existence from the effect they have on other particles and the trail that this leaves behind in a cloud chamber.

Moreover, no scientist has ever yet seen energy. Indeed, no one knows or can say what energy is. The late physics Nobel prizewinner, Richard P. Feynman, in his book *Six Easy Pieces*, devotes a chapter to the topic of conservation of energy.[48] In the course of that chapter he remarks:

> It is important to realize that in physics today, we have no knowledge of what energy *is*. We do not have a picture that energy comes in little blobs of a definite amount. It is not that way. However, there are formulas for calculating some numerical quantity, and when we add it all together it gives . . . always the same number. It is an abstract thing in that it does not tell us the mechanism or the *reasons* for the various formulas.[49]

But scientists do not refuse belief in the existence of energy because they do not know what it is. They can see and measure its effects.

Moreover, the thesis that only like things can act upon each other, and therefore an immaterial mind cannot act upon a material brain, is not borne out by the rest of nature. Popper makes the point:

> Perhaps the clearest physical example against the thesis that only like things can act upon each other is this. In modern physics, the action of bodies upon bodies is *mediated* by fields—by gravitational and electrical fields. Thus like does not act upon

[48] Ch. 4, pp. 69–86.

[49] pp. 71–2.

like, but bodies act first upon fields which they modify, and then the (modified) field acts upon another body.[50]

Added to this is our daily experience of receiving information in our minds which then affects our brains, emotions and bodies; and information is non-material.

Perhaps we need to pause and think just here, because we are so used to receiving information, by letter, newspaper, radio, television, social media, telephone, word of mouth, etc. that, if not careful, we could confuse information with the material carrier used to convey the information.

Suppose a mother whose son has gone to study in an Australian university. One day she receives a letter in the post from one of his friends. The first page tells that her son came out top in his examinations and received a prize at a special ceremony in the university. The second page tells that on the way back to his lodgings the car in which he was travelling crashed into a lorry. The driver of the car was killed and her son was injured and is now in hospital.

. . . if not careful, we could confuse information with the material carrier used to convey the information.

As mother's mind grasps the information on the first page, it has a powerful effect on her body: great smiles erupt all over her face and her heart thumps with joy. As her mind takes in the information on the second page, it too has a powerful effect on her body: she freezes with fear and tears start from her eyes.

Obviously, the information is affecting her material brain and body. But what exactly was the information that entered her mind? It wasn't the paper the words were written on: the two pieces of paper did not enter her head. Nor did the ink in which the information was written; nor indeed did the letters and the words: they were still on the paper long after she had grasped the information they were carrying.

The words were in her native English language, and she therefore easily understood the meaning they were conveying. But the words themselves were not the information. A non-English speaker could have looked at the words and received no information at all; but for

[50] *Self and Its Brain*, 182.

that person the information could be transferred from English words to, say, Chinese.

It is true that as Mother read the letter, photons carried the shapes of the letters and words to her eyes where they were converted into electrical signals which passed down the optic nerve to the visual cortex in her brain. But these signals were not the information; they only carried it. Similar protons and electrical signals would have conveyed the letters and words to her visual cortex had the words been in Spanish or Russian. But her mind would not have been able to extract from them the information that they carried.

What then was the information? It was not any of the material things that carried it. It was not a form of matter, then; it was immaterial. It began in the mind of the person who wrote the letter. He decided it must be conveyed to the student's mother. The question then arose: what form of matter should he use to carry the information: sound waves by telephone? E-mail by computer? Pen, ink and paper? He chose the latter. The material carrying the information reaches Mother. Her mind grasped the non-material meaning, and she had no further need of the material which conveyed it. But this immaterial meaning grasped by the mind then had a powerful effect on her brain and body.

So then a non-material entity or force can affect a material substance. It is our everyday experience that it can do so. The dualistic interactionists are right: a non-material mind can act on a material brain and body.

So far, then, on this topic we have listened to the voice of intuition and the voice of science and philosophy. To complete this part of our study we ought now briefly to listen to the voice of what many believe to be divine revelation.

The voice of revelation

Theists, by definition, have no difficulty with the idea that a non-material entity can act upon a material body. 'God', said Christ, 'is spirit' (John 4:24). It was his word of command that created matter, and his word that was the source of the information that we find encoded in matter. It is his energy, his powerful word, that maintains the universe in being and in cohesion (Heb 1:3; 11:3; Col 1:16–17). It is his word, and not simply the second law of thermodynamics, that controls the mechanisms that will bring the earth to its end (2 Pet 3:5–7).

And as for man, the Bible teaches his dualistic nature. Man is not simply flesh, that is, matter, but also spirit. The Bible does not despise man's body, as some religions and philosophies do. Matter is good, and the human body an integral and glorious part of the human personality. The incarnation of the Son of God in a human body assures us of that. And the bodily resurrection of Christ is the central fundamental doctrine of the Christian faith.

But the Bible teaches that man is more than his body. God, who is himself spirit, forms the spirit of each man within him (Zech 12:1). It is the spirit of a human being within him that knows and understands those things that are typically human (1 Cor 2:11). Man's spirit is not to be thought of as something thin, weak, and virtually lifeless, any more than God is. The Bible uses several terms in order to indicate the richness of man's inner life: spirit, soul, heart, mind and conscience. Because we are a fallen race, man's spirit is naturally dead to God, like a telephone line that has gone dead and obstructs communication. Therefore man's spirit needs to be regenerated by the Spirit of God (Eph 2:1–10; John 3:1–16).

The Bible does not despise man's body, as some religions and philosophies do. Matter is good, and the human body an integral and glorious part of the human personality. The incarnation of the Son of God in a human body assures us of that.

When it comes to life, spirit is more important than flesh (John 6:63): when the spirit departs, the body dies. The human spirit can exist apart from the body. Hence Christ at his death committed his spirit into the hands of God (Luke 23:46), as also did Stephen, the first Christian martyr (Acts 7:59). The spirits of just men and women who have physically died are with God (Heb 12:23). The brigand who was crucified by the side of Christ, was upon repentance assured by Christ: 'Today you will be with me in paradise' (Luke 23:43). The goal of human redemption shall be reached when the regenerate human spirit is eventually 'clothed upon' with a redeemed and glorified body (2 Cor 5:1–5; Rom 8:11, 18–23).

Thus far, then, we have thought, first of what a wonderful thing the human race is, and particularly of humanity's power over nature.

Then we have thought of what humans are: they are not just matter like nature is. They have, indeed they are, immaterial spirits. It makes sense, therefore, to talk of humanity's power over nature.

Now we must move on and consider another fact about the human race; and this time it will not be so pleasant.

THE PARAMETERS OF HUMAN POWER

Man's conquest of Nature, if the dreams of some scientific planners are realized, means the rule of a few hundreds of men over billions upon billions of men. There neither is nor can be any simple increase of power on Man's side. Each new power won *by* man is a power *over* man as well.

—C. S. Lewis, *The Abolition of Man*

SAFEGUARDING HUMANITY'S RIGHTS AND FREEDOMS

At the start of the previous chapter we celebrated humanity's exalted status as ruler of the earth and the impressive power over nature that humans have in the course of the centuries achieved. We need to ask now, therefore, what are the parameters of humanity's power? Are there any? Are humans subject to any moral and spiritual laws that stand above them, that put a limit, not so much to what they can do, but to what they may do? Or does the acquisition of power itself confer on those that achieve it the right to exercise that power over nature and over their fellow humans as they decide best without any higher authority, moral or spiritual, to set limiting parameters to their use of power?

We need to ask these questions, because humanity's acquisition of power over nature has on the one hand conferred on us all innumerable benefits; but on the other our abuse of power has in time past undeniably wrought a great deal of damage. And now that we have begun to unlock the very secrets of life, the potential for good is enormous; so also is the potential for evil.

This has been particularly true of the twentieth century, not to mention the early decades of the twenty-first. Never in all the history of humankind has one century witnessed such spectacular progress in science and technology with all their attendant benefits. But never before has humanity in one single century perpetrated so much evil.

The sombre lesson of history

In the course of the twentieth century multi-millions were slaughtered; by two world wars, and countless other wars fought with ever more efficient armaments; by both right-wing and left-wing dictators, by Hitler and Pol Pot and the government of Indonesia; by religious and political persecution, by Mafia and terrorist organisations; by newly discovered atomic violence unleashed on Hiroshima and

Nagasaki, and by the sub-human savagery of Rwanda and the Democratic Republic of Congo and the Balkan states; by democratic nations who boosted their economies by manufacturing arms and selling them to undemocratic governments who have no respect for human rights; by industrialists who have made fortunes by manufacturing millions of landmines which they then sold to Afghanistan and Angola and other countries where they blew the legs off thousands of innocent civilians including children.

Millions have been impoverished by the exploitation of the majority world by more prosperous nations, and by corruption in countries in the majority world which puts millions of dollars of international aid into the pockets of their dictators while those dictators leave their own people in squalor and poverty. Nor has corruption been rife only in those countries: prime ministers and presidents of several countries in every part of the world, along withtheir associates, have been obliged to resign over charges of corruption.

And then there is the question of the damage that is being done to earth's ecosystem by the ruthless exploitation of the world's rainforests by huge multinational business conglomerates; and of the pollution of the planet and its atmosphere that appears to be creating an ever-increasing hole in the ozone layer that is meant to protect earth from ultraviolet radiation.

Let's not point the finger only at impersonal government and commercial organisations, but point it, where necessary, also at ourselves. After all, it is not simply humankind as an impersonal whole that is responsible for the stewardship of earth and its resources.

But for the sake of balance and fairness, let's not point the finger only at impersonal government and commercial organisations, but point it, where necessary, also at ourselves. After all, it is not simply humankind as an impersonal whole that is responsible for the stewardship of earth and its resources. Our own time, energies and abilities are also part, however small, of the planet's resources, and we each have a responsibility to use them as best we can for our own benefit and other people's.

One family member's greedy selfishness in the use of the family's resources is in principle the same as the greed of the multinational corporations in their aggressive acquisition of the world's resources. Laziness at school, or at work, if we have employment, is a waste of our own time, energy and abilities, let alone those of the factory or business or school or university at which we work. Immoderate drinking of alcohol is a perverse use of earth's resources and an abuse of the health of our bodies and brains. And so likewise is the abuse of drugs. And the deliberate rejection of traditional sexual morality in the last fifty years and more has put an enormous drain on the medical resources and health services in many countries as they attempt to cope with a range of sexually-transmitted diseases.

Humanity's conquest of nature, then, and the way humans have used their stewardship of earth's resources in the course of the twentieth century has been a very mixed blessing.

Prospect for the future

But now humanity has succeeded in cracking the genetic code and has completed the mapping of the whole human genome. That has put enormous power into the hands of humankind, or rather into the hands of some men and women—the experts—over the rest of their fellow humans, a power unparalleled in all previous history. The question is: how will that power be used? We can be sure it will be used to produce great benefits; but not only benefits, if past history is any guide. Already there have been disturbing signs.

Originally, when geneticists deciphered part of the human genome and discovered what genes in what sector control what part of the body's organs, they applied to take out a patent on their knowledge of this part of the genome. That could have meant, that, if a person became ill, and the necessary cure involved his doctors using this knowledge of that part of the genome, then the patient must pay the patent-holder for permission to have his own body's genetic mechanism treated.

In 1998 *New Scientist* was reporting an interesting case in point. Under the title, 'Selling the family secrets', it announced that 'Iceland plans to put its people's genetic history in the hands of a single company. The deal could put privacy at risk, with damaging consequences for genetics research everywhere'.[1] Later in the article

[1] Coghlan, 'Selling the family secrets', 20–1.

Richard Lewontin, professor of zoology and biology at Harvard University, is quoted as commenting:

> There's this general feeling that genes are being exploited for private profit. The population of Iceland has been turned into a tool for this one company, and that seems completely objectionable.

New Scientist also reported that in addition to the criticisms of the proposal by many Icelanders themselves, the European Union's Data Protection Commissioners criticised it for failing to 'protect the privacy, dignity and rights of people whose records are entered into databases for genetics research'.

Since those early days, some progress has been made in keeping genes accessible for research; let's hope that trend continues. It would, of course, be foolish to become alarmist and to impede responsible genetic research that promises us so many medical benefits. But at the same time we must envisage the dark side of what the future could bring about if there are no ethical controls placed on humanity's exploitation of our power over nature. Suppose the day comes when the genetic engineers who have mapped and decoded the whole of the human genome are under the control of some totalitarian government; and through them the government has the power to decide what kind of people shall be allowed to marry and produce children; or what foetuses should be permitted to be born. Then, obviously humanity's power over nature will certainly not mean every man and woman's power over nature, but the power of a comparatively few men and women over the vast majority.

As C. S. Lewis remarks:

> In reality, of course, if any one age really attains, by eugenics and scientific education, the power to make its descendants what it pleases, all men who live after it are the patients of that power. . . . And if . . . the age which had thus attained maximum power over posterity were also the age most emancipated from [moral] tradition, it would be engaged in reducing the power of its predecessors almost as drastically as that of its successors. . . . The real picture is that of one dominant age . . . which resists all previous ages most successfully and dominates all subsequent ages most irresistibly, and thus is the real master of the

> human species. But then within this master generation . . . the power will be exercised by a minority. . . . Man's conquest of Nature, if the dreams of some scientific planners are realized, means the rule of a few hundreds of men over billions upon billions of men. There neither is nor can be any simple increase of power on Man's side. Each new power won *by* man is a power *over* man as well.[2]

Long before any such hypothetical ultimate scenario comes into existence, therefore, we need to give careful thought to the question: by what moral constraints and by what principles is humanity's power over nature to be ethically controlled and directed?

If, for instance, government-controlled geneticists were to decree that only normal foetuses should be allowed to be born, by what standards would they define normality? Would they allow a future Helen Keller to be born? She was both blind and deaf and yet triumphed over her twin disabilities and became an inspiration to thousands. In the past many of our greatest musicians and artists have been less than 100 per cent emotionally balanced. If future geneticists were able to read the genes and tell that such foetuses, if born, would suffer emotional maladjustment, would they order them to be aborted and so, not only deprive them of life but (unknowingly) rob the world of their brilliant and enriching talent?

Considerations of this kind emphasise the seriousness of the question with which we began: What are the parameters of humanity's power? Are there any? Are we subject to any moral and spiritual laws that stand above us, that put a limit not so much to what we can do, but to what we may do?

The question of human dignity and rights

Take the question of human rights, the rights not of mankind as a whole, or of nations as a whole, but of each individual human being. For the lesson of history should be kept constantly before us, that empires come and go, tribes and ethnic groups merge together and then over time dissolve and re-assemble in different patterns; cultures

2 *Abolition of Man*, 36.

blossom and then fade. The individual human being is the constant. If we would assess the value of mankind, we must start with the value of each individual that makes up humankind. Nations are in some sense impersonal agglomerates; and history has shown all too often that it is possible for people to be obsessed with the power of nations and yet utterly unconcerned with the misery and destruction that such power-lust can eventually inflict on hundreds of thousands of individual human beings.

On what, then, are the rights of the individual human being based? Theism is quick with its answer: they are based on God and on God's character. Each individual is made in the image of God, and as such has intrinsic, inalienable dignity and rights. To maltreat an individual human being is to insult his Maker: 'Whoever sheds the blood of man, by man shall his blood be shed, for God made man in his own image' (Gen 9:6); 'Whoever oppresses a poor man insults his Maker' (Prov 14:31).

But atheists must by definition deny this basis of human rights, and must found those rights on some other source. Who, then, gives to the individual his rights? The humanist Sidney Cook says: 'It is not God but the human community that endows its members with rights.'[3]

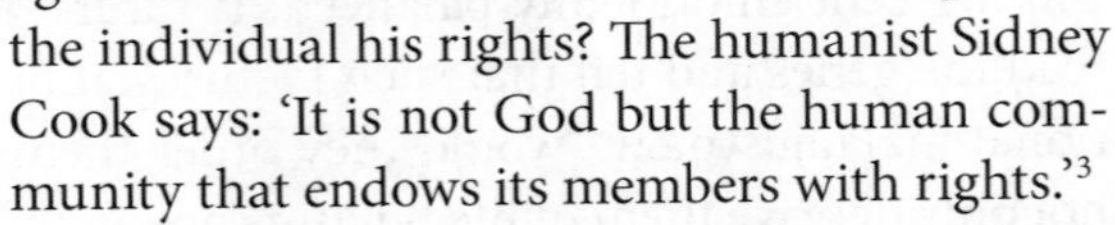

The witness of history is that communities and governments often act unreasonably. And in those times the question urgently arises: are communities, are governments, the final and absolute authority?

Now this theory may appear to be adequate in times when communities and their governments act reasonably. But the witness of history is that communities and governments often act unreasonably. And in those times the question urgently arises: are communities, are governments, the final and absolute authority? Have they the ultimate right to decide which individual or which ethnic group has a right to life, and which shall be eliminated? Is the State the supreme source of all law, or are there laws above even the State, which set the parameters of the State's exercise of power?

Sophocles' play *Antigone*, from which we earlier quoted that famous ode on man's conquest of nature, has for its central theme this

[3] 'Solzhenitsyn and Secular Humanism', 6.

very question: are the laws of the State, important as they are, the supreme laws, or are there other laws above those of the State? Antigone puts it this way:

> Nor did I deem that thou, a mortal man,
> Could'st by a breath annul and override
> The immutable unwritten laws of Heaven.
> They were not born to-day nor yesterday;
> They die not; and none knoweth whence they sprang.
> I was not like, who feared no mortal's frown,
> To disobey these laws and so provoke
> The wrath of Heaven.[4]

Worth reading, too, is the famous Hebrew story on this theme in Daniel 3. It relates to the time of Nebuchadnezzar (sometimes spelt Nebuchadrezzar), king of Babylon, 605–562 BC. Concerned for the stability of his empire, Nebuchadnezzar summoned to Babylon all the officers of state and leading civil servants. He then had erected a golden image of his god, and assembled all the officers and civil servants to a public ceremony in honour of this god. As the State orchestra struck up suitably patriotic music, all the officers and civil servants were required to bow down and worship the image. That image was, of course, a symbol of the deification of the State and of its head, Nebuchadnezzar; and the officers and civil servants were being compelled to recognise that the power of the State was absolute.

At that time, however, thousands of Jews had been deported to Babylon and were living there in enforced exile. Three young Jews had become civil servants, and thus were commanded along with their colleagues to bow down and worship the image of the State. Loyal subjects of the king though they were, they were not prepared to deify the State, and to offer to its image that absolute homage that should be given to God alone. So they refused to bow down, and thus took their stand not only for God, but for the fundamental dignity and freedom of conscience of every human being. For this they were thrown into a furnace. What happened next should be read in the words of the story itself.

---

[4] *Antigone* ll. 453–60 (Storr).

The Christians of the first and second centuries AD were faced with a similar challenge. Christ had been unjustly crucified by the Roman governor Pilate in the reign of the Emperor Tiberius. Yet Christians were taught by the Christian apostles to respect and obey the State:

> Let every person be subject to the governing authorities. For there is no authority except from God, and those that exist have been instituted by God. Therefore whoever resists the authorities resists what God has appointed, and those who resist will incur judgment. For rulers are not a terror to good conduct, but to bad. Would you have no fear of the one who is in authority? Then do what is good, and you will receive his approval, for he is God's servant for your good. But if you do wrong, be afraid, for he does not bear the sword in vain. For he is the servant of God, an avenger who carries out God's wrath on the wrongdoer. Therefore one must be in subjection, not only to avoid God's wrath but also for the sake of conscience. For because of this you also pay taxes, for the authorities are ministers of God, attending to this very thing. Pay to all what is owed to them: taxes to whom taxes are owed, revenue to whom revenue is owed, respect to whom respect is owed, honour to whom honour is owed. (Rom 13:1–7)

Christians were not to be anarchists or revolutionaries. But then some of the Roman emperors, in order to unify all the various nations, cultures and religions in their vast empire, decided to demand all their subjects to pay the emperor divine honours. Here, then, once more was the absolutizing of the State and the deification of man.

The Christians refused, and were executed.[5] But the Christians kept alive the belief that though human government is established by God it is both false and dangerous to absolutize the power of the State. God alone is the Absolute Power, and the dignity of each man and woman derives from God and not from society or the State.

[5] See the letter sent by Pliny, the Roman governor of Bithynia (AD 111–113), to Trajan the Roman emperor enquiring what should be done to Christians who refused to offer sacrifice to the emperor; and the emperor's reply. *Letters of Pliny*, x. 96 [97] and 97 [98].

Man is potentially God?

Humanists, as we have said, reject God. They are nonetheless concerned for human dignity, rights and freedom; they simply deny that these basic human values derive from God. Instead they—or some of them—put forward a striking alternative: man is himself God, or is, at least, on his way to becoming God.

Professor Paul Kurtz wrote: 'God himself is man deified.'[6] Professor Erich Fromm (1900–80), who was in his day a leading humanist psychologist, entitled one of his books *You Shall Be as Gods*. The title is interesting, for it comes from the Bible's account of man's temptation in the garden of Eden. (Fromm was a Jew and a descendant of a long line of rabbis, but at the age of twenty-six he abandoned Judaism, became a convinced humanist-atheist, and saw little distinction between the humanist and Marxist worldviews.) Indeed the promise 'You shall be as Gods' is, in the Bible, part of the temptation by which the serpent persuaded Eve and Adam to disobey God and grasp at independence from him (Gen 3:5). It would be important at this point to read the whole story.

The Christian understanding of this event is that this temptation was at the root of man's fall with all the alienation, pain, sin, and death that has resulted from it (Rom 5:12–21; 2 Cor 11:1–3; but compare also 1 Cor 15:42–49).

Fromm's interpretation is very different:

> The Christian interpretation of the story of man's act of disobedience as his 'fall' has obscured the clear meaning of the story. The biblical text does not even mention the word 'sin'; man challenges the supreme power of God, and he is able to challenge it because he is potentially God.[7]

To the Christian, Fromm's interpretation is very striking. Certainly it is evidence for the way that this idea 'You shall be as Gods'

---

[6] *Fullness of Life*, 19.

[7] p. 23. The story in Genesis 3 goes on to tell how immediately Adam and Eve succumbed to the temptation and disobeyed God, they became aware of their nakedness, felt alienated from God, fled from him, incurred God's curse, were driven out of the garden, and became subject to death. Whether Fromm's interpretation is true to the whole of the story can be left to the reader to decide.

has all down the centuries simmered in humanity's subconscious; and has particularly showed itself from time to time in the temptation to self-deification on the part of aspirants to world power, like the pharaohs, Nebuchadnezzar the Babylonian, Darius the Persian (see Daniel 6), Alexander the Great, some of the Roman emperors, and in the absolutization of recent totalitarian governments. According to the Bible, it will show itself in its full strength eventually when a future politician manages to grasp control of world power, and (in biblical language) 'will oppose and exalt himself against all that is called God or that is worshipped, so that he sits in the temple of God, setting himself forth as God' (2 Thess 2:4).

This idea 'You shall be as Gods' has all down the centuries simmered in humanity's subconscious; and has particularly showed itself from time to time in the temptation to self-deification on the part of aspirants to world power.

But Fromm's interpretation is interesting for another reason. According to Christ the goal of redemption is the union of the redeemed with God through his Son. Christ, in prayer to his Father, put it like this:

> I do not ask for these only [i.e. his apostles], but also for those who will believe in me through their word, that they may all be one, just as you, Father, are in me, and I in you, that they also may be in us, so that the world may believe that you have sent me. The glory that you have given me I have given to them, that they may be one even as we are one, I in them and you in me, that they may become perfectly one, so that the world may know that you sent me and loved them even as you loved me. (John 17:20–23)

And other New Testament passages express the same goal in similar terms:

> For those whom he foreknew he also predestined to be conformed to the image of his Son, in order that he might be the firstborn among many brothers. (Rom 8:29)

> Beloved, we are God's children now, and what we will be has not yet appeared; but we know that when he appears we shall be like him, because we shall see him as he is. (1 John 3:2)

So Fromm's atheistic concept of man's potential deity is, superficially, strikingly similar to what the Bible holds out as God's intention for redeemed humanity. Actually the two schemes are light-years apart. Fromm's atheistic concept is that, having denied God's existence, man has the potential to become God himself, instead of God; or, if God should happen to exist, in opposition to God, and to do so by developing the full potential of his own unaided human powers.

The glorious status of sons of God in union with Christ and God, which God's word, rather than the serpent's promise, holds out to mankind, is granted to man not through his own efforts but as a gift of God's grace and power through repentance, faith, regeneration, union with Christ, and eventual glorification.

Nevertheless, God's word and the promise of the serpent are so superficially similar and yet so significantly different that one can't help suspecting that one is a counterfeit of the other. The first and crucial difference between the two of them, however, is this: the one denies the fall of man, the other presupposes it.

THE QUESTION OF HUMANITY'S FATAL FLAW AND ITS CURE

Without any doubt there is something wrong with the human race. The very briefest knowledge of the long centuries of human history provide constant evidence of serious defects in our character and in our behaviour; nor have the succeeding centuries of his scientific and technological progress given any grounds for thinking that humanity has now mastered these deep-seated defects, or that we are on our way to mastering them: the last century has given more lurid evidence of this basic flaw than any that have gone before.

Nor is it simply or even chiefly in violent outbursts of savagery, slaughter, genocide, ethnic cleansing and such like crimes that man's malaise is seen; but rather in the unreasonable behaviour on the part of us all that hurts those whom we love most, undermines children's psychological security, disrupts family life, breaks up marriages and leads to social tension; and in the corruption that is endemic in commerce and bureaucracy.

What a wonder is man, sang Sophocles' ode.[8] He certainly is. But he is seriously flawed.

However, there would be no point in dwelling on the all too well known evils that flow from humanity's basic flaw; rather our main aim should be, as we look to the future, to consider if there is any reasonable hope of a cure. Or must humans go on forever as they have done throughout history, and are doing now in this twenty-first century?

But to decide upon a cure, if one exists, we should need first to arrive at a correct and realistic diagnosis of the basic trouble and not content ourselves with simply prescribing treatment for the various symptoms of humanity's malaise. In other words we must ask if humanity's misbehaviour is simply a superficial indisposition of a basically healthy moral constitution, like an occasional headache in the body; or if it is the temporary reaction to some moral infection or poison injected by society into an individual's otherwise healthy moral character, like the body's reaction to influenza or malaria; or if humanity's evil behaviour, in whatever form it manifests itself, is but a symptom of some basic defect in our moral make-up.

To this question atheists will, of course, give very different answers from what theists, and particularly Christians, will give. But our task is to try to understand both sets of answers. So let's begin with atheistic points of view.

Our behaviour is determined

The human race like the rest of nature is a closed system of cause and effect. This is the doctrine of behaviourists like B. F. Skinner whom we discussed earlier in Chapter 5. Said B. F. Skinner: 'The hypothesis that man is not free is essential to the application of scientific method to the study of human behaviour'.[9] And again, 'We must expect to discover that what a man does is the result of specifiable conditions and that once these conditions have been discovered, we can anticipate and to some extent determine his actions.'[10]

Now it is true that, for one reason and another, we all develop habits, good and bad, and the bad ones are very difficult to break.

---

8 See p. 175.

9 *Science and Human Behaviour*, 447.

10 *Science and Human Behaviour*, pp. 186-7.

And it is also true that some people develop irresistible psychological compulsions that drive them, say, constantly to wash their hands scores of times a day. But bad habits can be broken, and compulsive behaviour, with the help of experts, can be cured.

But this is not what Skinner is talking about. He is saying that all human beings are little more than biological machines, which have no choice but to behave according to the fixed cause-and-effect laws of physics and biochemistry. If this were true, humanity's condition would be serious indeed, for men and women would not even be able to behave as moral beings. Having no free choice, they would be no better than animals. They could not be held to be guilty of anything. They would not be morally responsible.

And the cure of their (to other people) unacceptable behaviour, would be to treat them, not as human beings, but as malfunctioning machines. Even when they were, if ever, cured, it would be a very sad state of affairs. For even a malfunctioning human being is of higher worth and dignity than a well-trained dog or a smoothly running car or a human robot.

But we need not take behaviourism's diagnosis seriously; comparatively few atheists accept it nowadays. And few behaviourists themselves live what they preach. If someone robs them, they hold the thief morally responsible, blame him and, if need be, prosecute him.

There is nothing basically wrong with man at all

The humanist psychologist Professor Carl Rogers[11] says:

> For myself, though I am very well aware of the incredible amount of destructive, cruel, malevolent behaviour in today's world—from the threat of war to the senseless violence in the streets—I do not find that this evil is inherent in human nature.[12]
>
> I see members of the human species, like members of other species, as essentially constructive in their fundamental nature, but damaged by their experience.[13]

---

[11] He was one of the four leaders of the so-called 'third force' psychology, the other three being Abraham Maslow, Rollo May and Erich Fromm.

[12] 'Notes on Rollo May', 8.

[13] 'Notes on Rollo May', 8.

If, then, people are basically good, what is it, according to this theory, that spoils them? The answer is, apparently, society.

The humanist psychologist Abraham Maslow says:

> Sick people are made by a sick culture; healthy people are made possible by a healthy culture.[14]

And speaking of the noble impulses and instincts that people have within them, Maslow says that they 'are easily warped by cultures—you never find them in their pure state. The people within a culture may, deep within themselves, hold the universal constant of justice. Within the framework of a bad culture it can be twisted into an instrument of evil'.[15]

There is, of course, a lot of truth in this. When unscrupulous demagogues stoke the fires of nationalism, ordinary, otherwise kindly, people can be forced by public pressure to connive at, or even perpetrate, horrible crimes. Rogers adds: 'experience leads me to believe that it is cultural influences which are the major factor in our evil behaviours.'[16]

Consider what some examples of this would be.

Marxism has constantly proclaimed the exploitation of the proletariat by the bourgeois capitalists. It says that man's alienation from the means of production and the fruits of his labour have been the cause of his alienation from himself; and that the cure of this perversion of man's character is the destruction of capitalism and its replacement with a better society created by man, and yet in turn helping to mould and develop his character.

The psychological damage done to children and young people is described by Lawrence K. Frank:

> The 'evil' in man becomes increasingly explicable as a product of what is done to and for the child and youth who, faced with these threats, these humiliations and denials, attempts to protect and maintain himself by distorted patterns of belief, action and feeling. These disturbances of personality appear, like disease, to be the efforts of the organism-personality to maintain

[14] *Towards a Psychology of Being*, 6

[15] In Welch et al., *Humanistic Psychology*, 189.

[16] 'Notes on Rollo May', 8.

itself in the face of a menacing environment, efforts that may be self-destructive as well as anti-social.[17]

Again, there is a great deal of truth in these explanations of the cause of many of the distortions of human personality and behaviour. Society, sometimes even parents, or siblings or harsh schoolteachers, could be to blame. And that being so, the cure would be to change society. But though there is a good deal of truth in these diagnoses, and some truth in the proposed cure, it is questionable whether either the diagnosis or the cure is fully adequate.

If the cause of the individual's bad behaviour is society, we have to ask how society became bad in the first place.

To start with, if the cause of the individual's bad behaviour is society, we have to ask how society became bad in the first place. Admittedly a crowd of five hundred people generates a dynamic that those five hundred people by themselves would not have developed. But if the crowd were made up of people entirely good, the crowd would not develop an evil dynamic, would it?

The humanist psychologist, Rollo May, himself makes the point:

> But you say that you 'believe that it is cultural influences which are the major factor in our evil behaviour'. This makes culture the enemy. But who makes up the culture except persons like you and me?[18]

And the Marxist diagnosis and suggested cure likewise invite questions. Granted that the oppression of the proletariat by bourgeois capitalists was evil, how did these bourgeois capitalists themselves become evil in the first place? Secondly, the Marxist prediction was that when private property was abolished there would no longer be any need for the commandment 'You shall not steal' because when everybody owned everything no one would be tempted to steal anything. Did no one, then, misappropriate public property under socialism?

And thirdly, the increased economic prosperity of the previously oppressed proletariat has, in many countries, been followed,

17 'Potentialities of Human Nature', 65.

18 'Problem of Evil', 12.

as wealth often is, by increased immorality, divorce, family break-up, one-parent families and all their attendant social ills. Does experience prove that control of the means of production necessarily leads to purity of life?

And then, from the evolutionary point of view, there is another difficulty with putting all the blame for the individual's bad behaviour on society. Evolutionary theory suggests that the human race is, as far as its origin goes, nothing but matter that by its inherent powers has evolved, without any forethought or intention, to produce humankind. This has led the sociobiologists, as we saw earlier (see p. 131) to suppose that human ethical behaviour can, and should, be genetically based simply on the biochemical processes of our genes. Many evolutionists, however, as again we saw, have argued that it is impossible to base human moral behaviour on mere biological systems; and not only impossible but unnecessary, because at a certain point in their evolution humans developed language which made possible a whole world of social interaction; and it is this social interaction that gave rise to, and now controls, humanity's moral sense. The Marxist psychologist Joseph Nahem says:

> Most decisive in its influence on our thoughts, feelings, and behaviour is society and social relations. As Marx stated, 'In its reality, it (the human essence) is the *ensemble* of the social relations.' Human beings are distinguished from animals by their social labour, their social communication, their social groupings, by their social acquisition and use of language, and by their involvement in the ideas, attitudes, morality and behaviour of their society.[19]

But if now the claim is that humanity, left to itself, is good, but bourgeois society (according to Marxism) or society as a whole (according to humanism) damages, perverts, and corrupts it, the evolutionary claim becomes incoherent.

The difficulty in coming to a satisfactory diagnosis has been highlighted by the humanist psychologist Rollo May:

> Today we know a great deal about bodily chemistry and the control of physical diseases; but we know very little about why peo-

[19] *Psychology and Psychiatry Today*, 45 (citing Marx's *Theses on Feuerbach*, 84).

> ple hate, why they cannot love, why they suffer anxiety and guilt, and why they destroy each other. As we stand beneath the fateful shadow of the H-bomb, however, we have become vividly aware that there can be desperate perils in a scientifically one-sided study of nature and man.[20]

Along the same lines Carl Rogers remarks:

> It is quite unfortunate that we have permitted the world of psychological science to be narrowed to behaviours observed, sounds emitted, marks scratched on paper, and the like. In an attempt to be ultra-scientific, psychology has endeavoured to walk in the footsteps of a Newtonian physics.[21]

Quite so. Science with all its amazing technology and instrumentation can measure the electrochemical activities in the brain. But if, as the dualists and the Bible maintain, meaning, morals and values belong to the immaterial mind and spirit of human beings, how could science hope to measure them anyway?

However, to assert that there is a non-material element in humans is distasteful to atheists because it smacks too much of God and religion; and it is not merely that atheists feel that there is no evidence for God's existence; many of them have another concern.

Religion is a significant contributory cause of the distortion of human personality

Professor Wendell W. Watters was Clinical Professor of Psychiatry at McMaster University; and in the November/December 1987 issue of *The Humanist* he published an article entitled 'Christianity and Mental Health'. In it he writes:

> I want you to entertain the hypothesis that Christian doctrine, the existential soother par excellence, is incompatible with the principles of sound mental health and contributes more to the genesis of human suffering than to its alleviation.[22]

---

[20] *Psychology and the Human Dilemma*, 188.

[21] In Welch et al., *Humanistic Psychology*, 322.

[22] 'Christianity and Mental Health', 3.

> In my view, all religions are inhuman anachronisms, but here I am only dealing with Christianity and, more specifically, with the noxious nature of Christian doctrine at the personal and interpersonal levels.[23]

> A true Christian must always be in a state of torment, since he or she can never really be certain that God has forgiven him or her for deeply felt negative feelings—in spite of the Catholic confessional and the fundamental trick of self-deception known as being saved or born again.[24]

> The true Christian is running furiously on a treadmill to get away from whole segments of his or her human nature which he or she is taught to fear or about which he or she is taught to feel guilty. The Christian is brain washed to believe that he or she was born wicked, should suffer as Christ suffered, and should aspire to a humanly impossible level of perfection nonetheless.[25]

Now these are weighty criticisms and deserve to be taken seriously.

The first thing to be said about them would be that the Bible itself agrees with Watters that religion can be a very unhealthy thing; it labours in many places to point it out. The Christian apostle, Paul, is constantly warning his readers against teachings that are 'not sound' (literally, 'not healthy'; e.g. 1 Tim 1:10; 6:3). Among these unhealthy doctrines he includes forbidding marriage and requiring abstinence from foods that God created to be received with thanksgiving (1 Tim 4:3). He insists that 'God . . . richly provides us with everything to enjoy' (1 Tim 6:17). He decries the false asceticism recommended by so many religions, which he calls the basic principles of this world. He pleads:

> Why do you submit to regulations—'Do not handle, Do not taste, Do not touch, (referring to things that all perish as they are used)—according to human precepts and teachings? These have indeed an appearance of wisdom in promoting self-made

23 'Christianity and Mental Health', 5.

24 'Christianity and Mental Health', 10.

25 'Christianity and Mental Health', 32.

> religion and asceticism and severity to the body, but they are of no value in stopping the indulgence of the flesh. (Col 2:20–23)

When, however, Watters says: 'A true Christian must always be in a state of torment, since he or she can never really be certain that God has forgiven him or her for deeply felt negative feelings',[26] one can only assume that he has gained this impression of true Christians from patients suffering from unreal, psychological guilt, or from some other mental or emotional disorder (for he is obviously not a Christian himself, and therefore cannot know by personal experience what true Christians feel).

It is true, of course, that Christians like anyone else, atheists included, can suffer emotional disturbances, neuroses, phobias and mental breakdowns; and Christians too can fail to distinguish between real guilt as distinct from unreal, psychological guilt feelings and imagine that they have committed the unpardonable sin.

But as for true Christians being unable to be certain that God has forgiven them for deeply felt negative feelings, that is scarcely the fault of the Bible: it constantly declares that true Christians are not only forgiven, but can also know with absolute certainty that they have been forgiven for now and for ever, not on the ground of their feelings, good or bad, but on the ground of God's love, undeserved grace, and unchanging declaration. Since Watters has obviously found people suffering mental anguish as the result of the opposite, contrary impression, it could be helpful to quote a number of biblical passages and let them speak for themselves:

> I am writing to you, little children, because your sins are forgiven for his name's sake. (1 John 2:12)

> I will remember their sins and their lawless deeds no more. (Heb 10:17)

> Therefore, since we have been justified by faith, we have peace with God . . . and we rejoice in hope of the glory of God. (Rom 5:1–2)

> God's love has been poured into our hearts through the Holy Spirit who has been given to us. For while we were still weak, at

[26] 'Christianity and Mental Health', 10.

> the right time Christ died for the ungodly. For one will scarcely die for a righteous person—though perhaps for a good person one would dare even to die—but God shows his love for us in that while we were still sinners, Christ died for us. Since, therefore, we have now been justified by his blood, much more shall we be saved by him from the wrath of God. For if while we were enemies we were reconciled to God by the death of his Son, much more, now that we are reconciled, shall we be saved by his life. (Rom 5:5–10)

> Truly, truly, I say to you, whoever hears my word and believes him who sent me has eternal life. He does not come into judgment, but has passed from death to life. (John 5:24)

> My sheep hear my voice, and I know them, and they follow me. I give them eternal life, and they will never perish, and no one will snatch them out of my hand. (John 10:27–28)

> I write these things to you who believe in the name of the Son of God that you may know that you have eternal life. (1 John 5:13)

> He saved us, not because of works done by us in righteousness, but according to his own mercy. (Titus 3:5)

It is important, then, to take Watters' criticisms seriously. But it would also be right to put alongside them the comments of another psychiatrist, this time from Harvard. Professor Robert Coles declares:

> Nothing I have discovered about the make-up of human beings contradicts in any way what I learn from the Hebrew prophets such as Isaiah, Jeremiah and Amos, and from the book of Ecclesiastes, and from Jesus and the lives of those he touched. Anything that I can say as a result of my research into human behaviour is a mere footnote to those lives in the Old and New Testaments.[27]

Comparisons, then, of these widely different accounts of their scientific findings by these two psychiatrists, Watters and Coles, might suggest that psychiatric verdicts depend a great deal on the individual psychiatrist's personal worldview.

---

27 Cited by P. Yancey in *Soul Survivor*, 111.

But Watters is also concerned about the damage that the Christian doctrine of original sin does to people's mental health. It is time, therefore, that we considered what is in fact the Christian diagnosis of humanity's fatal flaw and what is its proposed cure.

The Christian diagnosis of humanity's fatal flaw and its cure

The Bible is very honest and blunt. It does not try to blame human misbehaviour on society: it says that humanity himself is evil. That does not mean that humanity is as bad as we could possibly be in all aspects of our lives. In spite of being evil, humans retain many of the noble features that stem from our original creation by God. This is indicated in Christ's remark to his contemporaries: 'If you then, who are evil, know how to give good gifts to your children, how much more will the heavenly Father give the Holy Spirit to those who ask him!' (Luke 11:13).

Men and women, atheists as much as theists, know how to give good gifts to their children; they have loving paternal instincts and often care for others far beyond the confines of their families. The Bible neither denies it nor overlooks it. Neither does the Bible deny or disparage all the genuine efforts on the part of scientists, physicians, surgeons, psychiatrists, nurses, educationalists, economists, politicians and others to alleviate the ills and sufferings that afflict humans in our fallen state.

The fundamental fatal sin that perverted the human race from its very start was not only disobedience to the Creator but a deliberate attempt to grasp independence of God: to be as God, to be master of their own lives and to decide good and evil without regard to God's will or word.

But nonetheless it teaches that humanity is evil as a result of two things. First, humans belongs to a fallen race, and secondly, because each individual man and woman has personally and knowingly sinned.

The fundamental fatal sin that perverted the human race from its very start was not only disobedience to the Creator but a deliberate attempt to grasp independence of God: to be as God, to be master of their own lives and to decide good and evil without regard to God's will or word (Genesis 3). It was a revolt of the human spirit against the God who created the human spirit, a revolt which fundamentally changed the attitude of the creature to his creator, to other humans and to the creation around him.

Its distant repercussions are still to be seen in those who do not simply feel there is no evidence for God's existence and for that reason do not believe in him, but who maintain a positive anti-God stance. But it is seen also in people who use religion in an attempt to build for themselves, by the rigour of their own meritorious deeds, a bargaining position on the basis of which they can deserve God's acceptance, as if religion, or any other activity on the part of a creature, could merit acceptance by the Creator, when anything of good that any of us has comes from him anyway.

In truth, all of us without exception, as members of a fallen race, are born with this false attitude at the centre of our personalities, this fatal flaw, this false pride, which then tarnishes our otherwise noble deeds, as well as producing a lot of ignoble ones.

But this doctrine of original sin does not, as Watters suggests, mean that the Christian is brainwashed to believe that, though born wicked, he or she should aspire by his or her own efforts to a humanly impossible level of perfection nonetheless. It says quite bluntly and realistically that 'all have sinned and do come short of God's glory'; but it immediately adds that all can, if they will, 'be justified freely [the Greek means 'freely' in the sense of 'without payment or merit'] by his grace through the redemption that is in Christ Jesus. . . . We conclude that a man is justified by faith apart from the works of the law. . . . To him who does not work but believes on him who justifies the ungodly, his faith is reckoned for righteousness' (Rom 3:23–24, 28; 4:5 our trans).[28]

It says, moreover, to make things unmistakably clear, that just as the human race was spoiled and perverted at its beginning by its founding father's disobedience to God, so we individually can be forgiven, reconciled and accepted with God, not by our efforts at obedience, slender and imperfect as they are at their best, but by the obedience of another, that is Jesus Christ. The biblical statement is: 'For as by one man's disobedience [i.e., Adam's] the many were made

[28] For the relation of salvation to good works, see the discussion under 'The True Reward Motive', 164.

sinners, so by the one man's [i.e., Christ's] obedience the many will be made righteous' (Rom 5:19). God does not make his acceptance of anyone dependent on their attainment of a standard of perfection that it is humanly impossible for them to attain. The necessary perfection is given them as a gift: 'Christ . . . became to us', says the Christian apostle, Paul, 'wisdom from God, righteousness and sanctification and redemption' (1 Cor 1:30).

The apparent foolishness of the Christian cure

Anyone reading the New Testament seriously for the first time might well be struck by the apparent foolishness of its proclamation that the cure of humanity's evil lies in the story of a crucified man. To Greeks, versed in the intellectual profundities of Greek philosophy, it was bound to seem absurd, as it was also to Jews whose concept of deliverance from life's evils was national political liberation by a miracle-working Messiah.

The striking thing about this apparently foolish cure was that the first Christian preachers realised that at first hearing it must appear foolish to their audiences. But they preached it nonetheless, for, so they explain, they saw in it the wisdom of God (1 Cor 1:18–25).

When offered as a cure for humanity's fatal flaw, the cross of Christ points in the first place to what the diagnosis of humanity's basic trouble is. It lies not in a deficiency of intellect or reason; but in the misapprehension, fear and consequent hostility of the human heart towards God.

The ancient story tells how the serpent slandered God to man, suggesting that God was tantalising humankind, by first providing Adam and Eve with beautiful trees, and beautiful fruits, and then forbidding them to eat of them; suggesting also that God wished to keep the human race down, and not let humans rise to be as God (Gen 3:5). The slander was successful. But as soon as man took the forbidden fruit, he sensed shame and unease at his fallen condition, felt God was against him and fled to hide from God (Gen 3:7–10).

Ever since then there has lurked this slander, this suspicion of God, in the human heart: that God, if there is one, is bound to be against us, forbidding us natural pleasures and repressing us psychologically and restraining us from developing our full human potential. The result is the alienation of the human spirit from God, and in extreme cases the denial of anything that smacks of God, even to the extent of denying that humans have a spirit, and attempting to believe that humans are nothing but matter.

The slander was, and is, false. It is also irrational. How could it be reasonable to suppose that our creator—if there is such—would by definition be against us? At the same time, however, our awareness of the guilt and shame of our personal sins adds to the sense, this time quite rightly, that God, if he exists, must be against our sins.

The problem was: how could the spell of the slander be broken? How could the alienation and hostility be removed, and reconciliation be effected?

The problem was: how could the spell of the slander be broken? How could the alienation and hostility be removed, and reconciliation be effected? The answer, says the New Testament, was the incarnation of the Son of God and his death on the cross, by which means God might get through to man's heart and show him what God is really like. And the message is this: God was in Christ, says Christ's apostle, 'reconciling the world to himself, not counting their trespasses against them, and entrusting to us the message of reconciliation'.

> Therefore, we are ambassadors for Christ, God making his appeal through us. We implore you on behalf of Christ, be reconciled to God. For our sake he made him to be sin who knew no sin, so that in him we might become the righteousness of God. (2 Cor 5:19–21)

This then, according to the historical documents, was the diagnosis of humanity's fatal flaw and the means of its cure that the first Christians offered to the world. There was, of course, more to it than that. Far from God wanting to suppress human potential, Christ authorised his emissaries to offer the world the possibility of rising in the universe from being mere creatures of God, the product of his hands, so to speak, to becoming, through personal union with his Son, sons of God themselves, begotten by God with God's own life (John 1:12–13).

And there is yet more. Those ancient Hebrew lyrics that, as we studied earlier, celebrated the wonder of humanity set by God over all his works (p. 173), shall yet be fulfilled at a level which the ancient psalmist scarce dreamed of. Deliberately citing that psalm, the New Testament declares that God's intention for humanity has not been abandoned. It shall yet be realised in the man Jesus, when Christ and his glorified followers together reign over the universe (Heb 2:5–18; Rom 8:18–30).

This is the true evolution of the human race. Only the Bible calls it, not the evolution of humanity, but our creation, fall, redemption and ultimate glorification.

HUMAN DESTINY

Is humanity's destiny nothing but dust and ashes? Is it so that in spite of every individual's rational superiority over the mindless forces of nature, and in spite of humanity's increasing power over nature, mindless nature will eventually have the last word and consign everyone in every generation to mindless non-existence?

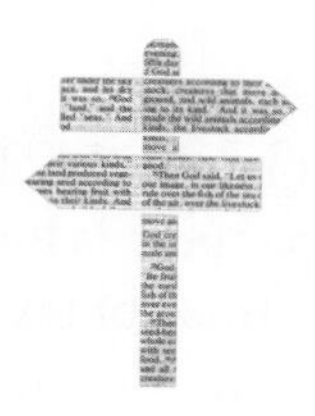

THE FOUNDATION OF A REALISTIC HOPE

The theme of our study throughout this book is one that extends through this entire series: the quest for reality and significance. We thought about the intrinsic dignity and value of human beings and the ability of the human mind to transcend itself, to transcend material things, to engage in abstract thought, to traverse the universe, and to conceive of the beginning of time and of the end of the world; and we concluded that it was difficult to account for this transcendent ability, if humans were nothing more than an advanced form of mindless matter.

We considered also humanity's inbuilt sense of a right to freedom, and a feeling of superiority over the non-rational forces of nature, however powerful those forces might be. We examined what attitudes and beliefs it is necessary for humans to maintain if we are to retain our freedom and not come to think of ourselves as prisoners in a materialistic universe.

Next, humanity's inbuilt sense of fairness, of right and wrong, made us enquire about its source, and ask where humankind got the idea from that this world ought to be a just place, when so often it isn't; and we then observed how crippled and ineffective morality becomes if no objective criterion exists to set its standards, and humanity has to be its own god.

We thought next of humanity's role and function in relation to the world around us and of our amazing and increasing power over nature; but then also of humanity's glaring abuse of that power over nature and over our fellow human beings, and of the dangers this poses in the light of humanity's ever increasing ability to manipulate nature. Humanity obviously suffers, we concluded, from some fatal flaw; and we pondered what its cause was. We saw, however, that there was hope of a cure, and of humanity's eventual full realisation of the function for which we were so evidently designed.

Now in this last chapter of this book we are to consider human destiny, and to ask what hope there is for humanity's future.

It would be tempting in this context to think about humanity's immediate and long-term economic and political future. We might ask whether and how the nations will solve the perennial problems that have constantly beset them, and still do beset them just as severely as they have always done. We might further speculate as to what form the modern urge for globalisation will take: whether it will content itself with the economic globalisation which the multinational commercial conglomerates are already vigorously pursuing, or whether this commercial globalisation will lead to a world authority for monetary control; and then, as humanists long since and adherents of New Age philosophies more recently have been advocating, to the setting up of a world government. And finally we might ponder whether, if it is ever achieved, such an anthropocentric, economic, monetary and political world-system built on humanist and atheistic principles would actually promote peace and freedom or if it would achieve peace only through a form of authoritarian, world totalitarianism.

But on this occasion we must resist the temptation to engage in such speculations, fascinating though they would be. Rather, we must concentrate on the far more important question: what hope is there for the future of each individual man and woman?

HOPE FOR THE INDIVIDUAL

It is right, of course, that we all work as best we can for the ongoing improvement of the human race, and doing that certainly involves forward thinking and planning. But it is all too easy to become so preoccupied with ideologies and schemes for producing some remote utopian future for humankind as a whole that we forget the supreme importance of the future of the people who are living here and now in this generation, and who are never likely to see the remote utopia if and when it comes.

When we talk of the future of the human race, it is good to stop and think what we mean by 'the human race' in this context. We don't mean all the generations of human beings that have ever lived or will live. We mean only some generations of human beings in the future. We all fervently hope for the coming of a time when the motto of the United Nations shall be fulfilled: the nations 'shall beat their swords into ploughshares, and their spears into pruning-hooks; nation shall not lift up sword against nation, neither shall they learn war any more' (Micah 4:3). But what about all the people who have lived and died, and those who will yet live and die before that time comes? Are we to say that for them, 'Of course, there was never going to be a worthwhile and satisfying future'? Are we to think with Professor Richard Dawkins that it should have been satisfaction enough for them to have understood that they were the product of mindless genes which had no other intention than to use them as disposable channels for passing on their genetic information to future generations? Or should they be content to be human throwaways which evolution used as temporary staging posts en route to utopia, and then discarded?

Some argue that life should be regarded as an ongoing banquet. Each generation comes in its turn as guests to the table and eats its full; and, being satisfied, can have no complaint when it is required gracefully to retire and let the next generation take its place at the table.

Some argue that life should be regarded as an ongoing banquet. Each generation comes in its turn as guests to the table and eats its full; and being satisfied, can have no complaint when it is required gracefully to retire and let the next generation take its place at the table.

But it is a shallow argument; for in each generation there are millions for whom life is anything but a banquet. They can see how enjoyable life could have been but in fact wasn't, because some Hitler or other for the sake of some promised utopia embroiled them and their country in disaster, loss, bereavement, misery and economic collapse, in addition to the normal pains and disappointments of life. They feel cheated, frustrated, wronged, unsatisfied, disappointed, and they depart this life broken-backed and broken-hearted. What use talking to them about hopes for the improvement of humankind-as-a-whole, or even of the next-but-one generation?

And even suppose that historical materialism by its irresistible workings eventually brought in an economic paradise: would not the dialectics of the situation inevitably change that paradise into something else? And what about the generations that enjoyed this paradise while it lasted? Would they not die as well as all previous generations have done?

When, therefore, we raise the topic of human destiny, realism demands that we face the question that has confronted every generation that has ever lived on the face of the earth: is death the end? Is humanity's destiny nothing but dust and ashes? Is it so that in spite of every individual's rational superiority over the mindless forces of nature, and in spite of humanity's increasing power over nature, mindless nature will eventually have the last word and consign everyone in every generation to mindless non-existence?

As usual when we ask questions like this, the answers given fall into two main groups: those from theists and those from atheists.[1]

Let us listen first, then, to some typical statements on the subject from the atheistic point of view:

The Humanist Manifesto II: 'As far as we know, the total personality is a function of the biological organism transacting in a social and cultural context. There is no credible evidence that life survives the death of the body.'[2]

Bertrand Russell: 'No fire, no heroism, no intensity of thought and feeling, can preserve an individual life beyond the grave.'[3]

A. J. Ayer: 'I take it . . . to be a fact that one's existence ends with death.'[4]

---

1 Nowadays in the West the conglomerate of philosophies that form the New Age movement, with the help of many old-time humanists, has revived the age-old theory of pantheism. Superficially this would appear to offer a third option to put alongside theism on the one side and atheism on the other. Indeed, nowadays many erstwhile atheists, having tasted the bleakness of atheistic materialism, view pantheism as an attractive alternative. It allows them to recognise an intelligence behind the universe, and to regard the universe and all its inhabitants as having a purpose.

But pantheism is scarcely a genuine alternative to atheism. For the god of pantheism is not a personal God with whom humans can have a personal relationship of love, trust and obedience. It is simply a life-force, like an intelligent form of energy, that is not only in every thing, but is everything. Everything is god, every human being is god. If, however, everything is god, then evil is god just like good is. Moreover New Agers hold many different and conflicting opinions among themselves. But if every New Ager is god, then god holds many conflicting opinions. Some New Agers will admit that in earlier years they held wrong ideas and did wrong things. But if pantheism is true, then they were already god at that time. So god held those wrong ideas and did those wrong things; and when they changed their minds, it was in fact god changing his. Pantheism is scarcely a serious intellectual, moral or spiritual alternative to atheism.

2 p. 16.

3 'A Free Man's Worship', 107.

4 *Humanist Outlook*, 9.

Ernest Nagel: 'Human destiny [is] an episode between two oblivions.'[5]

Humanist Manifesto II allows a certain 'immortality', but it consists solely in continuing 'to exist in our progeny and in the way that our lives have influenced others in our culture'.[6]

This last sentiment was widespread in the ancient pagan world. Parents took comfort in the thought that they would live on in their children. Emperors, kings, conquering generals and leading politicians had statues made of themselves to keep their memory fresh in the minds of posterity. Authors liked to think that their literary and philosophical works would be far more durable memorials than those made of marble or bronze.

All of this is clear enough evidence that there is an instinctive longing in the human heart for some kind of immortality. As atheists approach the end of life they understandably welcome the feeling that their lives have not been simply a few brief years of self-satisfying existence, but have contributed something of lasting good to someone. But it would seem to be poor comfort to be remembered when you yourself no longer exist to appreciate that you are being remembered.

This, then, is what atheists have to say about human destiny; and it is very little and very bleak. It is, moreover, an expression of their belief, not of proven fact.

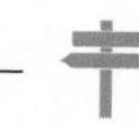

This, then, is what atheists have to say about human destiny; and it is very little and very bleak. It is, moreover, an expression of their belief, not of proven fact.

Atheists will assert that there is no positive evidence for survival after death, and therefore theists' belief in an after-life is simply wishful thinking. And maybe that is so. But it is not altogether certain that the atheistic denial of an afterlife does not sometimes have a strand of wishful thinking in it too. For any mature concept of life after death includes the emphatic assertion that the demands of morality and justice will prevail there as absolutely as they were meant to prevail here. Moral concerns do not end with death; but after death there shall come a judgment at which everyone shall give account of himself and herself to God, and that with

[5] 'Naturalism Reconsidered', [1954] in Peterson, *Essays in Philosophy*, 486.

[6] p. 17.

eternal consequences. It is certainly possible, then, that some atheists, at least, might have reasons for wishfully thinking that this will not be so.

The ancient Roman poet Lucretius was an enthusiastic adherent of Epicurean philosophy; and in his lengthy poem on the subject he tells us what lay behind his enthusiasm. Epicurean philosophy allowed him to think that science had proved that men and women did not survive death; and therefore he would never have to face a final judgment.[7] There could be others like him today.

We have listened, then, to typical atheistic views of human destiny; let us now hear what the theists, and particularly the Christians have to say.

HOPE OF RESURRECTION BASED ON THE CHARACTER OF GOD

First comes the statement of Christ himself:

> And as for the resurrection of the dead, have you not read what was said to you by God: 'I am the God of Abraham, and the God of Isaac, and the God of Jacob'? He is not God of the dead, but of the living. (Matt 22:31–32)

Here Christ bases the certainty of resurrection on the character of God and in particular on his loyalty to the men and women he has created. To create men and women and endow them with a moral sense and the faculty of love and loyalty; to bring them into the world without their consent; and then not be loyal to the instincts and moral character with which he himself endowed them—that would be the work of a morally irresponsible tyrant.

God is not such. Indeed his interest and loyal love are concerned not simply with the human race as a whole but with each individual. He does not say: 'I am the God of the Hebrew nation'; or even, 'I am the God of Abraham, Isaac, and Jacob'; but, 'I am the God of Abraham, and the God of Isaac, and the God of Jacob' (Exod 3:6). God has a one-to-one concern for every single man, woman and child.

[7] See his *De Rerum Natura*, Book 1.

Moreover when he identifies himself (in this passage from Exodus he is talking to Moses) he identifies and characterises himself by his relationship with particular individuals: 'I am the God of Abraham, and the God of Isaac, and the God of Jacob'. As far as this world was concerned, Abraham, Isaac and Jacob had long since passed away by the time that God spoke to Moses. But as far as God was concerned they had not passed away: to him they still lived. The relationship that God forms with people created in his image and redeemed by his grace is, like himself, eternal.

Here, then, is the first big difference between the atheistic and the theistic view of humanity's destiny. The atheist believes himself to be the unpurposed product of mindless impersonal forces that are not even aware of his existence. He cannot bring himself to believe that these mindless forces will repeat the accident that caused his birth and, when he dies, mindlessly resurrect him. All he can hope for is in terms of the survival of the human race as a whole.

He cannot suppose that the love and loyalty he feels for his family, friends and fellow-humans is felt in any way at all by the impersonal forces that brought mankind into existence. They are but temporary feelings of no permanent significance. They not only leave him without ultimate hope, they emphasise, by contrast, the unfeeling, impersonal, mindlessness of the universe in which his short, temporary existence is lived out.

RESURRECTION DEMANDED BY THE JUSTICE OF GOD

> Do not marvel at this, for an hour is coming when all who are in the tombs will hear his voice and come out, those who have done good to the resurrection of life, and those who have done evil to the resurrection of judgment. (John 5:28–29. See also Matt 12:36, 41–42)

Here Christ affirms that there will be a resurrection in order to satisfy the demands of justice. In this life countless acts of unfairness and injustice are perpetrated, the innocent suffer, and the perpetrators go free. But this life is not the end of the matter, nor could it be, for the evil that men and women do lives after them and infects and damages many subsequent generations. Its total effects cannot be measured until the end of time. But the justice of God will insist on a resurrection, and thus demonstrate that the universe he made is not simply an amoral machine, still less a moral madhouse.

RESURRECTION IS NECESSARY TO ACHIEVE THE GOAL ENVISAGED IN THE CREATION OF THE HUMAN RACE

God's purpose in creating the human race was never limited to humanity's existence on this temporary planet. Humans were originally designed as creatures made 'in the image of God'. This idea, expressed at a comparatively lowly level in the original creation, was always intended to be fulfilled at the highest possible level (Col 3:9–11; 2 Cor 3:18). Life on this planet was but the school that should develop and prepare man for the time when he shall be fully conformed to the image of God's Son. Christ's apostle, Paul, expresses it in this way:

> For all who are led by the Spirit of God are sons of God. For you did not receive the spirit of slavery to fall back into fear, but you have received the Spirit of adoption as sons, by whom we cry, 'Abba! Father!' The Spirit himself bears witness with our spirit that we are children of God, and if children, then heirs—heirs of God and fellow heirs with Christ, provided we suffer with him in order that we may also be glorified with him.
>
> For I consider that the sufferings of this present time are not worth comparing with the glory that is to be revealed to us. For the creation waits with eager longing for the revealing of the sons of God. For the creation was subjected to futility, not willingly, but because of him who subjected it, in hope that the creation itself will be set free from its bondage to corruption and obtain the freedom of the glory of the children of God. For we know that the whole creation has been groaning together in the pains of childbirth until now. And not only the creation, but we ourselves, who have the firstfruits of the Spirit, groan inwardly as we wait eagerly for adoption as sons, the redemption of our bodies. . . .
>
> And we know that for those who love God all things work together for good, for those who are called according to his

purpose. For those whom he foreknew he also predestined to be conformed to the image of his Son, in order that he might be the firstborn among many brothers. And those whom he predestined he also called, and those whom he called he also justified, and those whom he justified he also glorified.

What then shall we say to these things? If God is for us, who can be against us? He who did not spare his own Son but gave him up for us all, how will he not also with him graciously give us all things? Who shall bring any charge against God's elect? It is God who justifies. Who is to condemn? Christ Jesus is the one who died—more than that, who was raised—who is at the right hand of God, who indeed is interceding for us. Who shall separate us from the love of Christ? Shall tribulation, or distress, or persecution, or famine, or nakedness, or danger, or sword? . . .

No, in all these things we are more than conquerors through him who loved us. For I am sure that neither death nor life, nor angels nor rulers, nor things present nor things to come, nor powers, nor height nor depth, nor anything else in all creation, will be able to separate us from the love of God in Christ Jesus our Lord. (Rom 8:14–23, 28–35, 37–39)

CHRIST'S OWN RESURRECTION: THE BEGINNING OF THE RESTORATION OF THE UNIVERSE

Christ himself predicted his own resurrection (Matt 16:21; Luke 18:31–33) and the record of his actual resurrection shows us clearly what is meant by the term 'resurrection'.[8]

[8] For the authenticity of the New Testament documents, and for the evidence of early Gentile writers regarding the historicity of Christ, see F. F. Bruce, *New Testament Documents*.

For the evidence for the resurrection of Christ as seen through the eyes of a former director of the Institute of Advanced Legal Studies in the University of London, see 'Empty Tomb', in J. N. D. Anderson, *Christianity*, 84–108.

For further reading on the evidence for the resurrection and related issues, see William Lane Craig, *Reasonable Faith: Christian Truth and Apologetics* [1984] 3rd edn. (Wheaton: Crossway, 2008); Gary R. Habermas and Michael R. Licona, *The Case for the Resurrection of Jesus* (Grand Rapids: Kregel Publications, 2004); Timothy Keller, *The Reason for God* (London: Hodder & Stoughton, 2008); John Lennox, *Gunning for God: A Critique of the New Atheism* (Oxford: Lion, 2011); Lee Strobel, *The Case for Christ: A Journalist's Personal Investigation of the Evidence for Jesus* (Grand Rapids: Zondervan, 1998); and N. T. Wright, *The Resurrection of the Son of God* (Christian Origins and the Question of God series Book 3) (London: SPCK, 2003).

The resurrection of Christ is not a version of the widespread Middle-Eastern myth of a dying and rising god. It is not a nature-myth. Christ and his apostles were Jews, born in the first century AD into a nation that for centuries had confronted the religious mythologies of the surrounding nations and had finally and deliberately repudiated them, hence their emphasis on the fact that when Christ rose from the dead his tomb was found empty. Christ's physical human body had literally been resurrected and not only resurrected but transformed, thus setting the pattern for the resurrection of all who are spiritually united to him. Here is how the New Testament puts it:

> Now I would remind you, brothers, of the gospel I preached to you, which you received, in which you stand, and by which you are being saved, if you hold fast to the word I preached to you—unless you believed in vain.
>
> For I delivered to you as of first importance what I also received: that Christ died for our sins in accordance with the Scriptures, that he was buried, that he was raised on the third day in accordance with the Scriptures, and that he appeared to Cephas, then to the twelve. Then he appeared to more than five hundred brothers at one time, most of whom are still alive, though some have fallen asleep. Then he appeared to James, then to all the apostles. Last of all, as to one untimely born, he appeared also to me. (1 Cor 15:1–8)

> But in fact Christ has been raised from the dead, the firstfruits of those who have fallen asleep. For as by a man came death, by a man has come also the resurrection of the dead. For as in Adam all die, so also in Christ shall all be made alive. But each in his own order: Christ the firstfruits, then at his coming those who belong to Christ. Then comes the end, when he delivers the kingdom to God the Father after destroying every rule and every authority and power. For he must reign until he has put all his enemies under his feet. The last enemy to be destroyed is death. For 'God has put all things in subjection under his feet.' But when it says, 'all things are put in subjection', it is plain that he is excepted who put all things in subjection under him. When all things are subjected to him, then the Son himself will

also be subjected to him who put all things in subjection under him, that God may be all in all. (vv. 20–28)

But someone will ask, 'How are the dead raised? With what kind of body do they come?' You foolish person! What you sow does not come to life unless it dies. And what you sow is not the body that is to be, but a bare seed, perhaps of wheat or of some other grain. But God gives it a body as he has chosen, and to each kind of seed its own body. For not all flesh is the same, but there is one kind for humans, another for animals, another for birds, and another for fish. There are heavenly bodies and earthly bodies, but the glory of the heavenly is of one kind, and the glory of the earthly is of another. There is one glory of the sun, and another glory of the moon, and another glory of the stars; for star differs from star in glory.

So is it with the resurrection of the dead. What is sown is perishable; what is raised is imperishable. It is sown in dishonour; it is raised in glory. It is sown in weakness; it is raised in power. It is sown a natural body; it is raised a spiritual body. If there is a natural body, there is also a spiritual body. Thus it is written, 'The first man Adam became a living being'; the last Adam became a life-giving spirit. But it is not the spiritual that is first but the natural, and then the spiritual. The first man was from the earth, a man of dust; the second man is from heaven. As was the man of dust, so also are those who are of the dust, and as is the man of heaven, so also are those who are of heaven. Just as we have borne the image of the man of dust, we shall also bear the image of the man of heaven.

I tell you this, brothers: flesh and blood cannot inherit the kingdom of God, nor does the perishable inherit the imperishable. Behold! I tell you a mystery. We shall not all sleep, but we shall all be changed, in a moment, in the twinkling of an eye, at the last trumpet. For the trumpet will sound, and the dead will be raised imperishable, and we shall be changed. For this perishable body must put on the imperishable, and this mortal body must put on immortality. When the perishable puts on the imperishable, and the mortal puts on immortality, then shall come to pass the saying that is written:

> 'Death is swallowed up in victory.'
> 'O death, where is your victory?
> O death, where is your sting?'
>
> The sting of death is sin, and the power of sin is the law. But thanks be to God, who gives us the victory through our Lord Jesus Christ.
>
> Therefore, my beloved brothers, be steadfast, immovable, always abounding in the work of the Lord, knowing that in the Lord your labour is not in vain. (vv. 35–58)

Here then is hope not only for individual human beings but for nature itself. Certainly humanity and nature have been spoiled by humanity's spiritual revolt against our creator. But God's intention is not to destroy nature and humankind with it, and then start again with something unconnected and altogether different. His intention is to redeem and transform them, thus bringing them to a greater glory and a higher order than even unfallen man originally enjoyed. The resurrection of the man, Christ Jesus, not only sets the pattern of this final restoration; it is that restoration already begun.

HOPE FOR THIS LIFE

It is, of course, often asserted that hope of a resurrection and of life in the world to come reduces the significance of life in this world and gives people no hope for life in the here and now. The easy reply would be that for people who are already, say, forty years old, the promise that some ideology will in fifty years' time bring in an economic paradise, likewise offers them no hope either.

But the serious answer to the objection is that it is precisely the hope of resurrection that fills this present life with maximum significance. We need life's basic necessities, food, clothes, and shelter; but the acquisition of these things is not life's prime objective. Without petrol a car cannot go anywhere. But the prime purpose of a car's existence is not so that it can be filled with petrol.

Christ taught us that the prime objective of life is to 'seek first the kingdom of God and his righteousness' (Matt 6:31–34). That is to say, the prime purpose of life in the here and now, is 'soul-making', the development of our character that takes place as we seek to act and react according to God's kingly rule in all our affairs. For a believer in Christ, therefore, no circumstances, however bad, can remove the possibility of pursuing life's chief objective: to live, to love, obey and please God, and thus develop a character which, because there is a resurrection, will endure eternally. This, at least, is the Christian answer to the human quest for reality and significance.

APPENDIX: THE SCIENTIFIC ENDEAVOUR

The doing of successful science follows no set of cosy rules. It is as complex as the human personalities that are involved in doing it.

THE CLEAR VOICE OF SCIENCE

Science rightly has the power to fire the imagination. Who could read the story of how Francis Crick and James D. Watson unravelled the double helix structure of DNA without entering at least a little into the almost unbearable joy that they experienced at this discovery? Who could watch an operation to repair someone's eye with a delicately controlled laser beam without a sense of wonder at human creativity and invention? Who could see pictures from space showing astronauts floating weightless in the cabin of the International Space Station or watch them repair the Hubble telescope against the background of the almost tangible blackness of space without a feeling akin to awe? Science has a right to our respect and to our active encouragement. Getting young people into science and giving them the training and facilities to develop their intellectual potential is a clear priority for any nation. It would be an incalculable loss if the scientific instinct were in any way stifled by philosophical, economic or political considerations.

But since one of the most powerful and influential voices to which we want to listen is the voice of science, it will be very important for us, whether we are scientists or not, to have some idea of what science is and what the scientific method is before we try to evaluate what science says to us on any particular issue. Our aim, therefore, first of all is to remind ourselves of some of the basic principles of scientific thinking, some of which we may already know. Following this, we shall think about the nature of scientific explanation and we shall examine some of the assumptions that underlie scientific activity—basic beliefs without which science cannot be done.

Then what is science? It tends to be one of those things that we all know what it means until we come to try to define it. And then we find that precise definition eludes us. The difficulty arises because we use the word in different ways. First of all, science is used as shorthand for:

1. sciences—areas of knowledge like physics, chemistry, biology, etc.;
2. scientists—the people who work in these areas;
3. scientific method—the way in which scientists do their work.

Often, however, the word science is used in expressions like 'Science says . . .', or 'Science has demonstrated . . .', as if science were a conscious being of great authority and knowledge. This usage, though understandable, can be misleading. The fact is that, strictly speaking, there is no such thing as 'science' in this sense. Science does not say, demonstrate, know or discover anything—scientists do. Of course, scientists often agree, but it is increasingly recognised that science, being a very human endeavour, is very much more complex than is often thought and there is considerable debate about what constitutes scientific method.

SCIENTIFIC METHOD

It is now generally agreed among philosophers of science that there is no one 'scientific method', so it is easier to speak of the kind of thing that doing science involves than to give a precise definition of science.

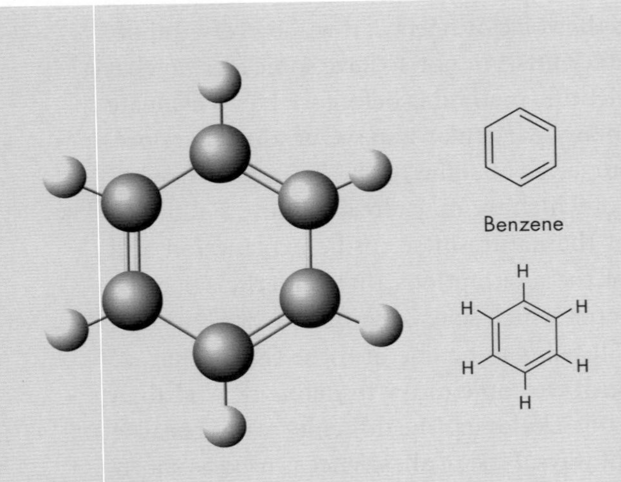

FIGURE Ap.1. Benzene Molecule.

In 1929 crystallographer Kathleen Lonsdale confirmed Kekulé's earlier theory about the flat, cyclic nature of benzene, an important milestone in organic chemistry.

Reproduced with permission of ©iStock/hromatos.

Certainly observation and experimentation have primary roles to play, as well as do the reasoning processes that lead scientists to their conclusions. However, a glance at the history of science will show that there is much more to it than this. We find, for example, that inexplicable hunches have played a considerable role. Even dreams have had their place! The chemist Friedrich August Kekulé was studying the structure of benzene and dreamed about a snake that grabbed its own tail, thus forming itself into a ring. As a result he was led to the idea that benzene might be like the snake. He had a look and found that benzene indeed contained a closed ring of six carbon atoms! The doing of successful science follows no set of cosy rules. It is as complex as the human personalities that are involved in doing it.

Observation and experimentation

It is generally agreed that a revolution in scientific thinking took place in the sixteenth and seventeenth centuries. Up to then one main method of thinking about the nature of the universe was to appeal to authority. For example, in the fourth century BC Aristotle had argued from philosophical principles that the only perfect motion was circular. Thus, if you wanted to know how the planets moved, then, since according to Aristotle they inhabited the realm of perfection beyond the orbit of the moon, they must move in circles. In a radical departure from this approach, scientists like Galileo insisted that the best way to find out how the planets moved was to take his telescope and go and have a look! And through that telescope he saw things like the moons of Jupiter which, according to the Aristotelian system, did not exist. Galileo comes to embody for many people the true spirit of scientific enquiry: the freedom to do full justice to observation and experimentation, even if it meant seriously modifying or even abandoning the theories that he had previously held. That freedom should be retained and jealously guarded by us all.

Data, patterns, relationships and hypotheses

In summary form, the most widespread view, often attributed to Francis Bacon and John Stuart Mill, is that the scientific method consists of:

1. the collection of data (facts, about which there can be no dispute) by means of observation and experiment, neither of them influenced by presuppositions or prejudices;
2. the derivation of hypotheses from the data by looking for patterns or relationships between the data and then making an inductive generalisation;
3. the testing of the hypotheses by deducing predictions from them and then constructing and doing experiments designed to check if those predictions are true;
4. the discarding of hypotheses that are not supported by the experimental data and the building up of the theory by adding confirmed hypotheses.

Scientists collect data, experimental observations and measurements that they record. As examples of data, think of a set of blood pressure measurements of your class just before and just after a school examination, or of the rock samples collected by astronauts from the surface of the moon.

There are, however, many other things that are equally real to us, but which scarcely can count as data in the scientific sense: our subjective experience of a sunset, or of friendship and love, or of dreams. With dreams, of course, heart rate, brain activity and eye movement can be observed by scientists as they monitor people who are asleep and dreaming, but their subjective experience of the dream itself cannot be measured. Thus we see that the scientific method has certain built-in limits. It cannot capture the whole of reality.

Scientists are in the business of looking for relationships and patterns in their data and they try to infer some kind of hypothesis or theory to account for those patterns. Initially the hypothesis may be an intelligent or inspired guess that strikes the scientists from their experience as being a possible way of accounting for what they have observed. For example, a scientist might suggest the (very reasonable) hypothesis that the blood pressure measurements in your class can be accounted for by the fact that examinations cause stress in most people! To test the hypothesis a scientist will then work out what he or she would expect to find if the hypothesis were true and then will proceed to devise an experiment or a series of experiments to check if such is indeed the case. If the experiments fail to confirm expectation, the hypothesis may be modified or discarded in favour of another and the process repeated. Once a hypothesis has been successfully tested by repeated experimentation then it is dignified by being called a theory.[1]

It is now generally agreed by scientists themselves and philosophers of science that our account so far of what the scientific method is, is not only highly idealised but also flawed. In particular, contrary to what is asserted about observation and experimentation above, it is now widely accepted that no scientist, however honest and careful, can come to his or her work in a completely impartial way, without presuppositions and assumptions. This fact will be of importance for our understanding of science's contribution to our worldview. It is easier, however, to consider that topic after we have first had a look at some of the logical concepts and procedures that underlie scientific argumentation and proof.

Induction

Induction is probably the most important logical process that scientists use in the formulation of laws and theories.[2] It is also a process that is familiar to all of us from a very early age whether we are scientists or not, though we may well not have been aware of it. When we as young children first see a crow we notice it is black. For all we know, the next crow we see may well be white or yellow. But after observing crows day after day, there comes a point at which our feeling that any other crow we see is going to be black is so strong that we would be prepared to say that all crows are black. We have taken what is called an inductive step based on our own data—we have seen, say, 435 crows—to make a universal statement about all crows. Induction, then, is the process of

---

[1] The terms *hypothesis* and *theory* are in fact almost indistinguishable, the only difference in normal usage being that a hypothesis is sometimes regarded as more tentative than a theory.

[2] Note for mathematicians: the process of induction described above is not the same as the principle of mathematical induction by which (typically) the truth of a statement $P(n)$ is established for all positive integers n from two propositions:

(1) $P(1)$ is true;

(2) for any positive integer k, we can prove that the truth of $P(k+1)$ follows from the truth of $P(k)$.

The key difference is that (2) describes an infinite set of hypotheses, one for each positive integer, whereas in philosophical induction we are generalising from a finite set of hypotheses.

generalising from a finite set of data to a universal or general statement.

A famous example of the use of induction in science is the derivation of Mendel's laws of heredity. Gregor Mendel and his assistants made a number of observations of the frequency of occurrence of particular characteristics in each of several generations of peas, like whether seeds were wrinkled or smooth, or plants were tall or short, and then made an inductive generalisation from those observations to formulate the laws that now bear his name.

Induction, then, is the process of generalising from a finite set of data to a universal or general statement.

But, as may well have occurred to you, there is a problem with induction. To illustrate this, let's turn our minds to swans rather than the crows we thought about just now. Suppose that from childhood every swan you have seen was white. You might well conclude (by induction) that all swans are white. But then one day you are shown a picture of an Australian black swan and discover that your conclusion was false. This illustrates what the problem with induction is. How can you ever really know that you have made enough observations to draw a universal conclusion from a limited set of observations?

But please notice what the discovery of the black swan has done. It has proved wrong the statement that all swans are white, but it has not proved wrong the modified statement that if you see a swan in Europe, the high probability is that the swan will be white.

Let's look at another example of induction, this time from chemistry.

Particular observations:

Time	Date	Substance	Litmus test result
0905	2015-08-14	sulphuric acid	turned red
1435	2015-09-17	citric acid	turned red
1045	2015-09-18	hydrochloric acid	turned red
1900	2015-10-20	sulphuric acid	turned red

Universal or general statement (law): litmus paper turns red when dipped in acid.

This law, based on induction from the finite set of particular observations that are made of particular acids at particular times in particular places, is claimed to hold for all acids at all times in all places. The problem with induction is, how can we be sure that such a general statement is valid, when, in the very nature of things, we can only make a finite number of observations of litmus paper turning red on the application of acid? The story of the black swan makes us aware of the difficulty.

Well, we cannot be absolutely sure, it is true. But every time we do the experiment and find it works, our confidence in the litmus test is increased to the extent that if we dipped some paper in a liquid and found it did not go red we would be likely to conclude, not that the litmus test did not work, but that either the paper we had was not litmus paper or the liquid was not acid! Of course it is true that underlying our confidence is the assumption that nature behaves in a uniform way, that if I repeat an experiment tomorrow under the same conditions as I did it today, I will get the same results.

Let's take another example that Bertrand Russell used to illustrate the problem of induction in a more complex situation: Bertrand Russell's inductivist turkey. A turkey observes that on its first day at the turkey farm it was fed at 9 a.m. For two months it collects observations and notes that even if it chooses days at random, it is fed at 9 a.m. It finally concludes by induction that it always will be fed at 9 a.m. It therefore gets an awful shock on Christmas Eve when, instead of being fed, it is taken out and killed for Christmas dinner!

So how can we know for certain that we have made enough observations in an experiment? How many times do we have to check that particular metals expand on heating to conclude that all metals expand on heating? How do we avoid the inductivist turkey shock? Of course we can see that the problem with the turkey is that it did not have (indeed could not have) the wider experience of the turkey farmer who could replace the turkey's incorrect inductivist conclusion with a more complicated correct one: namely the law that each turkey will experience a sequence of days of feeding followed by execution!

The point of what we are saying here is not to undermine science by suggesting that induction is useless, nor that science in itself cannot lead us to any firm conclusions. It simply teaches us to recognise the limits of any one method and to found our conclusions, wherever possible, on a combination of them.

The role of deduction

Once a law has been formulated by induction, we can test the validity of the law by using it to make predictions. For example, assuming Mendel's laws to be true, we can deduce from them a prediction as to what the relative frequency of occurrence, say, of blue eyes in different generations of a family, should be. When we find by direct observation that the occurrence of blue eyes is what we predicted it to be, our observations are said to confirm the theory, although this sort of confirmation can never amount to total certainty. Thus deduction plays an important role in the confirmation of induction.

Deduction plays an important role in the confirmation of induction.

It may be that what we have said about induction has given the impression that scientific work always starts by looking at data and reasoning to some inductive hypothesis that accounts for those data. However, in reality, scientific method tends to be somewhat more complicated than this. Frequently, scientists start by deciding what kind of data they are looking for. That is, they already have in their mind some hypothesis or theory they want to test, and they look for data that will confirm that theory. In this situation deduction will play a dominant role.

For example, as we mentioned above regarding observation and experimentation, in the ancient world, Greek philosophers supposed as a hypothesis that the planets must move in circular orbits around the earth, since, for them, the circle was the perfect shape. They then deduced what their hypothesis should lead them to observe in the heavens. When their observations did not appear to confirm their original hypothesis completely, they modified it. They did this by replacing the original hypothesis by one in which other circular motions are imposed on top of the original one (epicycles, they were called). They then used this more complicated hypothesis from which to deduce their predictions. This theory of epicycles dominated astronomy for a long time, and was overturned and replaced by the revolutionary suggestions of Copernicus and Kepler.

Kepler's work in turn again illustrates the deductive method. Using the observations the astronomer Tycho Brahe had made available, Kepler tried to work out the shape that the orbit of Mars traced against the background of 'fixed' stars. He did not get anywhere until he hit on an idea that was prompted by geometrical work he had done on the ellipse. That idea was to suppose as a hypothesis that the orbit of Mars was an ellipse, then to use mathematical calculations to deduce what should be observed on the basis of that hypothesis, and finally to compare those predictions with the actual observations. The validity of the elliptical orbit hypothesis would then be judged by how closely the predictions fit the observations.

This method of inference is called the deductive or hypothetico-deductive method of reasoning: deducing predictions from a hypothesis, and then comparing them with actual observations.

Since deduction is such an important procedure it is worth considering it briefly. Deduction is a logical process by which an assertion we want to prove (the conclusion) is logically deduced from things we already accept (the premises). Here is an example of logical deduction, usually called a syllogism:

P1: All dogs have four legs.
P2: Fido is a dog.

C: Fido has four legs.

Here statements P1 and P2 are the premises and C is the conclusion. If P1 and P2 are true then C is true. Or to put it another way, to have P1 and P2 true and C false, would involve a logical contradiction. This is the essence of a logically valid deduction.

Let's now look at an example of a logically invalid deduction:

P1: Many dogs have a long tail.
P2: Albert is a dog.

C: Albert has a long tail.

Here statement C does not necessarily follow from P1 and P2. It is clearly possible for P1 and P2 to be true and yet for C to be false.

It all appears to be so simple that there is danger of your switching off. But don't do that quite yet or you might miss something very important. And that is that deductive logic cannot establish the truth of any of the statements involved in the procedure. All that the logic can tell us (but this much is very important!) is that if the premises are true and the argument is logically valid, then the conclusion is true. In order to get this clear let us look at a final example:

P1: All planets have a buried ocean.
P2: Mercury is a planet.

C: Mercury has a buried ocean.

This is a logically valid argument even though statement P1 and statement C are (so far as we know) false. The argument says only that if P1 and P2 were true, then C should be true, which is perfectly valid. This sort of thing may seem strange to us at first, but it can help us grasp that logic can only criticise the argument and check whether it is valid or not. It cannot tell us whether any or all of the premises or conclusion are true. Logic has to do with the way in which some statements are derived from others, not with the truth of those statements.

Logic has to do with the way in which some statements are derived from others, not with the truth of those statements.

We should also note that deductive inference plays a central role in pure mathematics where theories are constructed by means of making deductions from explicitly given axioms, as in Euclidean geometry. The results (or theorems, as they are usually called) are said to be true if there is a logically valid chain of deductions deriving them from the axioms. Such deductive proofs give a certainty (granted the consistency of the axioms) that is not attainable in the inductive sciences.

In practice induction and deduction are usually both involved in establishing scientific theories. We referred above to Kepler's use of deduction in deriving his theory that Mars moved in an ellipse round the sun. However, he first thought of the ellipse (rather than, say, the parabola or the hyperbola) because the observations of Brahe led Kepler to believe the orbit of Mars was roughly egg-shaped. The egg shape was initially conjectured as a result of induction from astronomical observations.

Competing hypotheses can cover the same data

But here we should notice that when it comes to interpreting the data we have collected, different hypotheses can be constructed to cover that data. We have two illustrations of this.

Illustration from astronomy. Under the role of deduction above we discussed two hypotheses from ancient astronomy that were put forward to explain the motion of the planets. Successive refinements of the epicyclic model appeared to cover the data at the expense of greater and greater complication in that more and more circles were necessary. Kepler's proposal, by contrast, covered the data by the simple device of replacing the complex array of circles by one single ellipse, which simplified the whole business enormously. Now, if we knew nothing of gravity and the deduction of elliptical orbits that can be made from it by means of Newton's laws, how would we choose between the two explanations?

At this point, scientists might well invoke the principle sometimes called 'Occam's razor', after William of Occam. This is the belief that simpler explanations of natural phenomena are more likely to be correct than more complex ones. More precisely, the idea is that if we have two or more competing hypotheses covering the same data, we should choose the one that involves the least number of assumptions or complications. The metaphorical use of the word 'razor' comes from this cutting or shaving down to the smallest possible number of assumptions. Occam's razor has proved very useful but we should observe that it is a philosophical preference, and it is not something that you can prove to be true in every case, so it needs to be used with care.

> The principle sometimes called 'Occam's razor', after William of Occam . . . is the belief that simpler explanations of natural phenomena are more likely to be correct than more complex ones.

Illustration from physics. Another illustration of the way in which different hypotheses can account for the same data is given by a common exercise in school physics. We are given a spring, a series of weights and a ruler and asked to plot a graph of the length of the spring against the weight hanging on the end of it. We end up with a series, say, of 10 points on the paper that look as if they might (with a bit of imagination!) lie on a straight line. We take an inductive step and draw a straight line that goes through most of the points and we claim that there is a linear relationship between the length of spring and the tension it is put under by the weights (Hooke's law). But then we reflect that there is an infinite number of curves that can be drawn through our ten points. Changing the curve would change the relation between spring length and tension. Why not choose one of those other curves in preference to the straight line? That is, in the situation just described, there are many different hypotheses that cover the same set of data. How do you choose between them?

Application of Occam's razor would lead to choosing the most elegant or economical solution—a straight line is simpler than a complicated curve. We could also repeat the experiment with 100 points, 200 points, etc. The results would build up our confidence that the straight line was the correct answer. When we build up evidence in this way, we say that we have cumulative evidence for the validity of our hypothesis.

So far we have been looking at various methods employed by scientists and have seen that none of them yields 100% certainty, except in deductive proofs in mathematics where the certainty is that particular conclusions follow from particular axioms. However, we would emphasise once more that this does not mean that the scientific enterprise is about to collapse! Far from it. What we mean by 'not giving 100% certainty' can be interpreted as saying that there is a small probability that a particular result or theory is false. But that does not mean that we cannot have confidence in the theory.

Indeed there are some situations, as in the litmus-paper test for acid where there has been 100% success in the past. Now whereas this does not formally guarantee 100% success in the future, scientists will say that it is a fact that litmus paper turns red on being dipped in acid. By a 'fact', they mean, as palaeontologist Stephen Jay Gould has delightfully put it, 'confirmed to such a degree that it would be perverse to withhold provisional assent to it'.[3]

On other occasions we are prepared to trust our lives to the findings of science and technology even though we know we do not have 100% certainty. For example, before we travel by train, we know that it is theoretically possible for something to go wrong, maybe for the brakes or signalling to fail and cause the train to crash. But we also know from the statistics of rail travel that the probability of such an event is very small indeed (though it is not zero—trains have from time to time crashed). Since the probability of a crash is so small, most of us who travel by train do so without even thinking about the risk.

On the other hand we must not assume that we can accept all

[3] Gould, 'Evolution as Fact and Theory', 119.

proposed hypotheses arrived at by scientific method as absolute fact without testing them.

One of the criteria of testing is called falsifiability.

Falsifiability

Karl Popper put the emphasis not on the verifiability of a hypothesis but on its falsifiability. It is unfortunate that Popper's terminology can be a real source of confusion, since the adjective 'falsifiable' does not mean 'will turn out to be false'! The confusion is even worse when one realises, on the other hand, that the verb 'to falsify' means 'to demonstrate that something is false'! The term 'falsifiable' has in fact a technical meaning. A hypothesis is said to be falsifiable if you can think of a logically possible set of observations that would be inconsistent with it.

It is, of course, much easier to falsify a universal statement than to verify it. As an illustration, take one of our earlier examples. The statement 'All swans are white' is, from the very start, falsifiable. One would only have to discover one swan that was black and that would falsify it. And since we know that black swans do exist, the statement has long since been falsified.

> The term 'falsifiable' has in fact a technical meaning. A hypothesis is said to be falsifiable if you can think of a logically possible set of observations that would be inconsistent with it.

However, there can be problems. Most scientific activity is much more complex than dealing with claims like 'All swans are white'!

For example, in the nineteenth century observations of the planet Uranus appeared to indicate that its motion was inconsistent with predictions made on the basis of Newton's laws. Therefore, it appeared to threaten to demonstrate Newton's laws to be false. However, instead of immediately saying that Newton's laws had been falsified, it was suggested by French mathematician Urbain Le Verrier and English astronomer John Couch Adams (unknown to each other) that there might be a hitherto undetected planet in the neighbourhood of Uranus that would account for its apparently anomalous behaviour. As a result another scientist, German astronomer Johann Galle, was prompted to look for a new planet and discovered the planet Neptune.

It would, therefore, have been incorrect to regard the behaviour of Uranus as falsifying Newton's laws. The problem was ignorance of the initial conditions—there was a planet missing in the configuration being studied. In other words, some of the crucial data was missing. This story demonstrates one of the problems inherent in Popper's approach. When observation does not fit theory, it could be that the theory is false, but it could equally well be that the theory is correct but the data is incomplete or even false, or that some of the auxiliary assumptions are incorrect. How can you judge what is the correct picture?

Most scientists in fact feel that Popper's ideas are far too pessimistic and his methodology too counter-intuitive. Their experience and intuition tell them that their scientific methods in fact enable them to get a better and better understanding of the universe, that they are in this sense getting a tighter grip on reality. One benefit of Popper's approach, however, is its insistence that scientific theories be testable.

Repeatability and abduction

The scientific activity we have been thinking of so far is characterised by *repeatability*. That is, we have considered situations where scientists are looking for universally valid laws that cover repeatable phenomena, laws which, like Newton's laws of motion, may be experimentally tested again and again. Sciences of this sort are often called inductive or nomological sciences (Gk. *nomos* = law) and between them they cover most of science.

However there are major areas of scientific enquiry where repeatability is not possible, notably study of the origin of the universe and the origin and development of life.

Now of course we do not mean to imply that science has nothing to say about phenomena that are non-repeatable. On the contrary, if one is to judge by the amount of literature published, particularly, but not only, at the popular level, the origin of the universe and of life, for example, are among the most interesting subjects by far that science addresses.

But precisely because of the importance of such non-repeatable phenomena, it is vital to see that the way in which they are accessible to science is not the same in general as the way in which repeatable phenomena are. For theories about both kinds of phenomena tend to be presented to the public in the powerful name of science as though they had an equal claim to be accepted. Thus there is a real danger that the public ascribes the same authority and validity to conjectures about non-repeatable events that are not capable of experimental verification as it does to those theories that have been confirmed by repeated experiment.

Physical chemist and philosopher Michael Polanyi points out that the study of how something originates is usually very different from the study of how it operates, although, of course, clues to how something originated may well be found in how it operates. It is one thing to investigate something repeatable in the laboratory, such as dissecting a frog to see how its nervous system functions, but it is an altogether different thing to study something non-repeatable, such as how frogs came to exist in the first place. And, on the large scale, how the universe works is one thing, yet how it came to be may be quite another.

> How the universe works is one thing, yet how it came to be may be quite another.

The most striking difference between the study of non-repeatable and repeatable phenomena is that the method of induction is no longer applicable, since we no longer have a sequence of observations or experiments to induce from, nor any repetition in the future to predict about! The principal method that applies to non-repeatable phenomena is *abduction*.

Although this term, introduced by logician Charles Peirce in the nineteenth century, may be unfamiliar, the underlying idea is very familiar. For abduction is what every good detective does in order to clear up a murder mystery! With the murder mystery a certain event has happened. No one doubts that it has happened. The question is: who or what was the cause of it happening? And often in the search for causes of an event that has already happened, abduction is the only method available.

As an example of abductive inference, think of the following:

Data: Ivan's car went over the cliff edge and he was killed.

Inference: If the car brakes had failed, then the car would have gone over the cliff.

Abductive conclusion: There is reason to suppose that the brakes failed.

However, an alternative suggests itself (especially to avid readers of detective stories): if someone had pushed Ivan's car over the cliff, the result would have been the same! It would be fallacious and very foolish to assume that just because we had thought of one explanation of the circumstances, that it was the only one.

The basic idea of abduction is given by the following scheme:

Data: A is observed.
Inference: If B were true then A would follow.

Abductive conclusion: There is reason to suppose B may be true.

Of course, there may well be another hypothesis, C, of which we could say: if C were true A would follow. Indeed, there may be many candidates for C.

The detective in our story has a procedure for considering them one by one. He may first consider the chance hypothesis, B, that the brakes failed. He may then consider the hypothesis C that it was no chance event, but deliberately designed by a murderer who pushed the car over the cliff. Or the detective may consider an even more sophisticated hypothesis, D, combining both chance and design, that someone who wanted to kill Ivan had tampered with the brakes of the car so that they would fail somewhere, and they happened to fail on the clifftop!

Inference to the best explanation. Our detective story illustrates how the process of abduction throws up plausible hypotheses and forces upon us the question as to which of the hypotheses best fits the data. In order to decide that question, the hypotheses are compared for their explanatory power: how much of the data do they cover, does the theory make coherent sense, is it consistent with other areas of our knowledge, etc.?

In order to answer these further questions, deduction will often be used. For example, if B in the detective story is true, then we would expect an investigation of the brakes of the wrecked car to reveal worn or broken parts. If C is true we would deduce that the brakes might well be found in perfect order, whereas if D were the case, we might expect to find marks of deliberate damage to the hydraulic braking system. If we found such marks then D would immediately be regarded as the best of the competing explanations given so far, since it has a greater explanatory power than the others.

Thus, abduction together with the subsequent comparison of competing hypotheses may be regarded as an 'inference to the best explanation'. This is the essence not only of detective and legal work but also of the work of the historian. Both detective and historian have to infer the best possible explanation from the available data after the events in which they are interested have occurred.

For more on the application of abduction in the natural sciences, particularly in cosmology and biology, see the books by John Lennox noted at the end of this Appendix. Here we need to consider a few more of the general issues related to the scientific endeavour.

EXPLAINING EXPLANATIONS

Levels of explanation

Science explains. This, for many people encapsulates the power and the fascination of science. Science enables us to understand what we did not understand before and, by giving us understanding, it gives us power over nature. But what do we mean by saying that 'science explains'?

In informal language we take an explanation of something to be adequate when the person to whom the explanation is given understands plainly what he or she did not understand before. However, we must try to be more precise about what we mean by the process of 'explanation', since it has different aspects that are often confused. An illustration can help us. We have considered a similar idea in relation to roses. Let's now take further examples.

Suppose Aunt Olga has baked a beautiful cake. She displays it to a gathering of the world's top scientists and we ask them for an explanation of the cake. The nutrition scientists will tell us about the number of calories in the cake and its nutritional effect; the biochemists will inform us about the structure of the proteins, fats, etc. in the cake and what it is that causes them to hold together; the chemists will enumerate the elements involved and describe their bonding; the physicists will be able to analyse the cake in terms of fundamental particles; and the mathematicians will offer us a set of beautiful equations to describe the behaviour of those particles. Suppose, then, that these experts have given us an exhaustive description of the cake, each in terms of his or her scientific discipline. Can we say that the cake is now completely explained? We have certainly been given a description of how the cake was made and how its various constituent elements relate to each other. But suppose we now ask the assembled group of experts why the cake was made. We notice the grin on Aunt Olga's face. She knows the answer since, after all, she made the cake! But if she does not reveal the answer by telling us, it is clear that no amount of scientific analysis will give us the answer.

Thus, although science can answer 'how' questions in terms of causes and mechanisms, it cannot answer 'why' questions, questions of purpose and intention—teleological questions, as they are sometimes called (Gk. *telos* = end or goal).

However, it would be nonsensical to suggest that Aunt Olga's answer to the teleological question, that she made the cake for Sam's birthday, say, contradicted the scientific analysis of the cake! No. The two kinds of answer are clearly logically compatible.

And yet exactly the same confusion of categories is evidenced when atheists argue that there is no longer need to bring in God and the supernatural to explain the workings of nature, since we now have a scientific explanation for them. As a result, the general public has come to think that belief in a creator belongs to a primitive and unsophisticated stage of human thinking and has been rendered both unnecessary and impossible by science.

Although science can answer 'how' questions in terms of causes and mechanisms, it cannot answer 'why' questions, questions of purpose and intention.

But there is an obvious fallacy here. Think of a Ford motor car. It is conceivable that a primitive person who was seeing one for the first time and who did not understand the principles of an internal combustion engine, might imagine that there was a god (Mr Ford) inside the engine, making it go. He might further imagine that when the engine ran sweetly that was because Mr Ford inside the engine liked him, and when it refused to go that was because Mr Ford did not like him. Of course, if eventually this primitive person became civilised, learned engineering, and took the engine to pieces, he would discover that there was no Mr Ford inside the engine, and that he did not need to introduce Mr Ford as an explanation for the working of the engine. His grasp of the impersonal principles of internal combustion would be altogether enough to explain how the engine worked. So far, so good. But if he then decided that his understanding of the principles of the internal combustion engine made it impossible to believe in the existence of a Mr Ford who designed the engine, this would be patently false!

FIGURE Ap.2. Model T Ford Motor Car.

Introducing the world's first moving assembly line in 1913, Ford Motor Company built more than 15 million Model Ts from 1908 until 1927.

Reproduced with permission of ©iStock/Peter Mah

It is likewise a confusion of categories to suppose that our understanding of the impersonal principles according to which the universe works makes it either unnecessary or impossible to believe in the existence of a personal creator who designed, made and upholds the great engine that is the universe. In other words, we should not confuse the mechanisms by which the universe works with its Cause. Every one of us knows how to distinguish between the consciously willed movement of an arm for a purpose and an involuntary spasmodic movement of an arm induced by accidental contact with an electric current.

Michael Poole, Visiting Research Fellow, Science and Religion, at King's College London, in his published debate on science and religion with Richard Dawkins, puts it this way:

> There is no logical conflict between reason-giving explanations which concern mechanisms, and reason-giving explanations which concern the plans and purposes of an agent, human or divine. This is a logical point, not a matter of whether one does or does not happen to believe in God oneself.[4]

[4] Poole, 'Critique of Aspects of the Philosophy and Theology of Richard Dawkins', 49.

One of the authors, in a debate with Richard Dawkins, noted how his opponent was confusing the categories of mechanism and agency:

> When Isaac Newton, for example, discovered his law of gravity and wrote down the equations of motion, he didn't say, 'Marvellous, I now understand it. I've got a mechanism therefore I don't need God.' In fact it was the exact opposite. It was because he understood the complexity of sophistication of the mathematical description of the universe that his praise for God was increased. And I would like to suggest, Richard, that somewhere down in this you're making a category mistake, because you're confusing mechanism with agency. We have a mechanism that does XYZ, therefore there's no need for an agent. I would suggest that the sophistication of the mechanism, and science rejoices in finding such mechanisms, is evidence for the sheer wonder of the creative genius of God.[5]

In spite of the clarity of the logic expressed in these counterpoints, a famous statement made by the French mathematician Laplace is constantly misappropriated to support atheism. On being asked by Napoleon where God fitted in to his mathematical work, Laplace replied: 'Sir, I have no need of that hypothesis.' Of course, God did not appear in Laplace's mathematical description of how things work, just as Mr Ford would not appear in a scientific description of the laws of internal combustion. But what does that prove? Such an argument can no more be used to prove that God does not exist than it can be used to prove that Mr Ford does not exist.

To sum up, then, it is important to be aware of the danger of confusing different levels of explanation and of thinking that one level of explanation tells the whole story.

This leads us at once to consider the related question of reductionism.

---

5 Lennox's response to Dawkins's first thesis 'Faith is blind; science is evidence-based', 'The God Delusion Debate', hosted by Fixed Point Foundation, University of Alabama at Birmingham, filmed and broadcast live 3 October 2007, http://fixed-point.org/index.php/video/35-full-length/164-the-dawkins-lennox-debate. Transcript provided courtesy of ProTorah, http://www.protorah.com/god-delusion-debate-dawkins-lennox-transcript/.

Reductionism

In order to study something, especially if it is complex, scientists often split it up into separate parts or aspects and thus 'reduce' it to simpler components that are individually easier to investigate. This kind of reductionism, often called methodological or structural reductionism, is part of the normal process of science and has proved very useful. It is, however, very important to bear in mind that there may well be, and usually is, more to a given whole than simply what we obtain by adding up all that we have learned from the parts. Studying all the parts of a watch separately will never enable you to grasp how the complete watch works as an integrated whole.

Besides methodological reductionism there are two further types of reductionism, epistemological and ontological. *Epistemological reductionism* is the view that higher level sciences can be explained without remainder by the sciences at a lower level. That is, chemistry is explained by physics; biochemistry by chemistry; biology by biochemistry; psychology by biology; sociology by brain science; and theology by sociology. As Francis Crick puts it: 'The ultimate aim of the modern development in biology is in fact to explain all biology in terms of physics and chemistry.'[6] The former Charles Simonyi Professor of the Public Understanding of Science at Oxford, Richard Dawkins, holds the same view: 'My task is to explain elephants, and the world of complex things, in terms of the simple things that physicists either understand, or are working on.'[7] The ultimate goal of reductionism is to reduce all human behaviour, our likes and dislikes, the entire mental landscape of our lives, to physics.

> The ultimate goal of reductionism is to reduce all human behaviour, our likes and dislikes, the entire mental landscape of our lives, to physics.

However, both the viability and the plausibility of this programme are open to serious question. The outstanding Russian psychologist Leo Vygotsky (1896–1934) was critical of certain aspects of this reductionist philosophy as applied to psychology. He pointed out that such reductionism often conflicts

6 Crick, *Of Molecules and Men*, 10.

7 Dawkins, *Blind Watchmaker*, 15.

with the goal of preserving all the basic features of a phenomenon or event that one wishes to explain. For example, one can reduce water (H_2O) into H and O. However, hydrogen burns and oxygen is necessary for burning, whereas water has neither of these properties, but has many others that are not possessed by either hydrogen or oxygen. Thus, Vygotsky's view was that reductionism can only be done up to certain limits. Karl Popper says: 'There is almost always an unresolved residue left by even the most successful attempts at reduction.'[8]

Furthermore, Michael Polanyi argues the intrinsic implausibility of expecting epistemological reductionism to work in every circumstance.[9] Think of the various levels of process involved in building an office building with bricks. First of all there is the process of extracting the raw materials out of which the bricks have to be made. Then there are the successively higher levels of making the bricks, they do not make themselves; bricklaying, the bricks do not self-assemble; designing the building, it does not design itself; and planning the town in which the building is to be built, it does not organise itself. Each level has its own rules. The laws of physics and chemistry govern the raw material of the bricks; technology prescribes the art of brick making; architecture teaches the builders, and the architects are controlled by the town planners. Each level is controlled by the level above, but the reverse is not true. The laws of a higher level cannot be derived from the laws of a lower level (although, of course what can be done at a higher level will depend on the lower levels: for example, if the bricks are not strong there will be a limit on the height of a building that can be safely built with them).

Consider the page you are reading just now. It consists of paper imprinted with ink or, in the case of an electronic version, text rendered digitally. It is obvious that the physics and chemistry of ink and paper can never, even in principle, tell you anything about the significance of the shapes of the letters on the page. And this is nothing to do with the fact that physics and chemistry are not yet sufficiently advanced to deal with this question. Even if we allow these sciences another 1,000 years of development, we can see that it will make no

---

[8] Popper, 'Scientific Reduction'.

[9] Polanyi, *Tacit Dimension*.

difference, because the shapes of those letters demand a totally new and higher level of explanation than that of which physics and chemistry are capable. In fact, explanation can only be given in terms of the concepts of language and authorship—the communication of a message by a person. The ink and paper are carriers of the message, but the message certainly does not emerge automatically from them. Furthermore, when it comes to language itself, there is again a sequence of levels—you cannot derive a vocabulary from phonetics, or the grammar of a language from its vocabulary, etc.

As is well known, the genetic material DNA carries information. We shall describe this later on in some detail, but the basic idea is simply this. DNA, a substance found in every living cell, can be looked at as a long tape on which there is a string of letters written in a four-letter chemical language. The sequence of letters contains coded instructions (information) that the cell uses to make proteins. Physical biochemist and theologian Arthur Peacocke writes: 'In no way can the concept of "information", the concept of conveying a message, be articulated in terms of the concepts of physics and chemistry, even though the latter can be shown to explain how the molecular machinery (DNA, RNA and protein) operates to carry information.'[10]

In each of the situations we have described above, we have a series of levels, each one higher than the previous one. What happens on a higher level is not completely derivable from what happens on the level beneath it, but requires another level of explanation.

In this kind of situation it is sometimes said that the higher level phenomena 'emerge' from the lower level. Unfortunately, however, the word 'emerge' is easily misunderstood to mean that the higher level properties emerge automatically from the lower level properties. This is clearly false in general, as we showed by considering brick making and writing on paper. Yet notwithstanding the fact that both writing on paper and DNA have in common the fact that they encode a 'message', those scientists committed to materialistic philosophy insist that the information carrying properties of DNA must have emerged automatically out of mindless matter. For if, as materialism insists, matter and energy are all that there is, then it logically follows

[10] Peacocke, *Experiment of Life*, 54.

that they must possess the inherent potential to organise themselves in such a way that eventually all the complex molecules necessary for life, including DNA, will emerge.[11]

There is a third type of reductionism, called *ontological reductionism*, which is frequently encountered in statements like the following: The universe is nothing but a collection of atoms in motion, human beings are 'machines for propagating DNA, and the propagation of DNA is a self-sustaining process. It is every living object's sole reason for living'.[12]

Words such as 'nothing but', 'sole' or 'simply' are the telltale sign of (ontological) reductionist thinking. If we remove these words we are usually left with something unobjectionable. The universe certainly is a collection of atoms and human beings do propagate DNA. The question is, is there nothing more to it than that? Are we going to say with Francis Crick, who won the Nobel Prize jointly with James D. Watson for his discovery of the double helix structure of DNA: '"You", your joys and your sorrows, your memories and your ambitions, your sense of personal identity and free will, are in fact no more than the behaviour of a vast assembly of nerve cells and their associated molecules'?[13]

What shall we say of human love and fear, of concepts like beauty and truth? Are they meaningless?

Ontological reductionism, carried to its logical conclusion, would ask us to believe that a Rembrandt painting is nothing but molecules of paint scattered on canvas. Physicist and theologian John Polkinghorne's reaction is clear:

> There is more to the world than physics can ever express.
>
> One of the fundamental experiences of the scientific life is that of wonder at the beautiful structure of the world. It is the pay-off for all the weary hours of labour involved in the pursuit of research. Yet in the world described by science where would that wonder find its lodging? Or our experiences of beauty? Of moral obligation? Of the presence of God? These seem to me

[11] Whether matter and energy do have this capacity is another matter that is discussed in the books noted at the end of this appendix.

[12] Dawkins, *Growing Up in the Universe* (study guide), 21.

[13] Crick, *Astonishing Hypothesis*, 3.

> to be quite as fundamental as anything we could measure in the laboratory. A worldview that does not take them adequately into account is woefully incomplete.[14]

The most devastating criticism of ontological reductionism is that it is self-destructive. Polkinghorne describes its programme as ultimately suicidal:

> For, not only does it relegate our experiences of beauty, moral obligation, and religious encounter to the epiphenomenal scrapheap. It also destroys rationality. Thought is replaced by electrochemical neural events. Two such events cannot confront each other in rational discourse. They are neither right nor wrong. They simply happen. . . . The very assertions of the reductionist himself are nothing but blips in the neural network of his brain. The world of rational discourse dissolves into the absurd chatter of firing synapses. Quite frankly, that cannot be right and none of us believes it to be so.[15]

BASIC OPERATIONAL PRESUPPOSITIONS

So far we have been concentrating on the scientific method and have seen that this is a much more complex (and, for that reason, a much more interesting) topic than may first appear. As promised earlier, we must now consider the implications of the fact that scientists, being human like the rest of us, do not come to any situation with their mind completely clear of preconceived ideas. The widespread idea that any scientist, if only he or she tries to be impartial, can be a completely dispassionate observer in any but the most trivial of situations, is a fallacy, as has been pointed out repeatedly by philosophers of science and by scientists themselves. At the very least scientists must already

The widespread idea that any scientist, if only he or she tries to be impartial, can be a completely dispassionate observer in any but the most trivial of situations, is a fallacy.

[14] Polkinghorne, *One World*, 72–3.
[15] Polkinghorne, *One World*, 92–3.

have formed some idea or theory about the nature of what they are about to study.

Observation is dependent on theory

It is simply not possible to make observations and do experiments without any presuppositions. Consider, for example, the fact that science, by its very nature, has to be selective. It would clearly be impossible to take every aspect of any given object of study into account. Scientists must therefore choose what variables are likely to be important and what are not. For example, physicists do not think of taking into account the colour of billiard balls when they are conducting a laboratory investigation of the application of Newton's laws to motion: but the shape of the balls is very important—cubical balls would not be much use! In making such choices, scientists are inevitably guided by already formed ideas and theories about what the important factors are likely to be. The problem is that such ideas may sometimes be wrong and cause scientists to miss vital aspects of a problem to such an extent that they draw false conclusions. A famous story about the physicist Heinrich Hertz illustrates this.

Maxwell's electromagnetic theory predicted that radio and light waves would be propagated with the same velocity. Hertz designed an experiment to check this and found that the velocities were different. His mistake, only discovered after his death, was that he did not think that the shape of his laboratory could have any influence on the results of his experiment. Unfortunately for him, it did. Radio waves were reflected from the walls and distorted his results.

The validity of his observations depended on the (preconceived) theory that the shape of the laboratory was irrelevant to his experiment. The fact that this preconception was false invalidated his conclusions.

This story also points up another difficulty. How does one decide in this kind of situation whether it is the theory or the experiment that is at fault, whether one should trust the results of the experiment and abandon the theory and look for a better one, or whether one should keep on having faith in the theory and try to discover what was wrong with the experiment? There is no easy answer to this question. A great deal will depend on the experience and judgment of the scientists involved, and, inevitably, mistakes can and will be made.

Knowledge cannot be gained without making certain assumptions to start with

Scientists not only inevitably have preconceived ideas about particular situations, as illustrated by the story about Hertz, but their science is done within a framework of general assumptions about science as such. World-famous Harvard geneticist Richard Lewontin writes: 'Scientists, like other intellectuals, come to their work with a world view, a set of preconceptions that provides the framework for their analysis of the world.'[16]

And those preconceptions can significantly affect scientists' research methods as well as their results and interpretations of those results, as we shall see.

We would emphasise, however, that the fact that scientists have presuppositions is not to be deprecated. That would, in fact be a nonsensical attitude to adopt. For the voice of logic reminds us that we cannot get to know anything if we are not prepared to presuppose something. Let's unpack this idea by thinking about a common attitude. 'I am not prepared to take anything for granted', says someone, 'I will only accept something if you prove it to me.' Sounds reasonable—but it isn't. For if this is your view then you will never accept or know anything! For suppose I want you to accept some proposition A. You will only accept it if I prove it to you. But I shall have to prove it to you on the basis of some other proposition B. You will only accept B if I prove it to you. I shall have to prove B to you on the basis of C. And so it will go on forever in what is called an infinite regress—that is, if you insist on taking nothing for granted in the first place!

We must all start somewhere with things we take as self-evident, basic assumptions that are not proved on the basis of something else. They are often called *axioms*.[17] Whatever axioms we adopt, we then proceed to try to make sense of the world by building on those

[16] Lewontin, *Dialectical Biologist*, 267.

[17] It should be borne in mind, however, that the axioms which appear in various branches of pure mathematics, for example, the theory of numbers or the theory of groups, do not appear out of nowhere. They usually arise from the attempt to encapsulate and formalise years, sometimes centuries, of mathematical research, into a so-called 'axiomatic system'.

axioms. This is true, not only at the worldview level but also in all of our individual disciplines. We retain those axioms that prove useful in the sense that they lead to theories which show a better 'fit' with nature and experience, and we abandon or modify those which do not fit so well. One thing is absolutely clear: none of us can avoid starting with assumptions.

Gaining knowledge involves trusting our senses and other people

There are essentially two sources from which we accumulate knowledge:

1. directly by our own 'hands-on' experience, for example, by accidentally putting our finger in boiling water, we learn that boiling water scalds;
2. we learn all kinds of things from sources external to ourselves, for example, teachers, books, parents, the media, etc.

In doing so we all constantly exercise faith. We intuitively trust our senses, even though we know they deceive us on times. For example, in extremely cold weather, if we put our hand on a metal handrail outside, the rail may feel hot to our touch.

We have faith, too, in our minds to interpret our senses, though here again we know that our minds can be deceived.

We also normally believe what other people tell us—teachers, parents, friends, etc. Sometimes we check what we learn from them because, without insulting them, we realise that even friends can be mistaken, and other people may set out to deceive us. However, much more often than not, we accept things on authority—if only because no one has time to check everything! In technical matters we trust our textbooks. We have faith in what (other) scientists have done. And it is, of course, reasonable so to do, though those experts themselves would teach us to be critical and not just to accept everything on their say-so. They would remind us also that the fact that a statement appears in print in a book, does not make it automatically true!

Gaining scientific knowledge involves belief in the rational intelligibility of the universe

We all take so much for granted the fact that we can use human reason as a probe to investigate the universe that we can fail to see that this is really something to be wondered at. For once we begin to think about the intelligibility of the universe, our minds demand an explanation. But where can we find one? Science cannot give it to us, for the very simple reason that science has to assume the rational intelligibility of the universe in order to get started. Einstein himself, in the same article we quoted earlier, makes this very clear in saying that the scientist's belief in the rational intelligibility of the universe goes beyond science and is in its very nature essentially religious:

> Science can only be created by those who are thoroughly imbued with the aspiration toward truth and understanding. This source of feeling, however, springs from the sphere of religion. To this there also belongs the faith in the possibility that the regulations valid for the world of existence are rational, that is, comprehensible to reason. I cannot conceive of a genuine scientist without that profound faith.[18]

Einstein saw no reason to be embarrassed by the fact that science involves at its root belief in something that science itself cannot justify.

Allied to belief in the rational intelligibility of the universe is the belief that patterns and law-like behaviour are to be expected in nature. The Greeks expressed this by using the word cosmos which means 'ordered'. It is this underlying expectation of order that lies behind the confidence with which scientists use the inductive method. Scientists speak of their belief in the uniformity of nature—the idea that the order in nature and the laws that describe it are valid at all times and in all parts of the universe.

Many theists from the Jewish, Islamic or Christian tradition would want to modify this concept of the uniformity of nature by adding their conviction that God the Creator has built regularities

[18] Einstein, *Out of My Later Years*, 26.

FIGURE Ap.3. Milky Way Galaxy.

The Milky Way galaxy is visible from earth on clear nights away from urban areas. Appearing as a cloud in the night sky, our galaxy's spiral bands of dust and glowing nebulae consist of billions of stars as seen from the inside.

into the working of the universe so that in general we can speak of uniformity—the norms to which nature normally operates. But because God is the Creator, he is not a prisoner of those regularities but can vary them by causing things to happen that do not fit into the regular pattern.

Here, again, commitment to the uniformity of nature is a matter of belief. Science cannot prove to us that nature is uniform, since we must assume the uniformity of nature in order to do science. Otherwise we would have no confidence that, if we repeat an experiment under the same conditions as it was done before, we shall get the same result. Were it so, our school textbooks would be useless. But surely, we might say, the uniformity of nature is highly probable since assuming it has led to such stunning scientific advance. However, as C. S. Lewis has observed: 'Can we say that Uniformity is at any rate very probable? Unfortunately not. We have just seen that all probabilities depend on *it*. Unless Nature is uniform, nothing is either probable or improbable.'[19]

[19] Lewis, *Miracles*, 163.

Operating within the reigning paradigms

Thomas Kuhn in his famous book *The Structure of Scientific Revolutions* (1962) pictured science as preceding through the following stages: pre-science, normal science, crisis revolution, new normal science, new crisis, and so on. Pre-science is the diverse and disorganised activity characterised by much disagreement that precedes the emergence of a new science that gradually becomes structured when a scientific community adheres to a paradigm. The paradigm is a web of assumptions and theories that are more or less agreed upon and are like the steelwork around which the scientific edifice is erected. Well-known examples are the paradigms of Copernican astronomy, Newtonian mechanics and evolutionary biology.

Normal science is then practised within the paradigm. It sets the standards for legitimate research. The normal scientist uses the paradigm to probe nature. He or she does not (often) look critically at the paradigm itself, because it commands so much agreement, much as we look down the light of a torch to illuminate an object, rather than look critically at the light of the torch itself. For this reason the paradigm will be very resistant to attempts to demonstrate that it is false. When anomalies, difficulties and apparent falsifications turn up, the normal scientists will hope to be able to accommodate them preferably within the paradigm or by making fine adjustments to the paradigm. However, if the difficulties can no longer be resolved and keep on piling up, a crisis situation develops, which leads to a scientific revolution involving the emergence of a new paradigm that then gains the ground to such an extent that the older paradigm is eventually completely abandoned. The essence of such a paradigm shift is the replacing of an old paradigm by a new one, not the refining of the old one by the new. The best known example of a major paradigm shift is the transition from Aristotelian geocentric (earth-centred) astronomy to Copernican heliocentric (sun-centred) astronomy in the sixteenth century.

Although Kuhn's work is open to criticism at various points, he has certainly made scientists aware of a number of issues that are important for our understanding of how science works:

1. the central role that metaphysical ideas play in the development of scientific theories;
2. the high resistance that paradigms show to attempts to prove them false;
3. the fact that science is subject to human frailty.

The second of these points has both a positive and a negative outworking. It means that a good paradigm will not be overturned automatically by the first experimental result or observation that appears to speak against it. On the other hand, it means that a paradigm which eventually proves to be inadequate or false, may take a long time to die and impede scientific progress by constraining scientists within its mesh and not giving them the freedom they need to explore radically new ideas that would yield real scientific advance.

It is important to realise that paradigms themselves are often influenced at a very deep level by worldview considerations. We saw earlier that there are essentially two fundamental worldviews, the materialistic and the theistic. It seems to be the case in science that there is sometimes a tacit understanding that only paradigms which are based on materialism are admissible as scientific. Richard Dawkins, for example, says, 'the kind of explanation we come up with must not contradict the laws of physics. Indeed it will make use of the laws of physics, and nothing more than the laws of physics.'[20] It is the words 'nothing more than' that show that Dawkins is only prepared to accept reductionist, materialistic explanations.

Further reading

God and Stephen Hawking: Whose Design Is It Anyway? (Lion, 2011)

God's Undertaker: Has Science Buried God? (Lion, 2009)

Gunning for God: A Critique of the New Atheism (Lion, 2011)

Miracles: Is Belief in the Supernatural Irrational? VeriTalks Vol. 2. (The Veritas Forum, 2013)

Seven Days That Divide the World (Zondervan, 2011)

[20] Dawkins, *Blind Watchmaker*, 24.

SERIES BIBLIOGRAPHY

See also reading lists given on pp. 245n8, and 285.

BOOKS

A

Abbott, Edwin. *Flatland: A Romance of Many Dimensions*. London, 1884. Repr. Oxford: Oxford University Press, 2006.

Ambrose, E. J. *The Nature and Origin of the Biological World*. New York: Halsted Press, 1982.

Ammon, Otto. *Die Gesellschaftsordnung und ihre natürlichen Grundlagen*. Jena: Gustav Fisher, 1895.

Anderson, J. N. D. (Norman). *Christianity: The Witness of History*. London: Tyndale Press, 1969.

Anderson, J. N. D. (Norman). *The Evidence for the Resurrection*. 1950. Leicester: InterVarsity Press, 1990.

Anderson, J. N. D. (Norman). *Islam in the Modern World*. Leicester: Apollos, 1990.

Andreyev, G. L. *What Kind of Morality Does Religion Teach?* Moscow: 'Znaniye', 1959.

Aristotle. *Metaphysics*. Tr. W. D. Ross, *Aristotle's Metaphysics: A Revised Text with Introduction and Commentary*. Vol. 2. Oxford: Clarendon Press, 1924.

Aristotle. *Nicomachean Ethics*. Tr. W. D. Ross. Oxford: Clarendon Press, 1925. Repr. Kitchener, Ont.: Batoche Books, 1999. Also tr. David Ross. Oxford: Oxford University Press, 1980.

Arnold, Thomas. *Christian Life, Its Hopes, Its Fears, and Its Close: Sermons preached mostly in the chapel of Rugby School, 1841–1842*. 1842. New edn, London: Longmans, 1878.

Ashman, Keith M. and Philip S. Baringer, eds. *After the Science Wars*. London: Routledge, 2001.

Atkins, Peter. *Creation Revisited*. Harmondsworth: Penguin, 1994.

Augustine of Hippo. *Confessions*. AD 397–400. Tr. Henry Chadwick, *The Confessions*. Oxford, 1991. Repr. Oxford World's Classics. Oxford: Oxford University Press, 2008.

Avise, John C. *The Genetic Gods, Evolution and Belief in Human Affairs*. Cambridge, Mass.: Harvard University Press, 1998.

Ayer, A. J., ed. *The Humanist Outlook*. London: Pemberton, 1968.

B

Bacon, Francis. *Advancement of Learning.* 1605. Ed. G. W. Kitchin, 1915. Repr. London: Dent, 1930. http://archive.org/details/advancementlearn00bacouoft (facsimile of 1915 edn).

Bādarāyana, Śankarācārya and George Thibaut. *The Vedānta Sūtras of Bādarāyana.* Vol. 34 of *Sacred books of the East.* Oxford: Clarendon Press, 1890.

Baier, Kurt. *The Moral Point of View: A Rational Basis of Ethics.* Ithaca, N.Y.: Cornell University Press, 1958.

Behe, Michael J. *Darwin's Black Box: The Biochemical Challenge to Evolution.* 1988. 10th ann. edn with new Afterword, New York: Simon & Schuster, 2006.

Bentham, Jeremy. *An Introduction to the Principles of Morals and Legislation.* 1780, 1789. Dover Philosophical Classics. Repr. of Bentham's 1823 rev. edn, Mineola, N.Y.: Dover Publications, 2007.

Berdyaev, N. A. *The Beginning and The End.* Tr. R. M. French. London: Geoffrey Bles, 1952.

Berlinski, David. *The Deniable Darwin and Other Essays.* Seattle, Wash.: Discovery Institute, 2009.

Bickerton, Derek. *Language and Species.* 1990. Repr. Chicago: University of Chicago Press, 1992.

Biddiss, M. D. *Father of Racist Ideology: The Social and Political Thought of Count Gobineau.* New York: Weybright & Talley, 1970.

Bouquet, A. C. *Comparative Religion.* Harmondsworth: Penguin (Pelican), 1962.

Breck, John. *The Sacred Gift of Life: Orthodox Christianity and Bioethics.* Crestwood, N.Y.: St. Vladimir's Seminary Press, 1998.

Bronowski, Jacob. *The Identity of Man.* Harmondsworth: Penguin, 1967.

Brow, Robert. *Religion, Origins and Ideas.* London: Tyndale Press, 1966.

Bruce, F. F. *1 and 2 Corinthians.* New Century Bible Commentary. London: Oliphants, 1971.

Bruce, F. F. *The New Testament Documents: Are They Reliable?* 1943. 6th edn, Nottingham: Inter-Varsity Press, 2000.

Butterfield, Herbert. *Christianity and History.* London: Bell, 1949. Repr. London: Fontana, 1958.

C

Cairns-Smith, A. G. *The Life Puzzle.* Edinburgh: Oliver & Boyd, 1971.

Caputo, John D., ed. *Deconstruction in a Nutshell: A Conversation with Jacques Derrida.* Perspectives in Continental Philosophy No. 1. 1997. Repr. New York: Fordham University Press, 2004.

Cary, M. and T. J. Haarhoff. *Life and Thought in the Greek and Roman World.* 5th edn, London: Methuen, 1951.

Chalmers, David J. *The Conscious Mind: In Search of a Fundamental Theory.* Oxford: Oxford University Press, 1996.

Chamberlain, Paul. *Can We Be Good Without God?: A Conversation about Truth, Morality, Culture and a Few Other Things That Matter.* Downers Grove, Ill.: InterVarsity Press, 1996.

Chomsky, Noam. *Knowledge of Language: Its Nature, Origin and Use.* New York: Praeger, 1986.

Chomsky, Noam. *Language and Mind.* 1972. 3rd edn, Cambridge: Cambridge University Press, 2006.

Chomsky, Noam. *Syntactic Structures.* The Hague: Mouton, 1957.

Cicero, Marcus Tullius. *Cicero, Selected Political Speeches.* Tr. Michael Grant. Harmondsworth: Penguin Books, 1969.

Cicero, Marcus Tullius. *De Natura Deorum.* Tr. H. Rackham, Loeb Classical Library, No. 268. Cambridge, Mass.: Harvard University Press, 1933.

Cicero, Marcus Tullius. *The Nature of the Gods.* Tr. H. C. P. McGregor. London: Penguin, 1972.

Cicero, Marcus Tullius. *Pro Rabirio.*

Clement of Alexandria. Stromata [or, Miscellanies]. In Kirk, G. S., J. E. Raven and M. Schofield. *The Presocratic Philosophers: A Critical History with a Selection of Texts.* 1957. Rev. edn, Cambridge: Cambridge University Press, 1983. Online at http://www.ccel.org/ccel/ schaff/anf02.vi.iv.html, accessed 29 Sept. 2015.

Cornford, F. M. *Before and After Socrates.* 1932. Repr. Cambridge: Cambridge University Press, 1999. doi: 10.1017/CBO9780511570308, accessed 29 Sept. 2015.

Craig, Edward, gen. ed. *Concise Routledge Encyclopaedia of Philosophy.* London: Routledge, 2000.

Craig, William Lane. *Reasonable Faith: Christian Truth and Apologetics.* 1994. 3rd edn, Wheaton, Ill.: Crossway, 2008.

Crane, Stephen. *War Is Kind.* New York: Frederick A. Stokes, 1899. http://www.gutenberg.org/ebooks/9870, accessed 11 Sept. 2015.

Cranfield, C. E. B. *A Critical and Exegetical Commentary on the Epistle to the Romans.* Vol. 1. The International Critical Commentary. Edinburgh: T&T Clark, 1975.

Crick, Francis. *The Astonishing Hypothesis: The Scientific Search for the Soul.* New York: Scribner, 1994.

Crick, Francis. *Life Itself: Its Origin and Nature.* New York: Simon & Schuster, 1981.

Crick, Francis. *Of Molecules and Men.* 1966 Jessie and John Danz Lectures. Seattle, Wash.: University of Washington Press, 1966.

Cudakov. A. *Komsomol'skaja Pravda* (11 Oct. 1988).

Culler, Jonathan. *On Deconstruction: Theory and Criticism after Structuralism.* 1982. 25th ann. edn, Ithaca, N.Y.: Cornell University Press, 2007.

D

Darwin, Charles. *The Descent of Man, and Selection in Relation to Sex.* 1871. 2nd edn, New York: A. L. Burt, 1874. Ed. James Moore and Adrian Desmond, Penguin Classics, London: Penguin Books, 2004.

Darwin, Charles. *On the Origin of Species*. 1859. Repr. World's Classics Edition, Oxford: Oxford University Press, 2008. Also cited is the 6th edn (1872) reprinted by New York University Press, 1988. Citations to one or the other edition are indicated as such.

Darwin, Francis. *The Life and Letters of Charles Darwin*. London: John Murray, 1887. doi: http://dx.doi.org/10.5962/bhl.title.1416, accessed 29 June 2015.

Davies, Paul. *The Cosmic Blueprint: New Discoveries in Nature's Creative Ability to Order the Universe*. 1988. Repr. West Conshohocken, Pa.: Templeton Foundation Press, 2004.

Davies, Paul. *The Fifth Miracle: The Search for the Origin and Meaning of Life*. 1999. Repr. New York: Touchstone, 2000.

Davies, Paul. *God and the New Physics*. London: J. M. Dent, 1983. Repr. London: Penguin Books, 1990.

Davies, Paul. *The Mind of God: Science and the Search for Ultimate Meaning*. 1992. Repr. London: Simon & Schuster, 2005.

Davies, Paul and John Gribbin. *The Matter Myth: Dramatic Discoveries that Challenge Our Understanding of Physical Reality*. London, 1991. Repr. London: Simon & Schuster, 2007.

Davis, Percival and Dean H. Kenyon. *Of Pandas and People: The Central Question of Biological Origins*. 1989. 2nd edn, Dallas, Tex.: Haughton Publishing, 1993.

Dawkins, Richard. *The Blind Watchmaker*. 1986. Rev. edn, 2006. Repr. London: Penguin, 2013.

Dawkins, Richard. *Climbing Mount Improbable*. New York: Norton, 1996.

Dawkins, Richard. *Growing Up in the Universe*. The Royal Institution Christmas Lectures for Children, 1991. Five one-hour episodes directed by Stuart McDonald for the BBC. 2-Disc DVD set released 20 April 2007 by the Richard Dawkins Foundation. Available on the Ri Channel, http://www.richannel.org/christmas-lectures/1991/richard-dawkins. Study Guide with the same title. London: BBC Education, 1991.

Dawkins, Richard. *River Out of Eden: A Darwinian View of Life*. 1995. Repr. London: Phoenix, 2004.

Dawkins, Richard. *The Selfish Gene*. 1976. Repr. 30th ann. edn, Oxford: Oxford University Press, 2006.

Dawkins, Richard. *Unweaving the Rainbow: Science, Delusion and the Appetite for Wonder*. 1998. Repr. London: Penguin Books, 2006.

Dawkins, Richard and John Lennox. 'The God Delusion Debate', hosted by Fixed Point Foundation, University of Alabama at Birmingham, filmed and broadcast live 3 October 2007, http://fixed-point.org/index.php/video/35-full-length/164-the-dawkins-lennox-debate. Transcript provided courtesy of ProTorah.com, http://www.protorah.com/god-delusion-debate-dawkins-lennox-transcript/.

Deacon, Terrence. *The Symbolic Species: The Co-Evolution of Language and the Human Brain*. London: Allen Lane, 1997.

Dembski, William A. *Being as Communion: A Metaphysics of Information*. Ashgate Science and Religion. Farnham, Surrey: Ashgate, 2014.

Dembski, William A. *The Design Inference: Eliminating Chance through Small Probabilities.* Cambridge Studies in Probability, Induction and Decision Theory. Cambridge: Cambridge University Press, 1998.

Dembski, William A., ed. *Uncommon Dissent: Intellectuals Who Find Darwinism Unconvincing.* Wilmington, Del.: Intercollegiate Studies Institute, 2004.

Dennett, Daniel. *Darwin's Dangerous Idea: Evolution and the Meanings of Life.* 1995; London: Penguin, 1996.

Denton, Michael. *Evolution: A Theory in Crisis.* 1986. 3rd rev. edn, Bethesda, Md.: Adler & Adler, 1986.

Derrida, Jacques. *Of Grammatology.* 1967 (French). Tr. G. C. Spivak, 1974. Repr. Baltimore, Md.: Johns Hopkins University Press, 1997.

Derrida, Jacques. *Positions.* 1972 (French). Tr. and ed. Alan Bass, 1981. 2nd edn 2002. Repr. London: Continuum, 2010.

Derrida, Jacques. *Writing and Difference.* 1967 (French). Tr. Alan Bass, Chicago, 1978. Repr. London: Routledge Classics, 2001.

Descartes, René. *Discourse on the Method of Rightly Conducting Reason and Reaching the Truth in the Sciences.* 1637. http://www.gutenberg.org/files/59/59-h/59-h.htm, accessed 11 Sept. 2015.

Descartes, René. *Meditations on First Philosophy.* Paris, 1641.

Deutsch, David. *The Fabric of Reality.* London: Penguin, 1997.

Dewey, John. *A Common Faith.* New Haven: Yale University Press, 1934.

Dostoevsky, F. *The Collected Works of Dostoevsky.* Tr. Rodion Raskolnikoff [German]. Munich: Piper, 1866.

Dostoevsky, Fyodor. *The Karamazov Brothers.* 1880 (Russian). Tr. and ed. David McDuff, Penguin Classics, 1993. Rev. edn, London: Penguin Books, 2003.

E

Eastwood, C. Cyril. *Life and Thought in the Ancient World.* Derby: Peter Smith, 1964.

Easwaran, Eknath. *The Bhagavad Gita.* 1985. Berkeley, Calif.: Nilgiri Press, 2007.

Easwaran, Eknath. *The Upanishads.* 1987. Berkeley, Calif.: Nilgiri Press, 2007.

Eccles, John C. *Evolution of the Brain, Creation of the Self.* 1989. Repr. London: Routledge, 2005.

Einstein, A. *Letters to Solovine: 1906–1955.* New York: Philosophical Library, 1987.

Einstein, A. *Out of My Later Years: The Scientist, Philosopher, and Man Portrayed Through His Own Words.* 1956. Secaucus, N.J.: Carol Publishing, 1995.

Eldredge, Niles. *Reinventing Darwin: The Great Debate at the High Table of Evolutionary Theory.* New York: Wiley, 1995.

Eldredge, Niles. *Time Frames: The Evolution of Punctuated Equilibria.* 1985. Corr. edn, Princeton, N.J.: Princeton University Press, 1989.

Ellis, John M. *Against Deconstruction.* Princeton, N.J.: Princeton University Press, 1989.

The Encyclopedia Britannica. 15th edn (*Britannica 3*), ed. Warren E. Preece and Philip W. Goetz. Chicago: Encyclopaedia Britannica, 1974–2012.

Engels, Friedrich. *Ludwig Feuerbach and the End of Classical German Philosophy.* German original first published in 1886, in *Die Neue Zeit.* Moscow: Progress Publishers, 1946.

Erbrich, Paul. *Zufall: Eine Naturwissenschaftlich-Philosophische Untersuchung.* Stuttgart: Kohlhammer, 1988.

Euripides. *The Bacchae.* Tr. James Morwood, *Bacchae and Other Plays.* Oxford World's Classics. 1999. Repr. Oxford: Oxford University Press, 2008.

Evans-Pritchard, E. E. *Nuer Religion.* 1956. 2nd edn, London: Oxford University Press, 1971.

F

Feuerbach, Ludwig. *The Essence of Christianity.* 1841. Ed. and tr. George Eliot (Mary Ann Evans). New York: Harper Torchbooks, 1957.

Feynman, Richard. *Six Easy Pieces.* 1963. Repr. London: Penguin Books, 1995.

Fischer, Ernst. *Marx in His Own Words.* Tr. Anna Bostock. London: Penguin Books, 1973.

Fish, Stanley. *Is There a Text in This Class? The Authority of Interpretive Communities.* Cambridge, Mass.: Harvard University Press, 1980.

Fish, Stanley. *There's No Such Thing as Free Speech, and It's a Good Thing Too.* New York: Oxford University Press, 1994.

Flew, Antony with Roy Abraham Varghese. *There Is a God: How the World's Most Notorious Atheist Changed His Mind.* London: HarperCollins, 2007.

Fox, S. W., ed. *The Origins of Prebiological Systems and of Their Molecular Matrices.* New York: Academic Press, 1965.

Frazer, J. G. *The Golden Bough.* 1890, 1900, 1906–15, 1937.

Fromm, Erich. *You Shall be as Gods: A Radical Interpretation of the Old Testament and its Tradition.* New York: Holt, Rinehart & Winston, 1966.

G

Gates, Bill. *The Road Ahead.* 1995. Rev. edn, Harmondsworth: Penguin, 1996.

Geisler, Norman L., Nix, William E., *A General Introduction to the Bible* (Chicago: Moody Press, 1986), 475. Gerson, Lloyd P. *Plotinus.* London: Routledge, 1994.

Gilligan, Carol. *In a Different Voice: Psychological Theory and Women's Development.* Cambridge, Mass.: Harvard University Press, 1982.

Goldschmidt, Richard. *The Material Basis of Evolution.* The Silliman Memorial Lectures Series. 1940. Repr. Yale University Press, 1982.

Gooding, David W. and John C. Lennox. *The Human Quest for Significance: Forming a Worldview* [in Russian]. Minsk: Myrtlefield Trust, 1999.

Gould, Stephen Jay. *The Lying Stones of Marrakech: Penultimate Reflections in Natural History.* 2000. Repr. Cambridge, Mass.: Harvard University Press, 2011.

Gould, Stephen Jay. *Wonderful Life: The Burgess Shale and the Nature of History.* 1989. Repr. London: Vintage, 2000.

Grant, Michael. *Jesus: An Historian's Review of the Gospels.* New York: Scribner, 1977.

Grene, Marjorie. *A Portrait of Aristotle*. London: Faber & Faber, 1963.

Groothuis, Douglas. *Truth Decay: Defending Christianity against the Challenges of Postmodernism*. Leicester: Inter-Varsity Press, 2000.

Guthrie, W. K. C. *The Greek Philosophers from Thales to Aristotle*. 1950. Repr. London: Methuen, 2013.

Guthrie, W. K. C. *Plato: the man and his dialogues, earlier period*. Vol. 4 of *A History of Greek Philosophy*. 1875. Repr. Cambridge: Cambridge University Press, 2000.

H

Haldane, J. B. S. *Possible Worlds*. 1927. London: Chatto & Windus, 1945.

Harrison, E. *Masks of the Universe*. 1985. 2nd edn, New York: Macmillan, 2003. Citations are to the first Macmillan edition.

Harvey, William. *On the Motion of the Heart and the Blood of Animals*. 1628. http://legacy.fordham.edu/halsall/mod/1628harvey-blood.asp, accessed 11 Sept. 2015.

Hawking, Stephen. *A Brief History of Time*. 1988. Updated and expanded 10th ann. edn, London: Bantam Press, 1998.

Hawking, Stephen and Leonard Mlodinow. *The Grand Design*. New York: Bantam Books, 2010.

Hegel, G. W. F. *Hegel's Logic*. Being Part One of the Encyclopaedia of the Philosophical Sciences (1830). Tr. William Wallace, 1892. Repr. Oxford: Clarendon Press, 1984–87.

Hegel, G. W. F. *The Phenomenology of the Mind* (Spirit). 1807. 2nd edn 1841. Tr. J. B. Baillie, London, 1910. Repr. Dover Philosophical Classics, New York: Dover Publications, 2003.

Hegel, G. W. F. *The Philosophy of History*. 1861. Tr. J. Sibree, 1857. Repr. New York: Dover Publications, 1956. Repr. Kitchener, Ont.: Batoche Books, 2001. http://www.efm.bris.ac.uk/het/hegel/history.pdf (facsimile), accessed 11 Sept. 2015.

Hegel, G. W. F. *Wissenschaft der Logik* [The Science of Logic]. Nurnberg, 1812–16.

Hemer, Colin. *The Book of Acts in the Setting of Hellenistic History*. Tübingen: J. C. B. Mohr, Paul Siebeck, 1989.

Hengel, Martin. *Judaism and Hellenism: Studies in their Encounter in Palestine during the Early Hellenistic Period*. Tr. John Bowden. London: SCM Press, 1974. Repr. Eugene, Oreg.: Wipf & Stock, 2003.

Hengel, Martin. *Studies in Early Christology*. Tr. Rollin Kearns. Edinburgh: T&T Clark, 1995.

Herodotus. *The Histories*. Tr. Robin Waterfield, 1998, Oxford World's Classics. Repr. New York: Oxford University Press, 2008.

Herzen, Alexander Ivanovich. *Byloe i dumy*. London, 1853. Tr. C. Garnett, *My Past and Thoughts, The Memoirs of Alexander Herzen*. Revised by H. Higgens, introduced by I. Berlin, 1968. Repr. London: Chatto and Windus, 2008.

Hesiod. *Theogony*. In Charles Abraham Elton, tr. *The remains of Hesiod*. London: Lackington, Allen, 1812. Also in Dorothea Wender, tr. *Hesiod and Theognis*. Harmondsworth: Penguin, 1973.

Hippolytus, *Refutation of all Heresies*. In Kirk, G. S., J. E. Raven and M. Schofield. *The Presocratic Philosophers: A Critical History with a Selection of Texts*. 1957. Rev. edn, Cambridge: Cambridge University Press, 1983.

Holmes, Arthur F. *Ethics*. Downers Grove, Ill.: InterVarsity Press, 1984; 2nd edn, 2007.

Honderich, Ted, ed. *The Oxford Companion to Philosophy*. Oxford, 1995. 2nd edn, Oxford: Oxford University Press, 2005.

Hooper, Judith. *Of Moths and Men*. New York: Norton, 2002.

Hooykaas, R. *Religion and the Rise of Modern Science*. 1972. Repr. Edinbugh: Scottish Academic Press, 2000.

Hospers, John. *An Introduction to Philosophical Analysis*. 1953. 4th edn, Abingdon: Routledge, 1997.

Houghton, John. *The Search for God—Can Science Help?* Oxford: Lion Publishing, 1995.

Hoyle, Fred. *The Intelligent Universe*. London: Joseph, 1983.

Hoyle, Fred and Chandra Wickramasinghe. *Cosmic Life-Force, the Power of Life Across the Universe*. London: Dent, 1988.

Hoyle, Fred and Chandra Wickramasinghe. *Evolution from Space: A Theory of Cosmic Creationism*. New York: Simon & Schuster, 1984.

Hume, David. *David Hume: A Treatise of Human Nature*. 1739–40. Ed. Lewis Amherst Selby-Bigge and P. H. Nidditch. Oxford: Clarendon Press, 1888. Repr. 1978. Repr. Oxford: Oxford University Press, 2014. doi: 10.1093/actrade/9780198245872.book.1, accessed 11 Sept. 2015.

Hume, David. *Dialogues Concerning Natural Religion*. 1779. Repr. ed. J. C. A. Gaskin, *Dialogues Concerning Natural Religion, and The Natural History of Religion*. Oxford World's Classics. Oxford: Oxford University Press, 2008. http://www.davidhume.org/texts/dnr.html, accessed 2 Aug. 2017. (Abbreviated as DNR.)

Hume, David. *An Enquiry Concerning Human Understanding*. London: A. Millar, 1748. Repr. Dover Philosophical Classics, Mineola, N.Y.: Dover Publications, 2012. http://www.davidhume.org/texts/ehu.html, accessed 2 Aug. 2017. (Abbreviated as EHU.)

Hume, David. *Treatise of Human Nature*. 1739–40. Eds. David Norton and Mary J. Norton, *David Hume: A Treatise of Human Nature: A critical edition*. Vol. 1 of The Clarendon Edition of The Works Of David Hume. Oxford: Oxford University Press, 2007. http://www.davidhume.org/texts/thn.html, accessed 2 Aug. 2017. (Abbreviated as THN.)

Hunt, R. N. Carew. *The Theory and Practice of Communism*. Baltimore: Penguin Books, 1966.

Hurley, Thomas. *Method and Results: Collected Essays*. Vol. I. London: Macmillan, 1898.

Husserl, Edmund. *Ideas: General Introduction to Pure Phenomenology*. Ger. orig. *Ideen zu einer reinen Phänomenologie und phänomenologischen Philosophie. Erstes Buch: Allgemeine Einführung in die reine Phänomenologie* (1913). Tr. W. R. Boyce Gibson. London: Macmillan, 1931.

Huxley, Julian. *Essays of a Humanist*. 1964. Repr. Harmondsworth: Penguin Books, 1969.

Huxley, Julian. *Religion Without Revelation*. New York: Mentor, 1957.

I

Isherwood, Christopher, ed. *Vedanta for Modern Man*. 1951. Repr. New York: New American Library, 1972.

J

Jacob, François. *Chance and Necessity: An Essay on the Natural Philosophy of Modern Biology*. Tr. Austryn Wainhouse. New York: Alfred A. Knopf, 1971.

Jacob, François. *The Logic of Life: A History of Heredity*. Tr. Betty E. Spillman. New York: Pantheon Books, 1973.

Jaeger, Werner. *The Theology of the Early Greek Philosophers*. The Gifford Lectures, 1936. Oxford: Oxford University Press, 1967.

James, E. O. *Christianity and Other Religions*. London: Hodder & Stoughton, 1968.

Jaroszwski, T. M. and P. A. Ignatovsky, eds. *Socialism as a Social System*. Moscow: Progress Publishers, 1981.

Jeremias, J. *New Testament Theology: The Proclamation of Jesus*. Tr. John Bowden. New York: Scribner, 1971.

Joad, C. E. M. *The Book of Joad: A Belligerent Autobiography* [= *Under the Fifth Rib*]. London: Faber & Faber, 1944.

Johnson, Phillip E. *Objections Sustained: Subversive Essays on Evolution, Law and Culture*. Downers Grove, Ill.: InterVarsity Press, 1998.

Jones, Steve. *In the Blood: God, Genes and Destiny*. London: Harper Collins, 1996.

Josephus, Flavius. *Antiquities of the Jews*. Tr. William Whiston, *The Works of Flavius Josephus*. 1737. Repr. Grand Rapids: Kregel, 1974. Repr. Peabody, Mass.: Hendrickson, 1995.

K

Kant, Immanuel. *Critique of Practical Reason*. 1788. Tr. and ed. Mary Gregor. Cambridge Texts in the History of Philosophy. 1997. Repr. Cambridge: Cambridge University Press, 2003.

Kant, Immanuel. *Critique of Pure Reason*. 1781. 2nd edn, 1787. Tr. Norman Kemp Smith. London: Macmillan, 1929. Repr. Blunt Press, 2007. Also Paul Guyer and Allen Wood, eds., Cambridge: Cambridge University Press, 1999.

Kant, Immanuel. *Groundwork of the Metaphysics of Morals*. 1785. In H. J. Paton, tr. *The Moral Law*. London: Hutchinson, 1972.

Kant, Immanuel. *The Metaphysics of Morals*. 1797. Tr. and ed. Mary J. Gregor. Cambridge Texts in the History of Philosophy. Cambridge: Cambridge University Press, 1996.

Kant, Immanuel. *Prolegomena to Any Future Metaphysics*. 1783. Tr. and ed. Gary Hatfield, *Prolegomena to Any Future Metaphysics with Selections from the Critique of Pure Reason*. Cambridge Texts in the History of Philosophy. 1997. Rev. edn, Cambridge: Cambridge University Press, 2004.

Kantikar, V. P. (Hemant) and W. Owen. *Hinduism—An Introduction: Teach Yourself*. 1995. Repr. London: Hodder Headline, 2010.

Kaye, Howard L. *The Social Meaning of Modern Biology, From Social Darwinism to Sociobiology*. 1986. Repr. with a new epilogue, New Brunswick, N.J.: Transaction Publishers, 1997.

Kenny, Anthony. *An Illustrated Brief History of Western Philosophy*. Oxford: Blackwell, 2006. First published as *A Brief History of Western Philosophy*, 1998.

Kenyon, D. H. and G. Steinman. *Biochemical Predestination*. New York: McGraw-Hill, 1969.

Kenyon, Frederic. *Our Bible and the Ancient Manuscripts*. 1895. 4th edn, 1938. Repr. Eugene, Oreg.: Wipf & Stock, 2011.

Kilner, J. F., C. C. Hook and D. B. Uustal, eds. *Cutting-Edge Bioethics: A Christian Exploration of Technologies and Trends*. Grand Rapids: Eerdmans, 2002.

Kirk, G. S., J. E. Raven and M. Schofield. *The Presocratic Philosophers: A Critical History with a Selection of Texts*. 1957. Rev. edn, Cambridge: Cambridge University Press, 1983.

Kirk, M. and H. Madsen. *After the Ball*. New York: Plume Books, 1989.

Knott, Kim. *Hinduism: A Very Short Introduction*. Oxford: Oxford University Press, 1998.

Koertge, Noretta, ed. *A House Built on Sand: Exposing Postmodernist Myths About Science*. Oxford: Oxford University Press, 1998.

Kolbanovskiy, V. N. *Communist Morality*. Moscow, 1951.

Krikorian, Yervant H., ed. *Naturalism and the Human Spirit*. 1944. Repr. New York: Columbia University Press, 1969.

Kuhn, Thomas. *The Structure of Scientific Revolutions*. 1962. 3rd edn, Chicago: University of Chicago Press, 1996.

Kurtz, Paul. *The Fullness of Life*. New York: Horizon Press, 1974.

Kurtz, Paul. *The Humanist Alternative*. Buffalo, N.Y.: Prometheus, 1973.

Kurtz, Paul, ed. *Humanist Manifestos I & II*. Buffalo, N.Y.: Prometheus, 1980.

Kurtz, Paul, ed. *Humanist Manifesto II*. Buffalo, N.Y.: Prometheus Books, 1980. http://americanhumanist.org/Humanism/Humanist_Manifesto_II, accessed 11 Sept. 2105.

L

Lamont, Corliss. *A Lifetime of Dissent*. Buffalo, N.Y.: Prometheus Books, 1988.

Lamont, Corliss. *The Philosophy of Humanism*. 1947. 8th edn, Emherst, N.Y.: Humanist Press, 1997.

Lapouge, G. Vacher de. *Les Sélections Sociales*. Paris: Fontemoing, 1899.

Leakey, Richard. *The Origin of Humankind*. London: Weidenfeld & Nicolson, 1994.

Leitch, Vincent B. *Deconstructive Criticism: An Advanced Introduction*. New York: Columbia University Press, 1982.

Lenin, V. I. *Complete Collected Works*. Tr. Andrew Rothstein. 4th Eng. edn, Moscow: Progress Publishers, 1960–78. http://www.marx2mao.com/Lenin/Index.html (facsimile), accessed 11 Sept. 2015. Repr. Moscow: Progress Publishers, 1982.

Lenin, V. I. *Materialism and Empirico-Criticism*. New York: International Publishers, 1927.

Lennox, John C. *Determined to Believe: The Sovereignty of God, Freedom, Faith and Human*. Oxford: Monarch Books, 2017.

Lennox, John C. *God and Stephen Hawking: Whose Design is it Anyway?* Oxford: Lion, 2010.

Lennox, John C. *God's Undertaker: Has Science Buried God?* Oxford, Lion Books, 2007, 2009.

Leslie, John. *Universes*. London: Routledge, 1989.

Levinskaya, Irina. *The Book of Acts in its First Century Setting*. Vol. 5. Diaspora Setting. Grand Rapids: Eerdmans, 1996.

Lewis, C. S. *The Abolition of Man*. London, 1945. Repr. London: Collins, Fount, 1978.

Lewis, C. S. *Christian Reflections*. London, 1967. Repr. New York: HarperCollins, 1998.

Lewis, C. S. *God in the Dock*. London, 1979. Repr. Grand Rapids: Eerdmans, 2014.

Lewis, C. S. *Mere Christianity*. London, 1952. Rev. edn with new introduction and foreword by Kathleen Norris, New York: HarperCollins, 2001.

Lewis, C. S. *Miracles*. 1947. Repr. London: Collins, 2012.

Lewis, C. S. *The Problem of Pain*. 1940. Repr. London: Collins, 2009.

Lewis, C. S. *Transposition and other Addresses*. London: Geoffrey Bles, 1949.

Lewontin, Richard. *The Dialectical Biologist*. Cambridge, Mass.: Harvard University Press, 1987.

Locke, John. *An Essay Concerning Human Understanding*. London, 1689. Ed. Peter H. Nidditch, Oxford: Oxford University Press, 1975.

Long, A. A. *Hellenistic Philosophy*. 1974. 2nd edn, Berkeley, Calif.: University of California Press, 1986.

Lossky, N. O. *History of Russian Philosophy*. London: Allen & Unwin, 1952.

Lucretius (Titus Lucretius Carus). *De Rerum Natura*. 50 BC. Tr. A. E. Stallings as *The Nature of Things*. London: Penguin, 2007. Also tr. and ed. William Ellery Leonard. 1916. Online at: http://www.perseus.tufts.edu/hopper/text?doc=Lucr or http://classics.mit.edu/Carus/nature_things.html.

Lumsden, Charles J. and Edward O. Wilson. *Promethean Fire: Reflections on the Origin of Mind*. Cambridge, Mass.: Harvard University Press, 1983.

M

Mabbott, J. D. *An Introduction to Ethics*. Hutchinson University Library. London: Hutchinson, 1966.

McKay, Donald. *The Clockwork Image: A Christian Perspective on Science*. London: Inter-Varsity Press, 1974.

Majerus, Michael. *Melanism: Evolution in Action*. Oxford: Oxford University Press, 1998.

Margenau, Henry and Roy Abraham Varghese, eds. *Cosmos, Bios, and Theos: Scientists Reflect on Science, God, and the Origins of the Universe, Life, and Homo Sapiens*. La Salle, Ill.: Open Court, 1992.

Marx, Karl. Marx's *Theses on Feuerbach*. 1845.

Mascall, E. L. *Words and Images, a study in the Possibility of Religious Discourse*. London: Longmans, 1957.

Mascarō, Juan, tr. *The Upanishads*. Harmondsworth: Penguin, 1965.

Maslow, Abraham. *Towards a Psychology of Being*. New York: Van Nostrand Reinhold, 1968.

Masterson, Patrick. *Atheism and Alienation*. Harmondsworth: Pelican Books, 1972.

May, Rollo. *Psychology and the Human Dilemma*. Princeton, N.J., 1967. Repr. New York: Norton, 1996.

Medawar, Peter. *Advice to a Young Scientist*. New York: Harper & Row, 1979.

Medawar, Peter. *The Limits of Science*. Oxford: Oxford University Press, 1985.

Medawar, Peter and Jean Medawar. *The Life Science*. London: Wildwood House, 1977.

Metzger, Bruce. *The Text of the New Testament, its Transmission, Corruption and Restoration*. 1964. 3rd edn, Oxford: Oxford University Press, 1992.

Mill, John Stuart. *Utilitarianism*. 1861, 1863. Repr. Mineola, N.Y.: Dover Publications, 2007.

Millard, Alan. *Reading and Writing in the Time of Jesus*. Sheffield: Sheffield Academic Press, 2000.

Miller, David, Janet Coleman, William Connolly, and Alan Ryan, eds. *The Blackwell Encyclopaedia of Political Thought*. 1987. Repr. Oxford: Blackwell, 1991.

Monod, Jacques. *Chance and Necessity: An Essay on the Natural Philosophy of Modern Biology*. 1970 (French). Tr. Austryn Wainhouse, 1971. Repr. London: Penguin Books, 1997. Citations are from Vintage Books 1972 edn.

Monod, Jacques. *From Biology to Ethics*. San Diego: Salk Institute for Biological Studies, 1969.

Morris, Simon Conway. *The Crucible of Creation: The Burgess Shale and the Rise of Animals*. 1998. New edn, Oxford: Oxford University Press, 1999.

Mossner, Ernest C., ed. *David Hume, A Treatise of Human Nature*. London: Penguin Classics, 1985.

Moule, C. F. D. *The Phenomenon of the New Testament: An Inquiry into the Implications of Certain Features of the New Testament*. London: SCM, 1967.

Murphy, John P. *Pragmatism: From Peirce to Davidson*. Boulder, Colo.: Westview Press, 1990.

N

Nagel, Thomas. *The Last Word*. Oxford: Oxford University Press, 1997.

Nagel, Thomas. *Mortal Questions*. Cambridge: Cambridge University Press. 1979.

Nahem, Joseph. *Psychology and Psychiatry Today: A Marxist View.* New York: International Publishers, 1981.

Nasr, Seyyed Hossein, and Oliver Leaman, eds. *History of Islamic Philosophy.* Part 1, Vol. 1 of *Routledge History of World Philosophies.* 1996. Repr. London: Routledge, 2001.

Nettleship, R. L. *Lectures on the Republic of Plato.* London: Macmillan, 1922.

Newton, Isaac. *Principia Mathematica.* London, 1687.

Nietzsche, Friedrich. *Beyond Good and Evil: Prelude to a Philosophy of the Future.* Leipzig, 1886. 1973. Repr. tr. R. J. Hollingdale, Harmondsworth: Penguin, 1975.

Noddings, Nel. *Caring: A Feminine Approach to Ethics and Moral Education.* 1984. Repr. Berkeley, Calif.: University of California Press, 2013.

Norris, Christopher. *Deconstruction: Theory and Practice.* 1982. 3rd edn, London: Methuen, 2002.

O

Olivelle, Patrick. *The Early Upanishads: Annotated Text and Translation.* 1996. Repr. Oxford: Oxford University Press, 1998.

O'Meara, Dominic J. *Plotinus: An Introduction to the Enneads.* Oxford: Clarendon Press, 1993.

P

Paley, William. *Natural Theology on Evidence and Attributes of Deity.* 1802. Repr. Oxford: Oxford University Press, 2006.

Patterson, Colin. *Evolution.* 1978. 2nd edn, Ithaca, N.Y.: Cornstock Publishing Associates, 1999.

Peacocke, Arthur. *The Experiment of Life.* Toronto: University of Toronto Press, 1983.

Pearsall, Judy and Bill Trumble, eds. *The Oxford English Reference Dictionary.* 2nd edn, Oxford: Oxford University Press, 1996.

Pearse, E. K. Victor. *Evidence for Truth: Science.* Guildford: Eagle, 1998.

Penfield, Wilder. *The Mystery of the Mind.* Princeton, N.J.: Princeton University Press, 1975.

Penrose, Roger. *The Emperor's New Mind.* 1986. Repr. with new preface, Oxford: Oxford University Press, 1999.

Penrose, Roger. *The Road to Reality: A Complete Guide to the Laws of the Universe.* London: Jonathan Cape, 2004.

Peterson, Houston, ed. *Essays in Philosophy.* New York: Pocket Library, 1959.

Pinker, Steven. *The Language Instinct: How the Mind Creates Language.* New York: Morrow, 1994.

Plantinga, Alvin. *Warranted Christian Belief.* Oxford: Oxford University Press, 2000.

Plato. *Apology.* Tr. Hugh Tredennick, 1954. Repr. Harmondsworth: Penguin Books, 1976. Also in *The Collected Dialogues of Plato including the letters.* 1961. Repr. with corrections, Princeton, N.J.: Princeton University Press, 1973.

Plato. *The Euthyphro.*

Plato. *The Last Days of Socrates.* Tr. Hugh Tredennick. Harmondsworth: Penguin Books, 1969.

Plato. *Phaedo.*

Plato. *Republic.* Tr. Desmond Lee. 2nd edn, Harmondsworth: Penguin, 1974. Also tr. Paul Shorey, Loeb Classical Library. Cambridge, Mass.: Harvard University Press, 1930. Also in *The Collected Dialogues of Plato including the letters*, 1961. Repr. with corrections, Princeton, N.J.: Princeton University Press, 1973.

Plato. *Timaeus.*

Pliny the Younger. *Letters.* Tr. Betty Radice as *The Letters of the Younger Pliny.* Harmondsworth: Penguin Books, 1963.

Plotinus. *Enneads.* Tr. Stephen MacKenna, 1917–30. Repr. London: Penguin, 2005.

Polanyi, Michael. *The Tacit Dimension.* New York: Doubleday, 1966.

Polkinghorne, John. *One World: The Interaction of Science and Theology.* London: SPCK, 1986.

Polkinghorne, John. *Reason and Reality: The Relationship between Science and Theology.* 1991. Repr. London: SPCK, 2011.

Polkinghorne, John. *Science and Creation: The Search for Understanding.* 1988. Rev. edn, West Conshohocken, Pa.: Templeton Foundation Press, 2009.

Polkinghorne, John. *Science and Providence: God's Interaction with the World.* 1989. Repr. West Conshohocken, Pa.: Templeton Foundation Press, 2011.

Popper, Karl R. *The World of Parmenides.* London: Routledge, 1998.

Popper, Karl R. and John C. Eccles. *The Self and Its Brain: An Argument for Interactionism.* 1977. Repr. Springer Berlin Heidelberg, 2012.

Pospisil, Leopold J. *Kapauku Papuans and their Law.* Yale University Publications in Anthropology 54. New Haven, 1958.

Pospisil, Leopold J. *The Kapauku Papuans of West New Guinea.* Case Studies in Cultural Anthropology. 1963. 2nd edn, New York: Holt, Rinehart and Winston, 1978.

Powers, B. Ward. *The Progressive Publication of Matthew.* Nashville: B&H Academic, 2010.

Poythress, Vern S. *Inerrancy and the Gospels: A God-Centered Approach to the Challenges of Harmonization.* Wheaton, Ill.: Crossway, 2012.

Pritchard, J. B., ed. *Ancient Near Eastern Texts Relating to the Old Testament.* Princeton, 1950. 3rd edn, Princeton, N.J.: Princeton University Press, 1969.

Putnam, Hilary. *Reason, Truth and History.* Cambridge: Cambridge University Press, 1981.

R

Rachels, James. *Elements of Moral Philosophy.* New York: McGraw-Hill, 1986.

Ragg, Lonsdale and Laura Ragg, eds. *The Gospel of Barnabas.* Oxford: Clarendon Press, 1907.

Ramsay, William. *St. Paul the Traveller and the Roman Citizen*. London: Hodder & Stoughton, 1895.

Randall, John H. *Cosmos*. New York: Random House, 1980.

Raphael, D. D. *Moral Philosophy*. 1981. 2nd edn, Oxford: Oxford University Press, 1994.

Rawls, John. *A Theory of Justice*. Cambridge, Mass.: Harvard University Press, 1971.

Redford, Donald B., ed. *The Oxford Encyclopaedia of Ancient Egypt*. Oxford: Oxford University Press, 2001. doi: 10.1093/acref/9780195102345.001.0001.

Reid, Thomas. *An Enquiry Concerning Human Understanding*. Oxford: Clarendon Press, 1777.

Reid, Thomas. *An Inquiry into the Human Mind on the Principles of Common Sense*. 1764. Repr. Cambridge: Cambridge University Press, 2011.

Renfrew, Colin. *Archaeology and Language: The Puzzle of Indo-European Origins*. 1987. Repr. Cambridge: Cambridge University Press, 1999.

Ricoeur, Paul. *Hermeneutics and the Human Sciences*. 1981. Ed. and tr. J. B. Thompson. Repr. Cambridge: Cambridge University Press, 1998.

Ricoeur, Paul. *Interpretation Theory: Discourse and the Surplus of Meaning*. Fort Worth, Tex.: Texas Christian University Press, 1976.

Ridley, Mark. *The Problems of Evolution*. Oxford: Oxford University Press, 1985.

Rodwell, J. M., tr. *The Koran*. Ed. Alan Jones. London: Phoenix, 2011.

Rorty, Richard. *Consequences of Pragmatism: Essays, 1972–1980*. Minneapolis, Minn.: University of Minnesota Press, 1982.

Rose, Steven. *Lifelines: Biology, Freedom, Determinism*. 1998. Repr. New York: Oxford University Press, 2003.

Ross, Hugh. *The Creator and the Cosmos*. Colorado Springs: NavPress, 1995.

Ross, W. D. *The Right and the Good*. Oxford: Clarendon Press, 1930. Repr. 2002.

Rousseau, Jean Jacques. *The Social Contract*. 1762.

Russell, Bertrand. *The Autobiography of Bertrand Russell*. 1967–69. Repr. London: Routledge, 1998.

Russell, Bertrand. *History of Western Philosophy*. 1946. New edn, London: Routledge, 2004.

Russell, Bertrand. *Human Society in Ethics and Politics*. New York: Mentor, 1962.

Russell, Bertrand. *The Problems of Philosophy*. 1912. Repr. New York: Cosimo Classics, 2010.

Russell, Bertrand. *Religion and Science*. Oxford: Oxford University Press, 1970.

Russell, Bertrand. *Understanding History*. 1943. New York: Philosophical Library, 1957.

Russell, Bertrand. *Why I Am Not a Christian and Other Essays on Religion and Related Subjects*. New York: Simon & Schuster, 1957.

Russell, L. O. and G. A. Adebiyi. *Classical Thermodynamics*. Oxford: Oxford University Press, 1993.

Ryle, Gilbert. *The Concept of Mind*. London, 1949. Repr. London: Routledge, 2009.

S

Sagan, Carl. *The Cosmic Connection: An Extraterrestrial Perspective*. New York: Anchor Press, 1973.

Sagan, Carl. *Cosmos: The Story of Cosmic Evolution, Science and Civilisation*. 1980. Repr. London: Abacus, 2003.

Sagan, Carl. *The Demon-Haunted World: Science as a Candle in the Dark*. London: Headline, 1996.

Sandbach, F. H. *The Stoics*. 1975. Rev. edn, London: Bloomsbury, 2013.

Sartre, Jean-Paul. *Being and Nothingness: An Essay on Phenomenological Ontology*. 1943. Tr. Hazel E. Barnes. 1956. Repr. New York: Pocket Books, 1984.

Sartre, Jean-Paul. *Existentialism and Human Emotions*. Tr. Bernard Frechtman. New York: Philosophical Library, 1957.

Sartre, Jean-Paul. *Existentialism and Humanism*. Tr. and ed. P. Mairet. London: Methuen, 1948.

Sartre, Jean-Paul. *The Flies*. 1943 (French). Tr. Stuart Gilbert. New York: Knopf, 1947.

Schaff, Adam. *A Philosophy of Man*. London: Lawrence and Wishart, 1963.

Scherer, Siegfried. *Evolution. Ein kritisches Lehrbuch*. Weyel Biologie, Giessen: Weyel Lehrmittelverlag, 1998.

Schmidt, W. *The Origin and Growth of Religion*. Tr. J. Rose. London: Methuen, 1931.

Scruton, Roger. *Modern Philosophy*. 1994; London: Arrow Books, 1996.

Searle, John R. *The Construction of Social Reality*. London: Penguin, 1995.

Searle, John R. *Minds, Brains and Science*. 1984 Reith Lectures. London: British Broadcasting Corporation, 1984.

Selsam, Howard. *Socialism and Ethics*. New York: International Publishers, 1943.

Sen, Amartya and Bernard Williams, eds. *Utilitarianism and Beyond*. Cambridge: Cambridge University Press, 1982. 8th repr. in association with La Maison Des Sciences De L'Homme, Paris, 1999.

Shakespeare, William. *As You Like It*.

Sherrington, Charles S. *The Integrative Action of the Nervous System*. 1906. Repr. with new preface, Cambridge: Cambridge University Press, 1947.

Sherwin-White, A. N. *Roman Society and Roman Law in the New Testament*. The Sarum Lectures 1960–61. Oxford: Clarendon Press, 1963. Repr. Eugene, Oreg.: Wipf & Stock, 2004.

Simplicius. *Commentary on Aristotle's Physics* [or, Miscellanies]. In Kirk, G. S., J. E. Raven, and M. Schofield. *The Presocratic Philosophers: A Critical History with a Selection of Texts*. 1957. Rev. edn, Cambridge: Cambridge University Press, 1983.

Simpson, George Gaylord. *The Meaning of Evolution: A Study of the History of Life and of Its Significance for Man*. The Terry Lectures Series. 1949. Rev. edn, New Haven, Conn.: Yale University Press, 1967.

Singer, Peter. *Practical Ethics*. 1979. 2nd edn, Cambridge: Cambridge University Press, 1993.

Singer, Peter. *Rethinking Life and Death: The Collapse of Our Traditional Ethics.* Oxford: Oxford University Press, 1994.

Sire, James. *The Universe Next Door.* Downers Grove, Ill.: InterVarsity Press, 1988.

Skinner, B. F. *Beyond Freedom and Dignity.* 1971; Harmondsworth: Penguin, 1974.

Skinner, B. F. *Lectures on Conditioned Reflexes.* New York: International Publishers, 1963.

Skinner, B. F. *Science and Human Behaviour.* New York: Macmillan, 1953.

Sleeper, Raymond S. *A Lexicon of Marxist-Leninist Semantics.* Alexandria, Va.: Western Goals, 1983.

Smart, J. J. C. and Bernard Williams. *Utilitarianism For and Against.* 1973. Repr. Cambridge: Cambridge University Press, 1998.

Smith, Adam. *An Enquiry into the Nature and Causes of the Wealth of Nations.* 1776. With introduction by Mark G. Spencer, Ware, UK: Wordsworth Editions, 2012.

Smith, John Maynard and Eörs Szathmary. *The Major Transitions in Evolution.* 1995. Repr. Oxford: Oxford University Press, 2010.

Smith, Wilbur. *Therefore Stand.* Grand Rapids: Baker, 1965.

Sober, E. *Philosophy of Biology.* 1993. Rev. 2nd edn, Boulder, Colo.: Westview Press, 2000.

Social Exclusion Unit. *Teenage Pregnancy.* Cmnd 4342. London: The Stationery Office, 1999.

Sophocles. *Antigone.* Tr. F. H. Storr, *Sophocles* Vol. 1. London: Heinemann, 1912.

Spencer, Herbert. *Social Statics.* New York: D. Appleton, 1851.

Stalin, Joseph. *J. Stalin Works.* Moscow: Foreign Languages Publishing House, 1953.

Stam, James H. *Inquiries into the Origin of Language: The Fate of a Question.* New York: Harper & Row, 1976.

Starkey, Mike. *God, Sex, and the Search for Lost Wonder: For Those Looking for Something to Believe In.* 1997. 2nd edn, Downers Grove, Ill.: InterVarsity Press, 1998.

Stauber, Ethelbert. *Jesus—Gestalt und Geschichte.* Bern: Francke Verlag, 1957.

Storer, Morris B., ed. *Humanist Ethics: Dialogue on Basics.* Buffalo, N.Y.: Prometheus Books, 1980.

Stott, John R. W. *The Message of Romans.* Leicester: Inter-Varsity Press, 1994.

Strabo. *Geography.* Tr. with introduction Duane W. Roller as *The Geography of Strabo*, Cambridge: Cambridge University Press, 2014. Tr. H. C. Hamilton and W. Falconer, London, 1903. Perseus, Tufts University, http://www.perseus.tufts.edu/hopper/text?doc=Perseus%3Atext%3A1999.01.0239, accessed 11 Sept. 2015.

Strickberger, Monroe. *Evolution.* 1990. 3rd edn, London: Jones and Bartlett, 2000.

Strobel, Lee. *The Case for Christ: A Journalist's Personal Investigation of the Evidence for Jesus.* Grand Rapids: Zondervan, 1998.

Suetonius. *Lives of the Caesars.* Tr. Catharine Edwards. 2000. Repr. Oxford World's Classics. Oxford: Oxford University Press, 2008.

Sunderland, Luther D. *Darwin's Enigma.* Green Forest, Ark.: Master Books, 1998.

Swinburne, Richard. *The Existence of God*. 1979. Repr. Oxford: Oxford University Press, 2004.

Swinburne, Richard. *Faith and Reason*. 1981. Repr. Oxford: Clarendon Press, 2002.

Swinburne, Richard. *Is There a God?* Oxford: Oxford University Press, 1996.

Swinburne, Richard. *Providence and the Problem of Evil*. Oxford: Oxford University Press, 1998.

T

Tacitus, Cornelius. *Annals*. Tr. Alfred John Church and William Jackson Brodribb as *Complete Works of Tacitus*. New York: Random House, 1872. Repr. 1942. Online in Sara Byrant, ed., Perseus Digital Library, Tufts University, Medford, MA: http://www.perseus.tufts.edu/hopper/text?doc=Perseus%3Atext%3A1999.02.0078%3Abook%3D15%3Achapter%3D44, accessed 2 Aug. 2017.

Tada, Joni Eareckson and Steven Estes. *When God Weeps: Why Our Sufferings Matter to the Almighty*. Grand Rapids: Zondervan, 1997.

Tax, Sol and Charles Callender, eds. *Issues in Evolution*. Chicago: University of Chicago Press, 1960.

Thaxton, Charles B., Walter L. Bradley and Roger L. Olsen. *The Mystery of Life's Origin*. Dallas: Lewis & Stanley, 1992.

Thibaut, George, tr. *The Vedānta Sūtras of Bādarāyana* with the Commentary by Śankara, 2 Parts. New York: Dover, 1962.

Torrance, T. F. *The Ground and Grammar of Theology*. Belfast: Christian Journals Limited, 1980; and Charlottesville: The University Press of Virginia, 1980. Repr. with new preface, Edinburgh: T&T Clark, 2001.

Torrance, T. F. *Theological Science*. Oxford: Oxford University Press, 1978.

U

Unamuno, Don Miguel de. *The Tragic Sense of Life*. Tr. J. E. Crawford. 1921. Repr. Charleston, SC: BiblioBazaar, 2007.

V

Von Neumann, John. *Theory of Self-Reproducing Automata*. Ed. and completed by Arthur W. Burks, Urbana: University of Illinois Press, 1966.

W

Waddington, C. H., ed. *Science and Ethics: An Essay*. London: Allen & Unwin, 1942.

Wallis, R. T. *Neoplatonism*. 1972. Repr. London: Duckworth, 1985.

Ward, Keith. *God, Chance and Necessity*. 1996. Repr. Oxford: Oneworld Publications, 2001.

Warner, Richard, and Tadeusz Szubka. *The Mind-Body Problem*. Oxford: Blackwell, 1994.

Weiner, Jonathan. *The Beak of the Finch*. London: Cape, 1994.

Welch, I. David, George A. Tate and Fred Richards, eds. *Humanistic Psychology.* Buffalo, N.Y.: Prometheus Books, 1978.

Wenham, John. *Easter Enigma—Do the Resurrection Stories Contradict One Another?* Exeter: Paternoster Press, 1984. Repr. as *Easter Enigma: Are the Resurrection Accounts in Conflict?*, Eugene, Oreg.: Wipf & Stock, 2005.

Wesson, Paul. *Beyond Natural Selection.* 1991. Repr. Cambridge, Mass.: Massachusetts Institute of Technology Press, 1997.

Westminster Shorter Catechism. 1647. [Widely available in print and online.]

Wetter, Gustav A. *Dialectical Materialism.* Westport, Conn.: Greenwood Press, 1977.

Whitehead, Alfred North. *Process and Reality.* Gifford Lectures 1927–28. London: Macmillan, 1929. Repr. New York: The Free Press, 1978.

Wilson, Edward O. *Consilience.* London: Little, Brown, 1998.

Wilson, Edward O. *Genes, Mind and Culture.* Cambridge, Mass.: Harvard University Press, 1981.

Wilson, Edward O. *On Human Nature.* Cambridge, Mass.: Harvard University Press, 1978.

Wilson, Edward O. *Sociobiology: The New Synthesis.* Cambridge, Mass.: Harvard University Press, 1975.

Wimsatt, William K. and Monroe Beardsley. *The Verbal Icon: Studies in the Meaning of Poetry.* 1954. Repr. Lexington, Ky.: University of Kentucky Press, 1982.

Wippel, John F., ed. *Studies in Medieval Philosophy.* Vol. 17 of *Studies in Philosophy and the History of Philosophy.* Washington D.C.: Catholic University of America Press, 1987.

Wittgenstein, L. *On Certainty.* Ed. G. E. M. Anscombe and G. H. von Wright; tr. Denis Paul and G. E. M. Anscombe. Oxford, 1969. Repr. New York: Harper & Row, 1972.

Wolpert, Lewis. *The Unnatural Nature of Science.* London: Faber & Faber, 1992.

Wolstenholme, Gordon, ed. *Man and His Future.* A Ciba Foundation Volume. London: J. & A. Churchill, 1963.

Wolters, Clifton, tr. *The Cloud of Unknowing.* 1961. Repr. London: Penguin, 1978.

Wolterstorff, Nicholas. *Divine Discourse: Philosophical Reflections on the Claim that God Speaks.* 1995. Repr. Cambridge: Cambridge University Press, 2000.

X

Xenophon. *Memorabilia.* Tr. E. C. Marchant. *Memorabilia. Oeconomicus. Symposium. Apology.* Vol. 4. Loeb Classical Library, Vol. 168. 1923. Repr. Cambridge, Mass.: Harvard University Press, 1997.

Y

Yancey, Philip. *Soul Survivor: How my Faith Survived the Church.* London: Hodder & Stoughton, 2001.

Yockey, Hubert. *Information Theory and Biology.* Cambridge: Cambridge University Press, 1992.

Z

Zacharias, Ravi. *Jesus Among Other Gods: The Absolute Claims of the Christian Message*. Nashville, Tenn.: Thomas Nelson, 2000.

Zacharias, Ravi. *The Real Face of Atheism*. Grand Rapids: Baker, 2004.

Zaehner, Z. C., ed. *The Concise Encyclopedia of Living Faiths*. 1959. 2nd edn, 1971. Repr. London: Hutchinson, 1982.

ARTICLES, PAPERS, CHAPTERS AND LECTURES

A

Adams, R. M. 'Religious Ethics in a Pluralistic Society.' In G. Outka and J. P. Reeder, Jr., eds. *Prospects for a Common Morality*. Princeton, N.J.: Princeton University Press, 1993.

Alberts, Bruce. 'The Cell as a Collection of Protein Machines: Preparing the Next Generation of Molecular Biologists.' *Cell* 92/3 (6 Feb. 1998), 291–4. doi: 10.1016/S0092-8674(00)80922-8.

Almond, Brenda. 'Liberty or Community? Defining the Post-Marxist Agenda.' In Brenda Almond, ed. *Introducing Applied Ethics*. Oxford: Wiley Blackwell, 1995.

Alpher, R. A., H. Bethe and G. Gamow. 'The Origin of Chemical Elements.' *Physical Review* 73/7 (Apr. 1948), 803–4. doi: 10.1103/PhysRev.73.803.

Anscombe, G. E. M. 'Modern Moral Philosophy.' *Philosophy* 33 (1958), 1–19.

Asimov, Isaac (interview by Paul Kurtz). 'An Interview with Isaac Asimov on Science and the Bible.' *Free Enquiry* 2/2 (Spring 1982), 6–10.

Auer, J. A. C. F. 'Religion as the Integration of Human Life.' *The Humanist* (Spring 1947).

Austin, J. L., P. F. Strawson and D. R. Cousin. 'Truth.' *Proceedings of the Aristotelian Society, Supplementary Volumes, Vol. 24, Physical Research, Ethics and Logic* (1950), 111–72. http://www.jstor.org/stable/4106745. Repr. in Paul Horwich, ed. *Theories of Truth*. Aldershot: Dartmouth Publishing, 1994.

B

Bada, Jeffrey L. 'Stanley Miller's 70th Birthday.' *Origins of Life and Evolution of Biospheres* 30/2 (2000), 107–12. doi: 10.1023/A:1006746205180.

Baier, Kurt E. M. 'Egoism.' In P. Singer, ed. *A Companion to Ethics*. Oxford: Blackwell, 1991. Repr. 2000, 197–204.

Baier, Kurt E. M. 'Freedom, Obligation, and Responsibility.' In Morris B. Storer, ed. *Humanist Ethics: Dialogue on Basics*. Buffalo, N.Y.: Prometheus Books, 1980, 75–92.

Baier, Kurt E. M. 'The Meaning of Life.' 1947. In Peter Angeles, ed. *Critiques of God*, Buffalo, N.Y.: Prometheus Books, 1976. Repr. in E. D. Klemke, ed. *The Meaning of Life*. New York: Oxford University Press, 1981, 81–117.

Baker, S. W. 'Albert Nyanza, Account of the Discovery of the Second Great Lake of the Nile.' *Journal of the Royal Geographical Society* 36 (1866). Also in *Proceedings of the Royal Geographical Society of London* 10 (13 Nov. 1856), 6–27.

Bates, Elizabeth, Donna Thal and Virginia Marchman. 'Symbols and Syntax: A Darwinian Approach to Language Development.' In Norman A. Krasnegor, Duane M. Rumbaugh, Richard L. Schiefelbusch and Michael Studdert-Kennedy, eds. *Biological and Behavioural Determinants of Language Development*. 1991. Repr. New York: Psychology Press, 2014, 29–65.

Behe, Michael J. 'Reply to My Critics: A Response to Reviews of *Darwin's Black Box: The Biochemical Challenge to Evolution*.' *Biology and Philosophy* 16 (2001), 685–709.

Berenbaum, Michael. 'T4 Program' In *Encyclopaedia Britannica*. https://www.britannica.com/event/T4-Program, accessed 2 Nov. 2017.

Berlinski, David. 'The Deniable Darwin.' *Commentary* (June 1996), 19–29.

Bernal, J. D. 'The Unity of Ethics.' In C. H. Waddington, ed. *Science and Ethics: An Essay*. London: Allen & Unwin, 1942.

Black, Deborah L. 'Al-Kindi.' In Seyyed Hossein Nasr and Oliver Leaman, eds. *History of Islamic Philosophy*. Part 1, Vol. 1 of *Routledge History of World Philosophies*. 1996. Repr. London: Routledge, 2001, 178–97.

Boghossian, Paul A. 'What the Sokal hoax ought to teach us: The pernicious consequences and internal contradictions of "postmodernist" relativism.' *Times Literary Supplement*, Commentary (13 Dec. 1996), 14–15. Reprinted in Noretta Koertge, ed. *A House Built on Sand: Exposing Postmodernist Myths about Science*. Oxford: Oxford University Press, 1998, 23–31.

Briggs, Arthur E. 'The Third Annual Humanist Convention.' *The Humanist* (Spring 1945).

Bristol, Evelyn. 'Turn of a Century: Modernism, 1895–1925.' Ch. 8 in C. A. Moser, ed. *The Cambridge History of Russian Literature*. 1989. Rev. edn, 1992. Repr. 1996, Cambridge: Cambridge University Press, 387–457.

C

Caputo, John D. 'The End of Ethics.' In Hugh LaFollette, ed. *The Blackwell Guide to Ethical Theory*. Oxford: Blackwell, 1999, 111–28.

Cartmill, Matt. 'Oppressed by Evolution.' *Discover* Magazine 19/3 (Mar. 1998), 78–83. Reprinted in L. Polnac, ed. *Purpose, Pattern, and Process*. 6th edn, Dubuque: Kendall-Hunt, 2002, 389–97.

Cavalier-Smith, T. 'The Blind Biochemist.' *Trends in Ecology and Evolution* 12 (1997), 162–3.

Chaitin, Gregory J. 'Randomness in Arithmetic and the Decline and Fall of Reductionism in Pure Mathematics.' Ch. 3 in John Cornwell, ed. *Nature's Imagination: The Frontiers of Scientific Vision*. Oxford: Oxford University Press, 1995, 27–44.

Chomsky, Noam. 'Review of B. F. Skinner.' *Verbal Behavior. Language* 35/1 (1959), 26–58.

Chomsky, Noam. 'Science, Mind, and Limits of Understanding.' Transcript of talk given at the Science and Faith Foundation (STOQ), The Vatican (Jan. 2014). No pages. http://www.chomsky.info/talks/201401--.htm, accessed 3 Aug. 2017.

Coghlan, Andy. 'Selling the family secrets.' *New Scientist* 160/2163 (5 Dec. 1998), 20–1.

Collins, Harry. 'Introduction: Stages in the Empirical Programme of Relativism.' *Social Studies of Science* 11/1 (Feb. 1981), 3–10. http://www.jstor.org/stable/284733, accessed 11 Sept. 2015.

Collins, R. 'A Physician's View of College Sex.' *Journal of the American Medical Association* 232 (1975), 392.

Cook, Sidney. 'Solzhenitsyn and Secular Humanism: A Response.' *The Humanist* (Nov./Dec. 1978), 6.

Cookson, Clive. 'Scientist Who Glimpsed God.' *Financial Times* (29 Apr. 1995), 20.

Cottingham, John. 'Descartes, René.' In Ted Honderich, ed. *The Oxford Companion to Philosophy*. Oxford, 1995. 2nd edn, Oxford: Oxford University Press, 2005.

Crick, Francis. 'Lessons from Biology.' *Natural History* 97 (Nov. 1988), 32–9.

Crosman, Robert. 'Do Readers Make Meaning?' In Susan R. Suleiman and Inge Crosman, eds. *The Reader in the Text: Essays on Audience and Interpretation*. Princeton, N.J.: Princeton University Press, 1980.

D

Davies, Paul. 'Bit before It?' *New Scientist* 2171 (30 Jan. 1999), 3.

Dawkins, Richard. 'Put Your Money on Evolution.' Review of Maitland A. Edey and Donald C. Johanson. *Blueprint: Solving the Mystery of Evolution*. Penguin, 1989. *The New York Times Review of Books* (9 Apr. 1989), sec. 7, 34–5.

Dembski, William. 'Intelligent Design as a Theory of Information.' *Perspectives on Science and Christian Faith* 49/3 (Sept. 1997), 180–90.

Derrida, Jacques. 'Force of Law: The "Mystical Foundation of Authority".' In Drucilla Cornell, Michel Rosenfeld and David Gray Carlson, eds. *Deconstruction and the Possibility of Justice*. 1992. Repr. Abingdon: Routledge, 2008.

Dirac, P. A. M. 'The Evolution of the Physicist's Picture of Nature.' *Scientific American* 208/5 (1963), 45–53. doi: 10.1038/scientificamerican0563-45.

Dobzhansky, Theodosius. 'Chance and Creativity in Evolution.' Ch. 18 in Francisco J. Ayala and Theodosius Dobzhansky, eds. *Studies in the Philosophy of Biology: Reduction and Related Problems*. Berkeley, Calif.: University of California Press, 1974, 307–36.

Dobzhansky, Theodosius. Discussion of paper by Gerhard Schramm, 'Synthesis of Nucleosides and Polynucleotide with Metaphosphate Esters.' In Sidney W. Fox, ed. *The Origins of Prebiological Systems and of Their Molecular Matrices*, 299–315. Proceedings of a Conference Conducted at Wakulla Springs, Florida, on 20–30 October 1963 under the auspices of the Institute for Space Biosciences, the Florida State University and the National Aeronautics and Space Administration. New York: Academic Press, 1965.

Dobzhansky, Theodosius. 'Evolutionary Roots of Family Ethics and Group Ethics.' In *The Centrality of Science and Absolute Values*, Vol. I of *Proceedings of the Fourth International Conference on the Unity of the Sciences*. New York: International Cultural Foundation, 1975.

Documents of the 22nd Congress of the Communist Party of the Soviet Union. 2 vols. Documents of Current History, nos. 18–19. New York: Crosscurrents Press, 1961.

Dose, Klaus. 'The Origin of Life: More Questions Than Answers.' *Interdisciplinary Science Reviews* 13 (Dec. 1988), 348–56.

Druart, Th.-A. 'Al-Fārābī and Emanationism.' In J. F. Wippel, ed. *Studies in Medieval Philosophy*. Vol. 17 of *Studies in Philosophy and the History of Philosophy*. Washington D.C.: Catholic University of America Press, 1987, 23–43.

Dyson, Freeman. 'Energy in the Universe.' *Scientific American* 225/3 (1971), 50–9.

E

Eddington, Arthur. 'The End of the World: From the Standpoint of Mathematical Physics.' *Nature* 127 (21 Mar. 1931), 447–53. doi: 10.1038/127447a0.

Edwards, William. 'On the Physical Death of Jesus Christ.' *Journal of the American Medical Association* 255/11 (21 Mar. 1986), 1455–63.

Eigen, Manfred, Christof K. Biebricher, Michael Gebinoga and William C. Gardiner. 'The Hypercycle: Coupling of RNA and Protein Biosynthesis in the Infection Cycle of an RNA Bacteriophage.' *Biochemistry* 30/46 (1991), 11005–18. doi: 10.1021/bi00110a001.

Einstein, Albert. 'Physics and Reality.' 1936. In Sonja Bargmann, tr. *Ideas and Opinions*. New York: Bonanza, 1954.

Einstein, Albert. 'Science and Religion.' 1941. Published in *Science, Philosophy and Religion, A Symposium*. New York: The Conference on Science, Philosophy and Religion in Their Relation to the Democratic Way of Life, 1941. Repr. in *Out of My Later Years*, 1950, 1956. Repr. New York: Open Road Media, 2011.

Eysenck, H. J. 'A Reason with Compassion.' In Paul Kurtz, ed. *The Humanist Alternative*. Buffalo, N.Y.: Prometheus Books, 1973.

F

Feynman, Richard P. 'Cargo Cult Science.' Repr. in *Engineering and Science* 37/7 (1974), 10–13. http://calteches.library.caltech.edu/51/2/CargoCult.pdf (facsimile), accessed 11 Sept. 2015. (Originally delivered as Caltech's 1974 commencement address in Pasadena, Calif.)

Fletcher, J. 'Comment by Joseph Fletcher on Nielsen Article.' In Morris B. Storer, ed. *Humanist Ethics: Dialogue on Basics*. Buffalo, N.Y.: Prometheus Books, 1980, 70.

Flew, Anthony. 'Miracles.' In Paul Edwards, ed. *The Encyclopedia of Philosophy*. New York: Macmillan, 1967, 5:346–53.

Flew, Anthony. 'Neo-Humean Arguments about the Miraculous.' In R. D. Geivett and G. R. Habermas, eds. *In Defence of Miracles*. Leicester: Apollos, 1997, 45–57.

Flieger, Jerry Aline. 'The Art of Being Taken by Surprise.' *Destructive Criticism: Directions. SCE Reports* 8 (Fall 1980), 54–67.

Fodor, J. A. 'Fixation of Belief and Concept Acquisition.' In M. Piattelli-Palmarini, ed., *Language and Learning: The Debate Between Jean Piaget and Noam Chomsky*. Cambridge, Mass.: Harvard University Press, 1980, 143–9.

Fotion, Nicholas G. 'Logical Positivism.' In Ted Honderich, ed. *The Oxford Companion to Philosophy*. 2nd edn, Oxford: Oxford University Press, 2005.

Frank, Lawrence K. 'Potentialities of Human Nature.' *The Humanist* (Apr. 1951).

Frankena, William K. 'Is morality logically dependent on religion?' In G. Outka and J. P. Reeder, Jr., eds. *Religion and Morality*. Garden City, N.Y.: Anchor, 1973.

G

Genequand, Charles. 'Metaphysics.' Ch. 47 in Seyyed Nossein Nasr and Oliver Leaman, eds. *History of Islamic Philosophy*. Vol. 1 of *Routledge History of World Philosophies*. London: Routledge, 1996, 783–801.

Genné, William H. 'Our Moral Responsibility.' *Journal of the American College Health Association* 15/Suppl (May 1967), 55–60.

Gilbert, Scott F., John Opitz and Rudolf A Raff. 'Resynthesizing Evolutionary and Developmental Biology.' *Developmental Biology* 173/2 (1996), 357–72.

Ginsburg, V. L. *Poisk* 29–30 (1998).

Gould, Stephen Jay. 'Evolution as Fact and Theory.' In Ashley Montagu, ed. *Science and Creationism*. Oxford: Oxford University Press, 1984.

Gould, Stephen Jay. 'Evolution's Erratic Pace.' *Natural History* 86/5 (May 1977), 12–16.

Gould, Stephen Jay. 'Evolutionary Considerations.' Paper presented at the McDonnell Foundation Conference, 'Selection vs. Instruction'. Venice, May 1989.

Gould, Stephen Jay. 'In Praise of Charles Darwin.' Paper presented at the Nobel Conference XVIII, Gustavus Adolphus College, St. Peter, Minn. Repr. in Charles L. Hamrum, ed. *Darwin's Legacy*. San Francisco: Harper & Row, 1983.

Gould, Stephen Jay. 'The Paradox of the Visibly Irrelevant.' *Annals of the New York Academy of Sciences* 879 (June 1999), 87–97. doi: 10.1111/j.1749-6632.1999.tb10407.x. Repr. in *The Lying Stones of Marrakech: Penultimate Reflections in Natural History*. 2000. Repr. Cambridge, Mass.: Harvard University Press, 2011.

Gribbin, John. 'Oscillating Universe Bounces Back.' *Nature* 259 (1 Jan. 1976), 15–16. doi: 10.1038/259015c0.

Grigg, Russell. 'Could Monkeys Type the 23rd Psalm?' *Interchange* 50 (1993), 25–31.

Guth, A. H. 'Inflationary Universe: A Possible Solution to the Horizon and Flatness Problems.' *Physical Review D* 23/2 (1981), 347–56.

Guttmacher Institute. 'Induced Abortion in the United States', Fact Sheet. New York: Guttmacher Institute, Jan. 2018. https://www.guttmacher.org/fact-sheet/induced-abortion-united-states, accessed 1 Feb. 2018.

H

Haldane, J. B. S. 'When I am Dead.' In *Possible Worlds*. [1927] London: Chatto & Windus, 1945, 204–11.

Hansen, Michèle; Jennifer J. Kurinczuk, Carol Bower and Sandra Webb. 'The Risk of Major Birth Defects after Intracytoplasmic Sperm Injection and in Vitro Fertilization.' *New England Journal of Medicine* 346 (2002), 725–30. doi: 10.1056/NEJMoa010035.

Hardwig, John. 'Dying at the Right Time: Reflections on (Un)Assisted Suicide.' In Hugh LaFollette, ed. *Ethics In Practice*. Blackwell Philosophy Anthologies. 2nd edn, Oxford: Blackwell, 1997, 101–11.

Hawking, S. W. 'The Edge of Spacetime: Does the universe have an edge and time a beginning, as Einstein's general relativity predicts, or is spacetime finite without boundary, as quantum mechanics suggests?' *American Scientist* 72/4 (1984), 355–9. http://www.jstor.org/stable/27852759, accessed 15 Sept. 2015.

Hawking, S. W. Letters to the Editors. Reply to letter by J. J. Tanner relating to article 'The Edge of Spacetime'. *American Scientist* 73/1 (1985), 12. http://www.jstor.org/stable/27853056, accessed 15 Sept. 2015.

Hawking, S. W. and R. Penrose. 'The Singularities of Gravitational Collapse and Cosmology.' *Proceedings of the Royal Society London A* 314/1519 (1970), 529–48. doi: 10.1098/rspa.1970.0021.

Hocutt, Max. 'Does Humanism Have an Ethic of Responsibility?' In Morris B. Storer, ed. *Humanist Ethic: Dialogue on Basics.* Buffalo, N.Y.: Prometheus Books, 1980, 11–24.

Hocutt, Max. 'Toward an Ethic of Mutual Accommodation.' In Morris B. Storer, ed. *Humanist Ethics: Dialogue on Basics.* Buffalo, N.Y.: Prometheus Books, 1980, 137–46.

Hookway, C. J. 'Scepticism.' In Ted Honderich, ed. *The Oxford Companion to Philosophy.* Oxford, 1995. 2nd edn, Oxford: Oxford University Press, 2005.

Hoyle, Fred. 'The Universe: Past and Present Reflections.' *Annual Reviews of Astronomy and Astrophysics* 20 (1982), 1–35. doi: 10.1146/annurev.aa.20.090182.000245.

Hursthouse, Rosalind. 'Virtue theory and abortion.' *Philosophy and Public Affairs* 20, 1991, 223–46.

Huxley, Julian. 'The Emergence of Darwinism.' In Sol Tax, ed. *The Evolution of Life: Its Origins, History, and Future.* Vol. 1 of *Evolution after Darwin.* Chicago: University of Chicago Press, 1960, 1–21.

Huxley, Julian. 'The Evolutionary Vision: The Convocation Address.' In Sol Tax and Charles Callender, eds. *Issues in Evolution.* Vol. 3 of *Evolution after Darwin.* Chicago: University of Chicago Press, 1960, 249–61.

I

Inwood, M. J. 'Feuerbach, Ludwig Andreas.' In Ted Honderich, ed. *The Oxford Companion to Philosophy.* Oxford, 1995. 2nd edn, Oxford: Oxford University Press, 2005.

J

Jeeves, Malcolm. 'Brain, Mind, and Behaviour.' In Warren S. Brown, Nancey Murphy and H. Newton Malony, eds. *Whatever Happened to the Soul: Scientific and Theological Portraits of Human Nature.* Minneapolis: Fortress Press, 1998.

Johnson, Barbara. 'Nothing Fails Like Success.' *Deconstructive Criticism: Directions. SCE Reports* 8 (Fall 1980), 7–16.

Josephson, Brian. Letters to the Editor. *The Independent* (12 Jan. 1997), London.

K

Kant, Immanuel. 'Beantwortung der Frage: Was ist Aufklärung?' *Berlinische Monatsschrift* 4 (Dec. 1784), 481–94. Repr. in *Kant's Gesammelte Schriften.* Berlin: Akademie Ausgabe, 1923, 8:33–42.

Khrushchev, Nikita. *Ukrainian Bulletin* (1–15 Aug. 1960), 12.

Klein-Franke, Felix. 'Al-Kindī.' In Seyyed Hossein Nasr and Oliver Leaman, eds. *History of Islamic Philosophy.* Vol. 1, Part 1 of *Routledge History of World Philosophies.* 1996. Repr. London: Routledge, 2001, 165–77.

Kurtz, Paul. 'A Declaration of Interdependence: A New Global Ethics.' *Free Inquiry* 8/4 (Fall 1988), 4–7. Also published in Vern L. Ballough and Timothy J. Madigan, ed. *Toward a New Enlightenment: The Philosophy of Paul Kurtz*. New Brunswick, N.J.: Transaction Publishers, 1994 (ch. 3, 'The Twenty-First Century and Beyond: The Need for a New Global Ethic and a Declaration of Interdependence').

Kurtz, Paul. 'Does Humanism Have an Ethic of Responsibility?' In Morris B. Storer, ed. *Humanist Ethics: Dialogue on Basics*. Buffalo, N.Y.: Prometheus Books, 1980, 11–24.

Kurtz, Paul. 'Is Everyone a Humanist?' In Paul Kurtz, ed. *The Humanist Alternative*. Buffalo, N.Y.: Prometheus Books, 1973.

L

Lamont, Corliss. 'The Ethics of Humanism.' In Frederick C. Dommeyer, ed. *In Quest of Value: Readings in Philosophy and Personal Values*. San Francisco: Chandler, 1963, 46–59. Repr. from ch. 6 of Corliss Lamont. *Humanism as a Philosophy*. Philosophical Library, 273–97.

Larson, Erik. 'Looking for the Mind.' (Review of David J. Chalmers. *The Conscious Mind: In Search of a Fundamental Theory*.) *Origins & Design* 18/1(34) (Winter 1997), Colorado Springs: Access Research Network, 28–9.

Leitch, Vincent B. 'The Book of Deconstructive Criticism.' *Studies in the Literary Imagination* 12/1 (Spring 1979), 19–39.

Lewis, C. S. 'The Funeral of a Great Myth.' In Walter Hooper, ed. *Christian Reflections*. Grand Rapids: Eerdmans, 1967, 102–116.

Lewis, C. S. 'The Weight of Glory.' In *Transposition and other Addresses*. London: Geoffrey Bles, 1949. Repr. in *The Weight of Glory and Other Addresses*. HarperOne, 2001.

Lewontin, Richard C. 'Billions and Billions of Demons.' *The New York Review of Books* 44/1 (9 Jan. 1997).

Lewontin, Richard C. 'Evolution/Creation Debate: A Time for Truth.' *BioScience* 31/8 (Sept. 1981), 559. Reprinted in J. Peter Zetterberg, ed. *Evolution versus Creationism*. Phoenix, Ariz.: Oryx Press, 1983. http://bioscience.oxfordjournals.org/content/31/8/local/ed-board.pdf, accessed 15 Sept. 2015.

Lieberman, Philip and E. S. Crelin. 'On the Speech of Neanderthal Man.' *Linguistic Inquiry* 2/2 (Mar. 1971), 203–22.

Louden, Robert. 'On Some Vices of Virtue Ethics.' Ch. 10 in R. Crisp and M. Slote, eds. *Virtue Ethics*. Oxford: Oxford University Press, 1997.

M

Mackie, J. L. 'Evil and Omnipotence.' *Mind* 64/254 (Apr. 1955), 200–12.

McNaughton, David and Piers Rawling. 'Intuitionism.' Ch. 13 in Hugh LaFollette, ed. *The Blackwell Guide to Ethical Theory*. Oxford: Blackwell, 2000, 268–87. Ch. 14 in 2nd edn, Wiley Blackwell, 2013, 287–310.

Maddox, John. 'Down with the Big Bang.' *Nature* 340 (1989), 425. doi: 10.1038/340425a0.

Marx, Karl. 'The Difference between the Natural Philosophy of Democritus and the Natural Philosophy of Epicurus.' In *K. Marx and F. Engels on Religion*. Moscow: Foreign Languages Publishing House, 1955.

Marx, Karl. 'Economic and Philosophical Manuscripts.' In T. B. Bottomore, tr. and ed. *Karl Marx: Early Writings*. London: Watts, 1963.

Marx, Karl. 'Theses on Feuerback.' In Frederick Engels, *Ludwig Feuerback*. New York: International Publishers, 1941.

May, Rollo. 'The Problem of Evil: An Open Letter to Carl Rogers.' *Journal of Humanistic Psychology* (Summer 1982).

Merezhkovsky, Dmitry. 'On the Reasons for the Decline and on the New Currents in Contemporary Russian Literature.' 1892 lecture. In Dmitry Merezhkovsky. *On the reasons for the decline and on the new currents in contemporary Russian literature*. Petersburg, 1893.

Meyer, Stephen C. 'The Explanatory Power of Design: DNA and the Origin of Information.' In William A. Dembski, ed. *Mere Creation: Science, Faith and Intelligent Design*. Downers Grove, Ill.: InterVarsity Press, 1998, 114–47.

Meyer, Stephen C. 'The Methodological Equivalence of Design and Descent.' In J. P. Moreland, ed. *The Creation Hypothesis*. Downers Grove, Ill.: InterVarsity Press, 1994, 67–112.

Meyer, Stephen C. 'Qualified Agreement: Modern Science and the Return of the "God Hypothesis".' In Richard F. Carlson, ed. *Science and Christianity: Four Views*. Downers Grove, Ill.: InterVarsity Press, 2000, 129–75.

Meyer, Stephen C. 'The Return of the God Hypothesis.' *Journal of Interdisciplinary Studies* 11/1&2 (Jan. 1999), 1–38. http://www.discovery.org/a/642, accessed 3 Aug. 2017. Citations are to the archived version, which is repaginated, http://www.discovery.org/scripts/viewDB/filesDB-download.php?command=download&id=12006, accessed 3 Aug. 2017.

Miller, J. Hillis. 'Deconstructing the Deconstructors.' Review of Joseph N. Riddel. *The Inverted Bell: Modernism and the Counterpoetics of William Carlos Williams. Diacritics* 5/2 (Summer 1975), 24–31. http://www.jstor.org/stable/464639, accessed 3 Aug. 2017. doi: 10.2307/464639.

Monod, Jacques. 'On the Logical Relationship between Knowledge and Values.' In Watson Fuller, ed. *The Biological Revolution*. Garden City, N.Y.: Doubleday, 1972.

N

Nagel, Ernest. 'Naturalism Reconsidered.' 1954. In Houston Peterson, ed. *Essays in Philosophy*. New York: Pocket Books, 1959. Repr. New York: Pocket Books, 1974.

Nagel, Thomas. 'Rawls, John.' In Ted Honderich, ed. *The Oxford Companion to Philosophy*. 1995. 2nd edn, Oxford: Oxford University Press, 2005.

Nagler, Michael N. 'Reading the Upanishads.' In Eknath Easwaran. *The Upanishads*. 1987. Repr. Berkeley, Calif.: Nilgiri Press, 2007.

Neill, Stephen. 'The Wrath of God and the Peace of God.' In Max Warren, *Interpreting the Cross*. London: SCM Press, 1966.

Newing, Edward G. 'Religions of pre-literary societies.' In Sir Norman Anderson, ed. *The World's Religions*. 4th edn, London: Inter-Varsity Press, 1975.

Nielsen, Kai. 'Religiosity and Powerlessness: Part III of "The Resurgence of Fundamentalism".' *The Humanist* 37/3 (May/June 1977), 46–8.

O

The Oxford Reference Encyclopaedia. Oxford: Oxford University Press, 1998.

P

Palmer, Alasdair. 'Must Knowledge Gained Mean Paradise Lost?' *Sunday Telegraph*. London (6 Apr. 1997).

Penzias, Arno. 'Creation is Supported by all the Data So Far.' In Henry Margenau and Roy Abraham Varghese, eds. *Cosmos, Bios, Theos: Scientists Reflect on Science, God, and the Origins of the Universe, Life, and Homo Sapiens*. La Salle, Ill.: Open Court, 1992.

Pinker, Steven, and Paul Bloom. 'Natural Language and Natural Selection.' *Behavioral and Brain Sciences* 13/4 (Dec. 1990), 707–27. doi: 10.1017/S0140525X00081061.

Polanyi, Michael. 'Life's Irreducible Structure. Live mechanisms and information in DNA are boundary conditions with a sequence of boundaries above them.' *Science* 160/3834 (1968), 1308–12. http://www.jstor.org/stable/1724152, accessed 3 Aug. 2017.

Poole, Michael. 'A Critique of Aspects of the Philosophy and Theology of Richard Dawkins.' *Christians and Science* 6/1 (1994), 41–59. http://www.scienceandchristianbelief.org/serve_pdf_free.php?filename=SCB+6-1+Poole.pdf, accessed 3 Aug. 2017.

Popper, Karl. 'Scientific Reduction and the Essential Incompleteness of All Science.' In F. J. Ayala and T. Dobzhansky, ed. *Studies in the Philosophy of Biology, Reduction and Related Problems*. London: MacMillan, 1974.

Premack, David. '"Gavagai!" or The Future History of the Animal Controversy.' *Cognition* 19/3 (1985), 207–96. doi: 10.1016/0010-0277(85)90036-8.

Provine, William B. 'Evolution and the Foundation of Ethics.' *Marine Biological Laboratory Science* 3 (1988), 27–8.

Provine, William B. 'Scientists, Face it! Science and Religion are Incompatible.' *The Scientist* (5 Sept. 1988), 10–11.

R

Rachels, James. 'Naturalism.' In Hugh LaFollette, ed. *The Blackwell Guide to Ethical Theory*. Oxford: Blackwell, 2000, 74–91.

Randall, John H. 'The Nature of Naturalism.' In Yervant H. Krikorian, ed. *Naturalism*, 354–82.

Raup, David. 'Conflicts between Darwin and Palaeontology.' *Field Museum of Natural History Bulletin* 50/1 (Jan. 1979), 22–9.

Reidhaar-Olson, John F. and Robert T. Sauer. 'Functionally Acceptable Substitutions in Two α-helical Regions of λ Repressor.' *Proteins: Structure, Function, and Genetics* 7/4 (1990), 306–16. doi: 10.1002/prot.340070403.

Rescher, Nicholas. 'Idealism.' In Jonathan Dancy and Ernest Sosa, eds. *A Companion to Epistemology*. 1992. Repr. Oxford: Blackwell, 2000.

Ridley, Mark. 'Who Doubts Evolution?' *New Scientist* 90 (25 June 1981), 830–2.

Rogers, Carl. 'Notes on Rollo May.' *Journal of Humanistic Psychology* 22/3 (Summer 1982), 8–9. doi: 10.1177/0022167882223002.

Rorty, Richard. 'Untruth and Consequences.' *The New Republic* (31 July 1995), 32–6.

Ruse, Michael. 'Is Rape Wrong on Andromeda?' In E. Regis Jr., ed. *Extraterrestrials*. Cambridge: Cambridge University Press, 1985.

Ruse, Michael. 'Transcript: Speech by Professor Michael Ruse,' Symposium, 'The New Antievolutionism', 1993 Annual Meeting of the American Association for the Advancement of Science, 13 Feb. 1993. http://www.arn.org/docs/orpages/or151/mr93tran.htm, accessed 3 Aug. 2017.

Ruse, Michael and Edward O. Wilson. 'The Evolution of Ethics.' *New Scientist* 108/1478 (17 Oct. 1985), 50–2.

Russell, Bertrand. 'A Free Man's Worship.' 1903. In *Why I Am Not a Christian*. New York: Simon & Schuster, 1957. Also in *Mysticism and Logic Including A Free Man's Worship*. London: Unwin, 1986.

Russell, Colin. 'The Conflict Metaphor and its Social Origins.' *Science and Christian Belief* 1/1 (1989), 3–26.

S

Sanders, Blanche. *The Humanist* 5 (1945).

Sanders, Peter. 'Eutychus.' *Triple Helix* (Summer 2002), 17.

Sayre-McCord, Geoffrey. 'Contractarianism.' In Hugh LaFollette, ed. *The Blackwell Guide to Ethical Theory*. Oxford: Blackwell, 2000, 247–67. 2nd edn, Wiley Blackwell, 2013, 332–53.

Scruton, Roger. *The Times* (Dec. 1997), London.

Searle, John. 'Minds, Brains and Programs.' In John Haugeland, ed. *Mind Design*. Cambridge, Mass.: Cambridge University Press, 1981.

Sedgh, Gilda, et al., 'Abortion incidence between 1990 and 2014: global, regional, and subregional levels and trends.' *The Lancet* 388/10041 (16 July 2016), 258–67. doi: http://dx.doi.org/10.1016/S0140-6736(16)30380-4.

Shapiro, James A. 'In the Details . . . What?' *National Review* (16 Sept. 1996), 62–5.

Simpson, George Gaylord. 'The Biological Nature of Man.' *Science* 152/3721 (22 Apr. 1966), 472–8.

Singer, Peter. 'Hegel, Georg Wilhelm Friedrich.' In Ted Honderich, ed. *The Oxford Companion to Philosophy*. Oxford, 1995. 2nd edn, Oxford: Oxford University Press, 2005.

Skorupski, John. 'Mill, John Stuart.' In Ted Honderich, ed. *The Oxford Companion to Philosophy*. Oxford, 1995. 2nd edn, Oxford: Oxford University Press, 2005.

Slote, Michael. 'Utilitarianism.' In Ted Honderich, ed. *The Oxford Companion to Philosophy*. Oxford, 1995. 2nd edn, Oxford: Oxford University Press, 2005.

Slote, Michael. 'Virtue Ethics.' In Hugh LaFollette, ed. *The Blackwell Guide to Ethical Theory*. Oxford: Blackwell, 2000, 325–47.

Sokal, Alan D. 'Transgressing the boundaries: towards a transformative hermeneutic of Quantum Gravity.' *Social Text* (Spring/Summer 1996), 217–52.

Sokal, Alan D. 'What the Social Text Affair Does and Does Not Prove.' In Noretta Koertge, ed. *A House Built on Sand: Exposing Postmodernist Myths About Science*. Oxford: Oxford University Press, 1998, 9–22.

Solzhenitsyn, Alexander. 'Alexandr Solzhenitsyn—Nobel Lecture.' *Nobelprize.org*. Nobel Media AB 2014. http://www.nobelprize.org/nobel_prizes/literature/laureates/1970/solzhenitsyn-lecture.html, accessed 15 Aug. 2017.

Spetner, L. M. 'Natural selection: An information-transmission mechanism for evolution.' *Journal of Theoretical Biology* 7/3 (Nov. 1964), 412–29.

Stalin, Joseph. Speech delivered 24 April 1924. New York, International Publishers, 1934.

Stolzenberg, Gabriel. 'Reading and relativism: an introduction to the science wars.' In Keith M. Ashman and Philip S. Baringer, eds. *After the Science Wars*. London: Routledge, 2001, 33–63.

T

Tarkunde, V. M. 'Comment by V. M. Tarkunde on Hocutt Article.' In Morris B. Storer, ed. *Humanist Ethics: Dialogue on Basics*. Buffalo, N.Y.: Prometheus Books, 1980, 147–8.

Taylor, Robert. 'Evolution is Dead.' *New Scientist* 160/2154 (3 Oct. 1998), 25–9.

W

Walicki, Andrzej. 'Hegelianism, Russian.' In Edward Craig, gen. ed. *Concise Routledge Encyclopedia of Philosophy*. London: Routledge, 2000.

Wallace, Daniel, "The Majority Text and the Original Text: Are They Identical?," Bibliotheca Sacra, April-June, 1991, 157-8.

Walton, J. C. 'Organization and the Origin of Life.' *Origins* 4 (1977), 16–35.

Warren, Mary Ann. 'On the Moral and Legal Status of Abortion.' Ch. 11 in Hugh LaFollette, ed. *Ethics in Practice: An Anthology*, 1997, 72–82. 4th edn, Oxford: Blackwell, 2014, 132–40.

Watters, Wendell W. 'Christianity and Mental Health.' *The Humanist* 37 (Nov./Dec. 1987).

Weatherford, Roy C. 'Freedom and Determinism.' In Ted Honderich, ed. *The Oxford Companion to Philosophy*. Oxford, 1995. 2nd edn, Oxford: Oxford University Press, 2005.

Wheeler, John A. 'Information, Physics, Quantum: The Search for Links.' In Wojciech Hubert Zurek. *Complexity, Entropy, and the Physics of Information*. The Proceedings of the 1988 Workshop on Complexity, Entropy, and the Physics of Information, held May–June, 1989, in Santa Fe, N. Mex. Redwood City, Calif.: Addison-Wesley, 1990.

Wigner, Eugene. 'The Unreasonable Effectiveness of Mathematics in the Natural Sciences', Richard Courant Lecture in Mathematical Sciences, delivered at New York University, 11 May 1959. *Communications in Pure and Applied Mathematics*, 13/1 (Feb. 1960), 1–14. Repr. in E. Wiger. *Symmetries and Reflections.* Bloomingon, Ind., 1967. Repr. Woodbridge, Conn.: Ox Bow Press, 1979, 222–37.

Wilford, John Noble. 'Sizing Up the Cosmos: An Astronomer's Quest.' *New York Times* (12 Mar. 1991), B9.

Wilkinson, David. 'Found in space?' Interview with Paul Davies. *Third Way* 22:6 (July 1999), 17–21.

Wilson, Edward O. 'The Ethical Implications of Human Sociobiology.' *Hastings Center Report* 10:6 (Dec. 1980), 27–9. doi: 10.2307/3560296.

Y

Yockey, Hubert. 'A Calculation of the Probability of Spontaneous Biogenesis by Information Theory.' *Journal of Theoretical Biology* 67 (1977), 377–98.

Yockey, Hubert. 'Self-Organisation Origin of Life Scenarios and Information Theory.' *Journal of Theoretical Biology* 91 (1981), 13–31.

STUDY QUESTIONS FOR TEACHERS AND STUDENTS

CHAPTER 1. THE BASIC VALUE OF A HUMAN BEING

The value of life

1.1 What value do you put on human life in and of itself? Is a human life so valuable that it would be wrong to mistreat it or to diminish it in any way or to destroy it? Or, are there circumstances under which you would accept that a human life can be destroyed, whether by a person themselves or by another?

1.2 Is the life of newborn babies so absolutely valuable that it would be wrong to kill them, even if their parents could not afford to keep them, or if for any reason they did not want them, or if the State wanted to curb excessive population growth?

1.3 Does the same apply to unborn babies? Why, or why not?

1.4 Not everyone values all lives equally. So, is there anything that can keep potentially conflicting personal preference from determining which lives are valued more than others?

1.5 Besides the historical examples provided, discuss two or more current events in which human life is not being valued, and perhaps not being valued equally.

1.6 Can you detect any common underlying causes that seem to be motivating both historical and recent events in which human life has been devalued?

1.7 What is the difference between a person or a thing having 'objective' or 'subjective' value? Can you give examples of each that are not drawn from this book?

Reductionist explanations and our direct experience of life

1.8 If human life is nothing but animated matter that came about without any conscious purpose, can it still have any intrinsic value? Why, or why not?

1.9 Do you agree with the following statement? If our brains came about through blind, purposeless forces, then the sensations of value that they produce have no intrinsic value.

1.10 Do you think that intuition is a valid route to knowledge? If so, what are its dangers? If not, what are its limitations?

1.11 Do you accept that there are particular things that make humans uniquely human? If so, what are those things?

1.12 Does the idea of a human 'soul' or 'spirit' strike you as old-fashioned, something you're comfortable with, or as a reasonable way of explaining some of your own knowledge and experience? Whatever your ideas are about the human soul or spirit, on what are you basing them?

The transcendence of human life

1.13 What does it mean that human life has the quality of transcendence about it?

1.14 Given Peter and Jean Medawar's statement, 'only human beings find their way by a light that illumines more than the patch of ground they stand on', what is the source of the 'light' by which you can see beyond yourself?

1.15 How do you understand the idea discussed here that human beings are 'made in the image of God'? If this is accurate, in what ways would it guarantee the inherent value of human life? If it is not, what, if anything, do you put in its place to guarantee such value?

CHAPTER 2. HUMAN FREEDOM AND THE DANGER OF ITS DEVALUATION

Freedom: everyone's birthright

2.1 Do you agree with the statement that: to attempt to remove someone's freedom is a crime against the essential dignity of what it means to be human? How would you defend your answer against someone who took the opposite view?

2.2 Please summarize, in your own words, what theists and atheists disagree over when it comes to the basic condition for realizing full human freedom.

The various kinds of atheism

2.3 In words, or in a chart, or in a sketch, how would you depict the range of atheist positions that you have encountered, in your own experience as well as in this section?

2.4 In your experience, how many of the people you know who do not believe in God are driven to that position by the arguments, and how many are motivated by the desire to be totally free from God (or the rules held to by those who believe he does exist)?

2.5 If you would call yourself an atheist or agnostic, are you more motivated by arguments, desire for personal freedom, or a combination of both?

2.6 If you are a theist, do you find any conflict between your desire to admit to God's rightful authority over your life and your own desire for autonomy? If so, how do you deal with that conflict?

Freedom and the danger of its devaluation

2.7 What were the basic views of the Stoic and Epicurean philosophers, and can you see parallels with their views in our own day?

2.8 Describe your reaction to the Apostle Paul's analysis of the human condition as he gives it in the section of his letter to the Romans quoted in the text.

2.9 Would you say that Paul's analysis is too bleak? If not, how do you see it mapping onto current trends in the world today? If it is, what are the specific points with which you disagree?

2.10 Summarize please, in a chart or a sketch or in a verbal description, the theory of the evolution of religion.

2.11 Please summarize, also in a chart or a sketch or in a verbal description, the way that belief in God fluctuated throughout the history of the nation of Israel, as recorded in the Bible.

2.12 What part does gratitude play in making your own life better or worse? Can you see parallels or contrasts with the human condition as a whole?

2.13 Does the Bible's description of a failure to be grateful to God strike you as a significant underlying cause behind human creatures' alienation from their creator? Why, or why not?

2.14 What is the difference between science and scientism?

CHAPTER 3. THE NATURE AND BASIS OF MORALITY

General considerations

3.1 Do you agree that morality sets humans apart from animals? If you do, is this the only thing that makes humans 'truly human'? If you don't, do you hold that anything sets us apart from animals in any real way?

3.2 What is the difference between ethics as a subject and ethics as a code of behaviour? Please give an example of each.

3.3 Is it right to break the letter of a moral law in order to keep the spirit of that law? What examples can you give that would support your answer?

3.4 Can you cite either historical examples that are not mentioned in the text, or personal examples, of when giving precedent to the higher of two competing moral laws was the right thing to do? On what basis would you decide which really is the higher of the two moral laws?

3.5 What is the possible effect of having only good theory and not right ethical practice? What would the effects be if we sought to behave rightly without sound theory? Please cite examples to illustrate each.

3.6 Why is a properly adjusted emotional sense necessary to right behaviour?

The source and nature of moral law

3.7 What do you personally hold to be the source and nature of moral law (assuming you think there is any such thing)?

3.8 Considering a time in your own life when you were treated unfairly, do you consider the sense of fairness/unfairness to indicate the reality of something deeper than personal preference or selfish desire?

3.9 Besides our innate sense of fairness, what other inbuilt senses are we born with? In what ways do they show us that there is something real about our sense of fairness?

3.10 What other moral virtues and vices do we find we were born with that we don't need to be taught?

3.11 How does the universal awareness of the natural law fit with the fact that not all people throughout history have kept it or have even desired to keep it (and have sometimes even enjoyed breaking it)?

3.12 Take a survey among your class or study group as to what you all hold in common as things you do not want done to yourselves or to those you love. Is there a significant divergence about the underlying principles within your group?

3.13 How close is your personal (or your group's) list to the basic rights and wrongs laid out in the Egyptian *Book of the Dead*?

3.14 What is the difference between conscience and shame? In what way or ways does each bear witness to the universal moral law?

3.15 How is God's writing of his law on the human heart different from programming a computer?

Morality: objective or subjective?

3.16 What are the basic questions that any theist would want to ask an atheist about his or her system of morality?

3.17 Do you hold that there are things that are always right or always wrong, independent of personal preferences or circumstances?

3.18 What would be the problem with a system of morality having only a subjective basis?

3.19 How effective would it be to regard moral rules like we do the rules of a game?

3.20 In your opinion, would it be useful to have a worldwide body such as the UN or other institution that could lay down the moral law for the entire world? If not, why not?

CHAPTER 4. COMPARATIVE MORALITIES

Moralities based on an evolutionary account of human origins

4.1 What is the basic argument for the view that science has destroyed the traditional basis of morality?

4.2 Is it possible to hold to the view that science undermines traditional morality and still live a morally exemplary life? What does the Bible's story of the two men who built two houses have to say to this question (see Matt 7:24–27)?

4.3 In what ways has 'Social Darwinism' been discredited?

4.4 How does 'sociobiology' differ from 'Social Darwinism?

Genes are the basic moral authority

4.5 Do you agree or disagree with Francis Crick's statement that 'Science in general and natural selection in particular', should become the basis on which we build a new culture? Please state your reasons for your answer.

4.6 If it is true that whatever anyone thinks about morality at any one time must be what that person's genes are making him or her think, is it possible for that thinking to have any authority (either for the individual or for the wider world)?

4.7 Do you agree with Richard Dawkins that it is possible for humans to rebel against their own selfish genes and choose differently from what they urge us to do? If so, what part of a human do you think is doing the rebelling?

Marxist morality

4.8 According to its founders and proponents, what is the basis of Marxist morality?

4.9 If humanity has no creator and evolution's materialistic forces are the ground and basis of man's intrinsic value, by what criterion shall one decide between Marx's and Hitler's evolutionary theories?

4.10 Is there anything within Marxism that places a moral duty upon people to struggle, suffer and die for future generations whom they will never see?

What might that be? Do you yourself think that such a demand is reasonable? Why or why not?

Humanity itself sets the moral law

4.11 What is the one thing upon which all secular humanists agree?

4.12 What difficulties does the idea that humans are themselves the ultimate rulemakers raise when people disagree?

4.13 Is the satisfaction of our needs an adequate standard by which to determine right and wrong? If so, who or what should arbitrate when the needs of two or more people come into conflict?

4.14 Of the various goals that various humanists have said morality should have, which do you take to be the most convincing? What problems do you perceive with the one you have chosen?

4.15 Although Bertrand Russell said, 'What the world needs is Christian love and compassion', he evidently did not accept its basis as being valid. If these virtues that Christianity extols are worth having, are there any good reasons for not examining their basis in the Bible for yourself? These may be your own reasons or those you have heard others raise.

God is the authority behind the moral law

4.16 Please summarize, in your own words, the five systems of morality surveyed in this chapter.

4.17 Is it more important to you to seek to live a life completely free from the restraint of an external authority, or to seek to discover the truth about the universe, whatever that might entail for your own personal freedom?

4.18 Does your own knowledge or experience of what many characterize as freedom in sexual life lead you to think that sexual freedom is always good? If not, what harm have you seen it cause? If you think it is generally a good thing, does the fact that one person's sexual freedom could actually violate another person's freedom and rights lead you to think that some level of restraint is necessary? On what would you base any such restraints?

4.19 Does the idea of 'as long as it doesn't hurt someone else' extend beyond the physical to the emotional and psychological? If so, should those categories of harm change the way we define the actions that do damage to another person?

4.20 In what ways can rules enhance, rather than hinder, the enjoyment of life?

4.21 State, in as few words as possible, the issue at stake in 'The Euthyphro Problem'. What, according to the Bible, is the answer to it?

4.22 Is it wrong to do things for the sake of reward? Is it better to act without the hope of reward? Why?

4.23 What is the difference between the true and the false reward motives?

4.24 If you believe in the God of the Bible, do you hold that he will ever remove a person's free will, even if it is for his or her own good? What is the basis of your answer?

CHAPTER 5. THE ROLE AND POWER OF HUMANS OVER NATURE

What a wonder humanity is!

5.1 What do you find to be the single most impressive feature of human beings?

5.2 How much does human progress in science, technology, the arts and the humanities set the species apart from other species?

5.3 What contemporary song lyrics do you know that sound similar notes of unease, angst or misgiving as those which Sophocles penned in the 400s BC?

The question of a human's body, brain, mind and self

5.4 Are humans nothing but a part of nature, or do we have any independence from nature?

5.5 Do you think that human beings have, in addition to their brains, a mind that is distinct from the brain?

5.6 Can you imagine a time in the future when it will be possible to develop artificial intelligence that will be indistinguishable from a human being? If so, do you think that will be a good thing or a dangerous one?

5.7 What are the basic positions of the opposing sides of the monist/dualist debate?

5.8 Why is our own direct experience so important when it comes to trying to understand what each one of us is?

Some monist explanations

5.9 How does the example of a wedding ring show that what a thing is made of is not an adequate explanation of what that thing is?

5.10 How does Behaviourism get its name?

5.11 Besides Karl Popper's example of the toothache, what other example can you give of what radical behaviourism means in practice?

5.12 What is epiphenomenalism?

5.13 What answer would those who hold Identity Theory give to answer the question: how could a non-material intention in my mind cause my material brain to raise my arm?

5.14 What are the main points of critique for Identity Theory?

5.15 Which, if any, of the monist explanations overviewed do you find convincing? Can you think of any way to modify any of them that would make it more convincing for you?

5.16 In what way are 'modified monist' views distinct from more traditional monist positions?

The heart of the monist/dualist debate

5.17 What is the key distinction between all monist explanations and dualistic interactionism?

5.18 What is the major objection of many scientists and philosophers to dualistic explanations?

5.19 How does the example of a mother receiving distressing news in a letter highlight the effect of information, not only on our brains, but on our emotions and bodies?

5.20 What examples could you give of a non-material entity or force affecting a material substance?

5.21 According to the Bible, what specifically is the source of information that we find encoded in matter?

5.22 What fundamental points of Christian doctrine agree with the idea of a distinction between body and mind?

5.23 Do you hold that the human spirit can exist independently of the body?

5.24 What shows that the Bible's teaching about the human spirit is not ultimately a negative teaching about the human body?

CHAPTER 6. THE PARAMETERS OF HUMAN POWER

Safeguarding humanity's rights and freedoms

6.1 Are humans subject to any moral and spiritual laws that stand above them that limit what they may do?

6.2 What is the difference between what humans can do and what they should do?

6.3 Does having power give those who have it the right to exercise that power over nature and over their fellow humans as they decide best, or are they accountable to any higher authority for how they use it?

6.4 Do you think that the positives of genetic programming and related research outweigh the potential dangers? Divide your class or study group according to those who see more dangers than benefits, draw up competing lists and debate their relative merits.

6.5 By what standard should we determine what constitutes a 'normal' foetus? Should we try to make any such determination at all?

6.6 If you hold that each individual has human rights that should not be violated, what do you take to be an adequate basis for those rights?

6.7 Why have governments sometimes not been the best guarantors of individual human rights? Please provide examples from history, as well as others from literature or films.

6.8 Describe the Christian view of how the desire of humans to 'be as gods' is at the root of humanity's problems.

6.9 In what ways does the Bible's idea of a redeemed humanity appear similar to some contemporary ideas of an ideal future humanity? In what ways are they crucially dissimilar?

The question of humanity's fatal flaw and its cure

6.10 How does the idea that human behaviour is predetermined seem to fit with the evidence of the world around us? In what ways does it undermine human responsibility and dignity?

6.11 According to those who say there is nothing basically wrong with the human race, what are the causes of the problems in our world? Do any of the examples overviewed strike you as convincing? If so, how convincing do you find them?

6.12 How does the evolutionary point of view undercut the argument that bad behaviour is only a product of a destructive society?

6.13 What reasons have sometimes been given for alleging that belief in God is one of the primary causes of harm for the human personality? Can you add any to the list? Would you try to refute them, or do you agree with them?

6.14 In what ways does the Bible itself answer some of the objections about the distortion of the human personality as a result of belief in God?

6.15 Which, if any, of the quotations from the Bible do you find intriguing in relation to the question of guilt and forgiveness of sins?

6.16 How would you summarize the Christian diagnosis of humanity's fatal flaw and its cure?

6.17 Does this answer seem more or less plausible than some of the alternatives overviewed? Why?

6.18 Setting to one side the question of whether the New Testament's cure seems foolish, if it were true, do you think it would be worth finding?

6.19 What does the New Testament teach that the cross of Jesus Christ is meant to answer about God's character and his desires for humanity?

CHAPTER 7. HUMAN DESTINY

Hope for the future and for the present, because of the resurrection

7.1 Is the motto that the United Nations has adopted from the Bible a realistic goal today?

7.2 Why is pantheism not a genuine alternative to atheism?

7.3 In what ways have various cultures and prominent persons throughout history expressed a longing for immortality?

7.4 Atheists sometimes say that the theist's belief in an afterlife is simply wishful thinking. Why might it be wishful thinking on the atheist's part that there is no afterlife?

7.5 On what is Christ basing the certainty of resurrection when he quotes God as saying that 'I am the God of Abraham, and the God of Isaac, and the God of Jacob' (Matt 22:31–32)?

7.6 How do the demands of justice demand a resurrection of all humans?

7.7 In what way is the resurrection necessary in order for God to fulfil the goal that he had in mind for humanity?

7.8 According to the New Testament, how does the resurrection of Jesus Christ set the pattern for the resurrection of all those who are spiritually united with him?

7.9 Besides what it promises for human beings, what does the resurrection promise for the rest of nature?

7.10 If it is true, how would the resurrection make a difference now in the lives of those who believe it? How might it show the significance of life now?

APPENDIX: THE SCIENTIFIC ENDEAVOUR

Scientific method

A.1 In what different ways have you heard the word 'science' used? How would you define it?

A.2 How is induction understood as part of our everyday experience and also of the scientific endeavour?

A.3 In what ways does deduction differ from induction, and what role does each play in scientific experiments?

A.4 Do you find the idea of 'falsifiability' appealing, or unsatisfactory? Why?

A.5 How does abduction differ from both induction and deduction, and what is the relationship among the three?

Explaining explanations

A.6 How many levels of explanation can you think of to explain a cake, in terms of how it was made, what it was made from, and why was it made? What can scientists tell us? What can 'Aunt Olga' tell us?

A.7 In what ways is reductionism helpful in scientific research, and in what ways could it be limiting, or even detrimental, to scientific research?

A.8 How do you react to physicist and theologian John Polkinghorne's statement that reductionism relegates 'our experiences of beauty, moral obligation, and religious encounter to the epiphenomenal scrapheap. It also destroys rationality'?

The basic operational presuppositions of the scientific endeavour

A.9 What is meant by the statement 'Observation is dependent on theory'?

A.10 What are some of the axioms upon which your thinking about scientific knowledge rests?

A.11 What does trust have to do with gaining knowledge?

A.12 What does belief have to do with gaining knowledge?

A.13 According to physicist and philosopher of science Thomas Kuhn, how do new scientific paradigms emerge?

SCRIPTURE INDEX

OTHER ANCIENT LITERATURE

GENERAL INDEX

ABOUT THE AUTHORS

David W. Gooding is Professor Emeritus of Old Testament Greek at Queen's University Belfast and a Member of the Royal Irish Academy. He has taught the Bible internationally and lectured on both its authenticity and its relevance to philosophy, world religions and daily life. He has published scholarly articles on the Septuagint and Old Testament narratives, as well as expositions of Luke, John, Acts, Hebrews, the New Testament's use of the Old Testament, and several books addressing arguments against the Bible and the Christian faith. His analysis of the Bible and our world continues to shape the thinking of scholars, teachers and students alike.

John C. Lennox is Professor Emeritus of Mathematics at the University of Oxford and Emeritus Fellow in Mathematics and the Philosophy of Science at Green Templeton College. He is also an Associate Fellow of the Saïd Business School. In addition, he is an Adjunct Lecturer at the Oxford Centre for Christian Apologetics, as well as being a Senior Fellow of the Trinity Forum. In addition to academic works, he has published on the relationship between science and Christianity, the books of Genesis and Daniel, and the doctrine of divine sovereignty and human free will. He has lectured internationally and participated in a number of televised debates with some of the world's leading atheist thinkers.

David W. Gooding (right) and John C. Lennox (left)

Photo credit: Barbara Hamilton

The Quest for Reality and Significance

Being Truly Human: ***The Limits of our Worth, Power, Freedom and Destiny***

In Book 1, Gooding and Lennox address issues surrounding the value of humans. They consider the nature and basis of morality, compare what morality means in different systems, and assess the dangerous way freedom is often devalued. What should guide our use of power? What should limit our choices? And to what extent can our choices keep us from fulfilling our potential?

Finding Ultimate Reality: ***In Search of the Best Answers to the Biggest Questions***

In Book 2, they remind us that the authority behind ethics cannot be separated from the truth about ultimate reality. Is there a Creator who stands behind his moral law? Are we the product of amoral forces, left to create moral consensus? Gooding and Lennox compare ultimate reality as understood in: Indian Pantheistic Monism, Greek Philosophy and Mysticism, Naturalism and Atheism, and Christian Theism.

Questioning Our Knowledge: ***Can we Know What we Need to Know?***

In Book 3, Gooding and Lennox discuss how we could know whether any of these competing worldviews are true. What is truth anyway, and is it absolute? How would we recognize truth if we encountered it? Beneath these questions lies another that affects science, philosophy, ethics, literature and our everyday lives: how do we know anything at all?

The Quest for Reality and Significance

Doing What's Right: ***Whose System of Ethics is Good Enough?***

In Book 4, Gooding and Lennox present particular ethical theories that claim to hold the basic principles everyone should follow. They compare the insights and potential weaknesses of each system by asking: what is its authority, its supreme goal, its specific rules, and its guidance for daily life? They then evaluate why even the best theories have proven to be impossible to follow consistently.

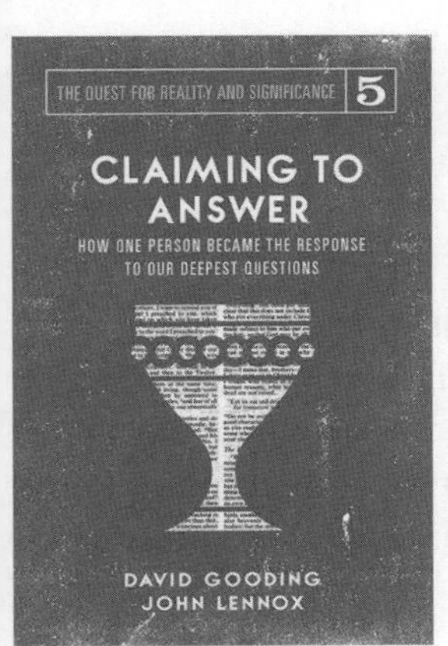

Claiming to Answer: ***How One Person Became the Response to our Deepest Questions***

In Book 5, they argue it is not enough to have an ethical theory telling us what standards we ought to live by, because we often fail in our duties and do what we know is wrong. How can we overcome this universal weakness? Many religions claim to be able to help, but is the hope they offer true? Gooding and Lennox state why they think the claims of Jesus Christ are valid and the help he offers is real.

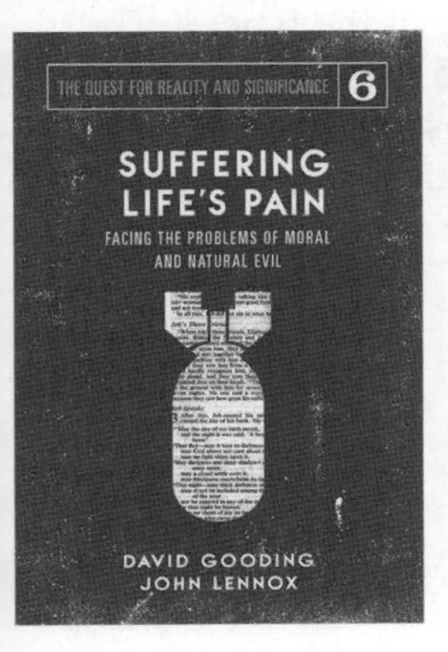

Suffering Life's Pain: ***Facing the Problems of Moral and Natural Evil***

In Book 6, they acknowledge the problem with believing in a wise, loving and just God who does not stop natural disasters or human cruelty. Why does he permit congenital diseases, human trafficking and genocide? Is he unable to do anything? Or does he not care? Gooding and Lennox offer answers based on the Creator's purpose for the human race, and his entry into his own creation.

Myrtlefield Encounters

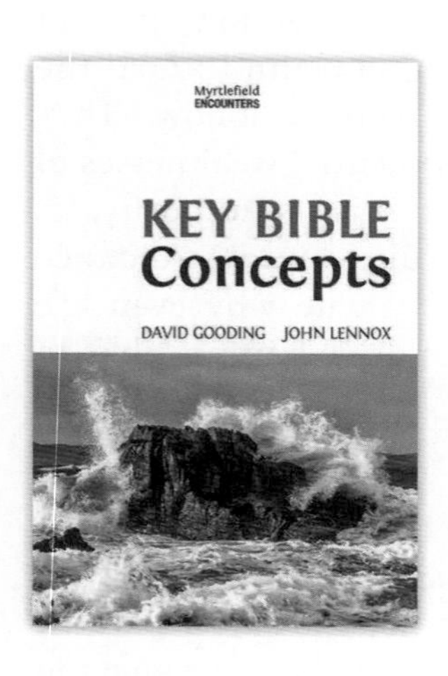

Key Bible Concepts
How can one book be so widely appreciated an
so contested? Millions revere it and man
ridicule it, but the Bible is often not allowed t
speak for itself. *Key Bible Concepts* explores an
clarifies the central terms of the Christian gospe
Gooding and Lennox provide succinc
explanations of the basic vocabulary of Christia
thought to unlock the Bible's meaning and it
significance for today.

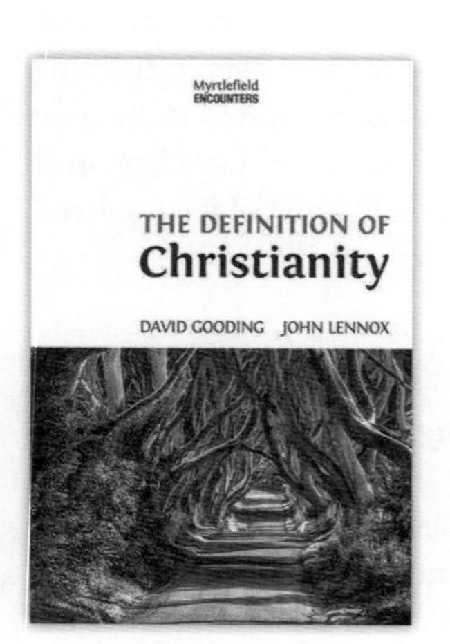

The Definition of Christianity
Who gets to determine what Christianit
means? Is it possible to understand its origina
message after centuries of tradition an
conflicting ideas? Gooding and Lennox thro
fresh light on these questions by tracing th
Book of Acts' historical account of the messag
that proved so effective in the time of Christ'
apostles. Luke's record of its confrontation
with competing philosophical and religiou
systems reveals Christianity's own original an
lasting definition.

Myrtlefield Encounters

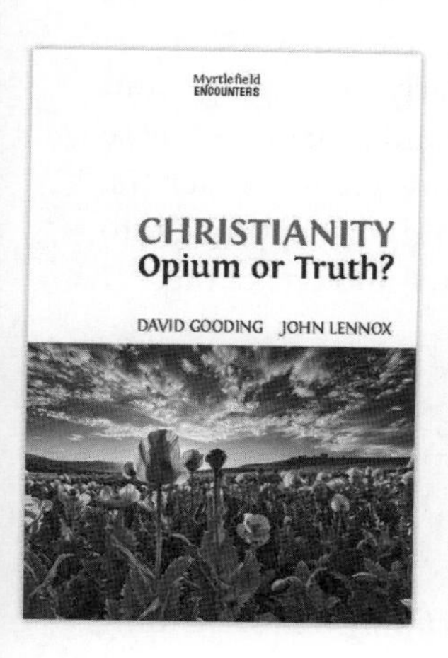

Christianity: Opium or Truth
Is Christianity just a belief that dulls the pain of our existence with dreams that are beautiful but false? Or is it an accurate account of reality, our own condition and God's attitude toward us? Gooding and Lennox address crucial issues that can make it difficult for thoughtful people to accept the Christian message. They answer those questions and show that clear thinking is not in conflict with personal faith in Jesus Christ.

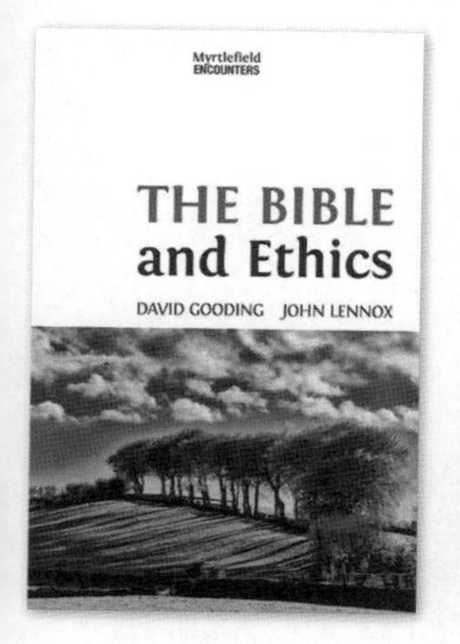

The Bible and Ethics
Why should we tell the truth or value a human life? Why should we not treat others in any way we like? Some say the Bible is the last place to find answers to such questions, but even its critics recognize the magnificence of Jesus' ethical teaching. To understand the ethics of Jesus we need to understand the values and beliefs on which they are based. Gooding and Lennox take us on a journey through the Bible and give us a concise survey of its leading events and people, ideas, poetry, moral values and ethics to bring into focus the ultimate significance of what Jesus taught about right and wrong.

Myrtlefield Expositions

Myrtlefield Expositions provide insights into the thought–flow and meaning of the biblical writings, motivated by devotion to the Lord who reveals himself in the Scriptures. Scholarly, engaging, and accessible, each book addresses the reader's mind and heart to increase faith in God and to encourage obedience to his Word. Teachers, preachers and all students of the Bible will find the approach to Scripture adopted in these volumes both instructive and enriching.

- The Riches of Divine Wisdom: *The New Testament's Use of the Old Testament*
- According to Luke: *The Third Gospel's Ordered Historical Narrative*
- True to the Faith: *The Acts of the Apostles: Defining and Defending the Gospel*
- In the School of Christ: *Lessons on Holiness in John 13–17*
- An Unshakeable Kingdom: *The Letter to the Hebrews for Today*

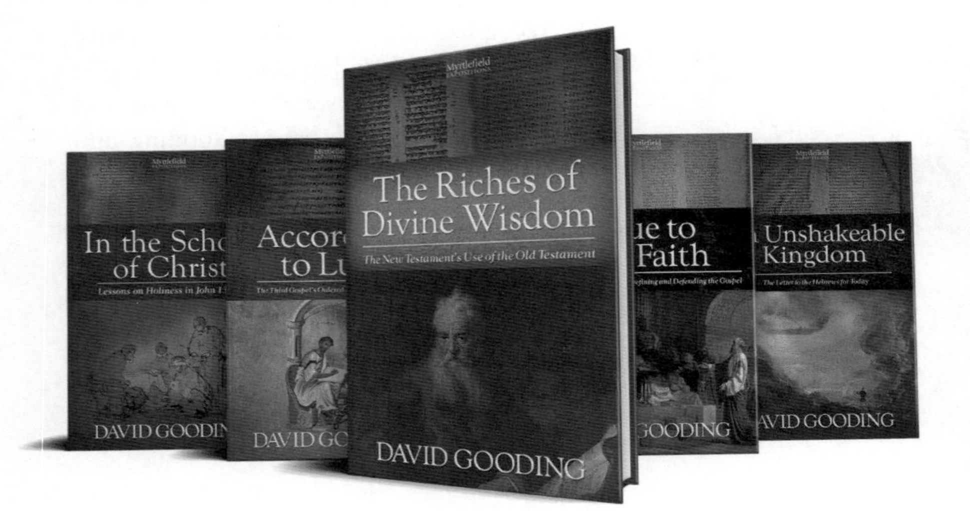

www.myrtlefieldhouse.com

Our website, www.myrtlefieldhouse.com, contains hundreds of resources in a variety of formats. You can read, listen to or watch David Gooding's teaching on over 35 Bible books and 14 topics.

You can also view the full catalogue of Myrtlefield House publications and download free e-book editions of the *Myrtlefield Expositions*, *Encounters* and *Discoveries* series.

The website is optimized for both computer and mobile viewing, making it easy for you to access the resources at home or on the go.

For more information about any of our publications or resources contact us at: info@myrtlefieldhouse.com

Clear, simple, fresh and highly practical—this David Gooding/John Lennox series is a goldmine for anyone who desires to live Socrates' 'examined life'.

Above all, the books are comprehensive and foundational, so they form an invaluable handbook for negotiating the crazy chaos of today's modern world.

Os Guinness, author of *Last Call for Liberty*

These six volumes, totalling almost 2000 pages, were written by two outstanding scholars who combine careers of research and teaching at the highest levels. David Gooding and John Lennox cover well the fields of Scripture, science, and philosophy, integrating them with one voice. The result is a set of texts that work systematically through a potpourri of major topics, like being human, discovering ultimate reality, knowing truth, ethically evaluating life's choices, answering our deepest questions, plus the problems of pain and suffering. To get all this wisdom together in this set was an enormous undertaking! Highly recommended!

Gary R. Habermas, Distinguished Research Professor & Chair,
Dept. of Philosophy, Liberty University & Theological Seminary

David Gooding and John Lennox are exemplary guides to the deepest questions of life in this comprehensive series. It will equip thinking Christians with an intellectual roadmap to the fundamental conflict between Christianity and secular humanism. For thinking seekers it will be a provocation to consider which worldview makes best sense of our deepest convictions about life.

Justin Brierley, host of the *Unbelievable?* radio show and podcast